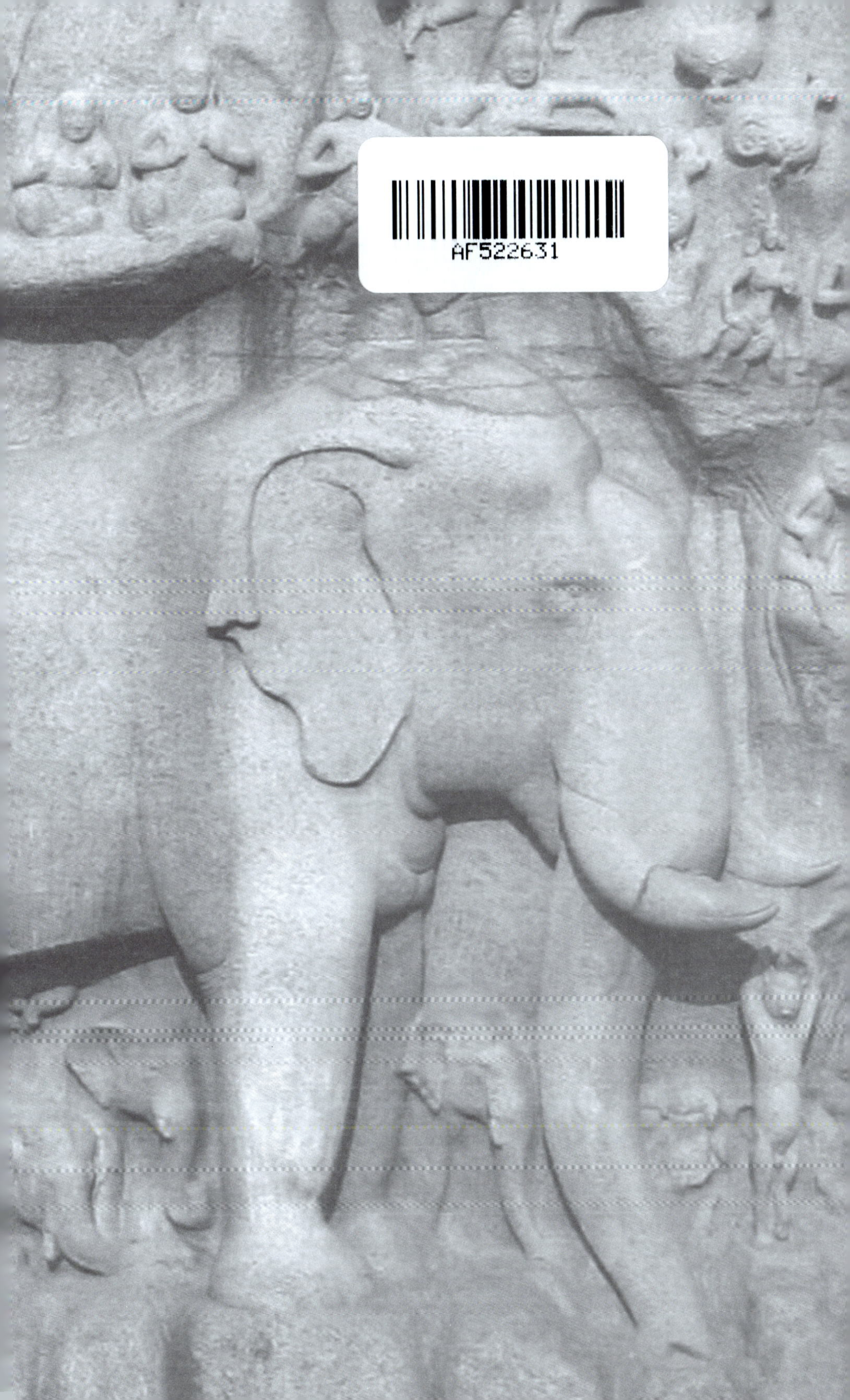
AF522631

THE
INDIAN CAT

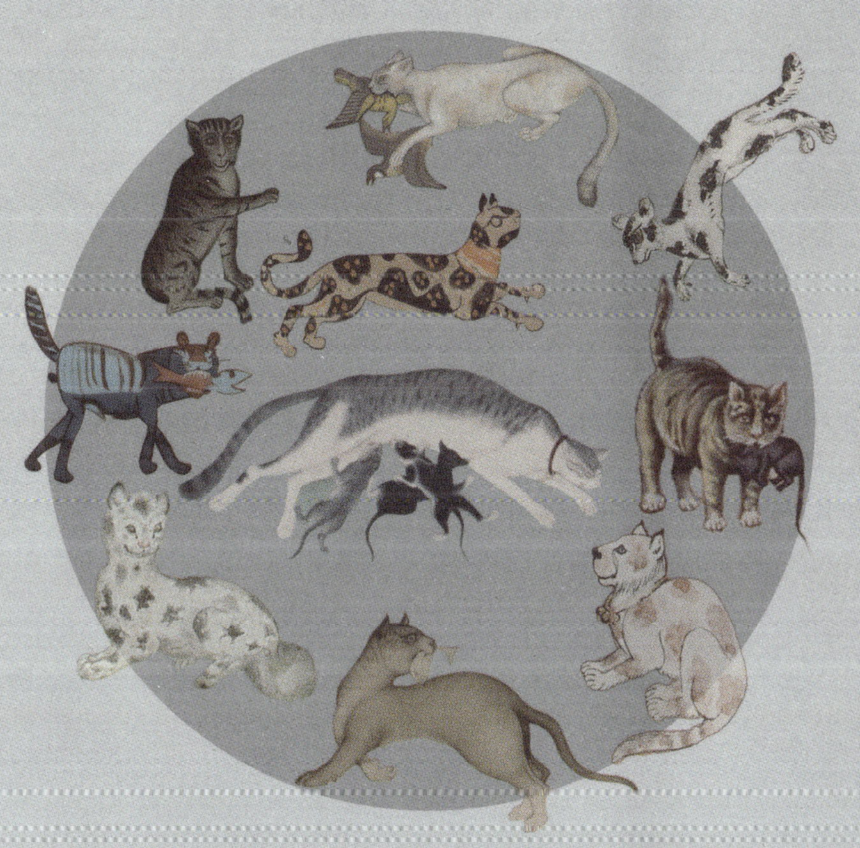

Also by B. N. Goswamy

Conversations

A Sacred Journey

The Great Mysore Bhagavata

The Spirit of Indian Painting

Domains of Wonder

Nainsukh of Guler

Essence of Indian Art

THE INDIAN CAT

STORIES, PAINTINGS, POETRY, AND PROVERBS

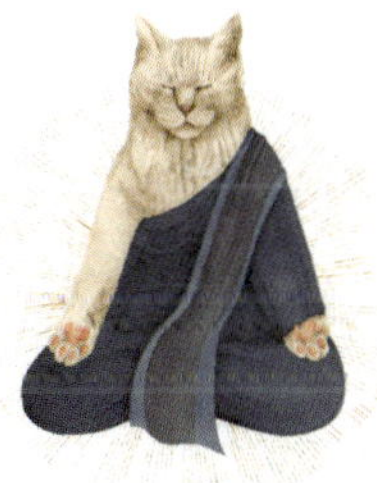

B. N. GOSWAMY

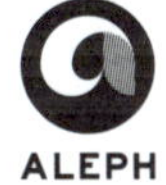

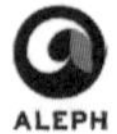

ALEPH BOOK COMPANY
An independent publishing firm
promoted by ***Rupa Publications India***

First published in India in 2023
by Aleph Book Company
7/16 Ansari Road, Daryaganj
New Delhi 110 002

The Acknowledgements on p. 226 constitute an extension of the copyright page.

Cover illustration © Jana Kulmatycka, Warsaw.
Endpapers designed by Girish Naphade, Chandigarh.

ISBN: 978-93-95853-30-9

3 5 7 9 10 8 6 4

Printed in India.

For
APU

and in memory of MAX whom he used to call
'a gentle poem on four feet'

CONTENTS

PREFATORY NOTE

It is best to begin with a confession, I think.

Strictly speaking, I am not a cat lover. I am therefore not even entitled perhaps to put together a book on cats. But, somehow, they have stayed in my awareness for long years. When a stray one sneaked into our house once, for instance, and Apu, my son, took to her, cold and shivering as she was when she came in. He fed her, held on to her, gave her a name—Katja it was if I remember aright—and, after returning from school, he would talk to her first, ahead of anyone else at home It was a few years before we shifted home and she decided against moving. As simple as that.

Then, years later, I had a faintly bristly encounter with a whole pride of cats at the home of a dear friend in Zurich: Ursula Dohrn. She loved cats, had many of them, and they had all become members of her family. Whenever I went to visit her, they were there, naturally and everywhere: if one was occupying the first seat on a sofa, another was lurking under the centre table, and yet another clambering onto her shoulder sometimes. For me it was not easy and, almost complainingly, I once told Ursula during a visit how hard it was to find a quiet moment with her without the cats participating in the conversation, nodding approval, or saying something in a whispered purr to her. Quickly, in a tone of mock-admonishment, Ursula shot back. 'You are an art historian, Brijinder, are you not?'

'I am; or so I think,' I replied.

'Then, you should love cats: all art historians do.'

This unsettled me a bit, but she went on. 'Annemarie Schimmel does: she has in fact even written more than one book on them.' I knew and held Professor Schimmel in great regard, but this fact I was not aware of. Even as I was registering it, Ursula came up with another name, another highly regarded art historian—Stella Kramrisch. 'She is a cat lover, is she not?' So she was, I knew, for I had seen a whole lot of them around her whenever I visited her, first in her Paoli home, and later in her apartment in the heart of Philadelphia. These firm statements showed me my place as far as Ursula's cats went. It wasn't over yet, however. For, the next day, a book was delivered to my apartment: a paperback edition of Annemarie Schimmel's work—much celebrated I was to learn—in German: *Die Orientalische Katze*, with the subtitle: *Mysticism and Poetry of the Orient.* Sent obviously by Ursula, but without a note. She was driving a point home.

I felt informed, but, as an art historian, not particularly persuaded. Or obligated. It was a bit later that I became involved: not so much with cats as with the idea of cats. A great Sanskrit scholar, C. Sivaramamurti, then director of the National Museum in Delhi, happened to bring up two terms in the course of a conversation that had the Sanskrit word for cats—*marjara*—built into them: *marjara-nyaya* and *marjara-vrata.* There was talk, in the context of Vaishnava bhakti or devotion, about different ways through which a devotee approaches his ishta deity. There are many *nyayas*—methods or theories—but the two most often cited are *markata-nyaya* and *marjara-nyaya.* The former refers to how the young one of a monkey—*markata* in Sanskrit—approaches God, and the latter to how the young one of a cat—*marjara*—does. Briefly put, '*markata-nyaya* refers to the behaviour of a baby monkey, who clings tightly to its mother wherever she goes. The mother monkey's arms are occupied as she leaps from tree to tree; she does not hold on to the baby; but as long as the baby holds firmly to her, it arrives safely'. Whereas '*marjara-nyaya* refers to the behaviour of kittens, who are likely to wander. The mother cat picks them up by the scruff of the neck and carries them wherever she wants them to be. The kitten is passive; she makes no effort but arrives safely by surrendering to the mother's protective grasp.' It is up to the devotee, then, to choose: to keep making an effort to cling for succour to his deity, or to leave everything to the deity, trusting him and surrendering to him completely. No recommendation is made, no preference indicated.

Never having heard of any of this before, I was fascinated. But even more fascinating for me was the use of the term *marjara-vrata*. In common usage it stands simply for 'a cat-like observance', but the term is not neutral. It really has come to stand for 'concealing one's malice or evil designs under the garb of piety or virtue'. It is an accusation that one person might fling at his rival while calling him a 'cheat', or a 'hypocrite'. In an episode in that ancient epic of ours, the *Mahabharata*, Duryodhana charges even the noble Yudhishthira with observing the *marjara-vrata*, not once, but repeatedly. Clearly, the cat had come to stand for 'hypocrisy'—'ye gods, that person whose standard of righteousness is always up, but whose sins are always concealed'—and the opprobrium seems to have endured over a very long time: cleverness, hypocrisy, avarice, inscrutability, thievery.

Interestingly enough, however, in our land at the same time there is no real dislike for cats. There are superstitions around her figure, for certain, and stories go on being repeated. But no fatwas have been passed; no papal bulls issued. Great poets like Mir and Ghalib loved their cats to distraction; the poet Jibanananda Das saw himself in a cat that went here and there, following the Sun; Vikram Seth saw her as full of mischief and cleverness but no evil. In fact, on a daily basis, the feline is 'addressed' almost with affection. She is 'maano', 'maaoon', 'mausi' (mother's sister), 'pisshi', 'biloongari', if one goes by usage, at least in the northern parts of our land.

It is somewhere out of these memories and stray thoughts and scattered observations—whether it was mock-admonishment that I received as an art historian, seductive and long-buried snippets that reading about cats yielded, or the fact that my son adopted recently two cats—that the present work has emerged. Of course, the reader is entitled to ask: 'So?' But he will at least find inside absorbing tales and images and poetry and proverbs, that I gathered together. All on cats. Indian cats.

A word of explanation to end with, however. Inadvertently, because one is so used to it in one's own life, the cat in my account is always taken to be a female. Lacking in logic as this is, the gender is open to change. Second word: the book is confined, strictly confined, to cats in India—domestic cats—not because they are unique, but because cats elsewhere—and they are everywhere—have their own histories, their own tales, their own place in life.

PERSPECTIVES

Some Clear Some Not So Clear

A Cat's a Cat; and That's That
—Common saying

A Cat is Not a Cat
A Cat is a fallen piece of cloud
rolled up in wakeful sleep.

A mixed metaphor
descending the stairs
with a questioning tail.

—S. Ganapathi

CAT: marjara in Sanskrit; majjar/manjar in Prakrit; gurba in Persian; billi in Hindi; billi or bi' bilai in Urdu; pucca in Malayalam; punnai in Tamil; pilli in Telugu; bekku in Kannada; bidala/pisshi in Bengali; maau/marjaar in Marathi; biladi in Gujarati; bror/boour in Kashmiri; maanjo/maano in Dogri; billi in Sindhi; birda/bidaal in Maithili; gant/bukkul in Konkani.

People who know them often say that cats can be 'quirky, aggressive, and confusing'. A bit like them perhaps, this book can also be quirky and confusing at times, but it is, at least, completely non-aggressive. Non-aggressive, because no theories are being advanced here; none challenged. Clarifying further: referring to the idioms that commonly feature cats, one could say that nothing 'comes out of the bag' in this book; no 'paw' is ready to scratch, no one is being 'set among the pigeons'. Nobody's 'tongue is being got'; no one hops on to 'a hot tin roof'. And there certainly is nothing with 'nine-tails' in this book. This is simply a look—a bit quirky perhaps—at how the cat is viewed in India: how it was in the past, and how it is today.

It is not easy. For there are no connected accounts, and not a single book on cats written in the past is around. So, one gleans and glues: shards of things and accounts and stories, in the hope that a picture of how cats were viewed in our land emerges. A large number of references to them can be found in fables which India has been so rich in, and still remembers. There are, for instance, the *Jataka* Tales—stories of the former lives of the Buddha when he was a Bodhisattva, constantly in the process of evolving; and these go back to the centuries between the third and fourth BCE. In these sometimes cats turn up as characters whose clever tricks or pretensions are—generally—foiled by the Bodhisattva who is always on the side of the wronged, the downtrodden. Not far from these tales is the core of the great classic which later came to be named the *Panchatantra*—'Five Strands', so to speak—a perennial favourite which has not only survived across centuries of time but which travelled all over the world and was translated, or transformed, in different languages at different periods of time. A version of this work, consisting as it does of 'animal fables that are as old as we are able to imagine', exists in practically every major language of India, but there also are close to two hundred known versions of the text in more than fifty languages of the world. Written somewhere close to 200 BCE, it came to be known from 'Java to Iceland', as has been said; and drawn upon by Aesop at one end and La Fontaine at the other. Nothing is known with certainty about the author but a learned pandit, Vishnu Sharma by name, is generally credited with having put the stories together to teach a king's sons, through clever lessons in verse and prose, how to deal with situations in the real world. In Islamic lands also, the *Panchatantra* had a huge following, the three versions of it that became best known in India being the eighth century Arabic version, *Kalila wa Dimna,* by Ibn al-Muqaffa, a fifteenth century version in Persian, the *Anvar-i Suhaili,* by the Sufi poet, Kashefi, and one translated by Abu'l Fazl entitled *Ayar-i Danish,* as commissioned by the emperor Akbar in 1588. Many of these stories we shall go into later in this very work.

Several other compendiums of stories, most of them in Sanskrit, followed, borrowings being common and overlapping with minor variations not infrequent: thus, the *Brihatkatha* of Gunadhyaya; the *Brihatkathamanjari* of Kshemendra. The most comprehensive among these time-honoured works, however, was the tenth-century

Kathasaritsagara by the Kashmiri scholar, Somadeva, written at the behest of King Ananta. Evidently, cats were never the subject proper of any of these works, but they surface every now and then, staring at you with those probing eyes, or sitting in quiet contemplation. A delicious group of interconnected stories also came together in the highly entertaining Sanskrit work, the *Shuka Saptati*—'Seventy Tales of the Parrot'—part philosophical, part erotic. The authorship of that widely popular work is still being argued among learned scholars, as also is its date, although on the latter there has emerged fair agreement that it comes from no earlier than the twelfth century. The net of the long story-within-story text is woven around a merchant who is about to proceed on a long journey and, concerned about how his wife might conduct herself in his absence, entrusts the task of keeping her on the straight path to a trained parrot who keeps telling her absorbing stories, one after another, night after night, just as she gets ready to go to her secret lover. The parrot succeeds but only after the enormous effort of inventing situation after situation in which men and animals and birds keep featuring, all in diverse contexts but all speaking the same tongue. In this group figures, naturally, a cat. Not unexpectedly, the Sanskrit text attained great popularity in other lands and was translated in different languages, including Persian, the best-known version of it being by the Sufi poet Nakhshabi who rendered it in a very poetic style in the *Tuti Nama* in the fourteenth century.

From these widely varied and singularly rich works—coming as they do from different centuries, from different regions of India, and in different languages—an outline of the cat as seen by Indian eyes slowly begins to emerge. 'She'—and one speaks almost thoughtlessly of cats as being feminine, for that is how the animal is most commonly referred to in our daily parlance: *billi* or *biluri*, for instance, or *mousi*, mother's sister, when stories about 'her' are told—has an irresistibly engaging human aspect: thinking, working things out, getting into situations and out of them, entertaining conflicting thoughts all at the same time. There is no getting away, however, from the fact that from most of the stories she emerges—broadly speaking—in a somewhat negative light. One can say with some confidence that there was not much ailurophilia, if that is the word, a fondness or love for cats, around. She may not have been seen as an embodiment of perfidy all the time, but she is clever, scheming, manipulative, even thieving. And, interestingly, the reader is always invited, all the entertainment apart, to take something from each story involving a cat: a moral, an advice, another look at the world around ourselves. Superstitions began—a bit naturally—clustering around her figure: to see a cat first thing in the morning is inauspicious, for instance; if a black cat crosses your path, you must turn back or else...and so on. At the same time, however, the exact opposite of this view of cats, was also around: that cats are God's creatures to be respected if not quite revered. The Buddhists were fairly partial to cats in general and one knows of monasteries where cats roam around fearlessly. But a considerable part of this view stemmed from Islam—which was very much at home in our land from a point of time onwards—in which, following old traditions, as in the Hadith where stories and incidents connected to the life of the great Prophet, who had a fondness for cats, were preserved and passed on from generation to generation, cats were loved. When a fifteenth century scholar like al-Suyuti writes that 'I have a cat whose foot-pads I dye with henna/ before I put henna on my own newborns. Then I tie cowrie shells to her collar/to repel the harm of evil eyes', people remember. As is remembered the name of a companion of the Prophet, Abu Huraira ('father of little cats') for his love of cats, while the Hadith speaks of the Prophet's own pet cat—Muezza by name—who was, once, sleeping on a sleeve of his great robe when the call for prayer came; he cut off that sleeve before picking up the robe, leaving her sleeping rather than disturbing her.

The view in Islam apart, running against the grain of the general attitude towards cats, as reflected in stories, there were also instances of great respect, and use, for cats in certain quarters. At one of the holiest shrines in India, the Sri Venkateswara temple at Tirumala in the Andhra area, the civet cat has been bred for generations on account of the fragrance derived from its '*punugo*' secretion that comes from its perineal gland which is used for the *abhishekam* ceremony of the Lord to whom the temple is dedicated. It is another matter that a case is being fought in a higher court whether the temple has the right to breed these cats on its premises while the animal falls under the Wild Life Protection Act. In Bengal, and Odisha, one of the deities widely worshipped by women, especially those who are pregnant, is Shashti who has a cat for her vehicle. She is the protectress of small children, it is believed, and several stories, current about her, and her interventions, are recited among women's groups. In major parts of North India, the belief persists that if you kill a cat by mistake, the only way to atone for that sin is to get a cat image cast in gold or silver and make an offering of it at a temple.

With all these practices and beliefs around, are there—a fair question—inconsistencies in our attitude towards cats, in the view we take of them? But in our land inconsistencies are nothing to be surprised about: we live with, even thrive on, them. But also, on the one hand one reminds oneself of contradictions being a natural human condition perhaps, and on the other the view that Walt Whitman took: 'Do I contradict myself?/Very well, then I contradict myself,/(I am large. I contain multitudes.)' In a country as large and as diverse as India, one knows that coexistence is the rule rather than an exception. 'You, Lord, are large, and you are small', an ancient and widely recited Sanskrit hymn reads: 'you are thin, and you are thick; you are filled with qualities, and you are devoid of them.' Nothing can define You, in other words, to the exclusion of everything else.

As in India, interestingly, there is nothing uniform in the way cats were seen, or regarded, as was the case, one finds, in many other cultures too. This may not be the place to go into the history of the cat everywhere, for the feline having been featured in the history of many nations, and being the subject of legend, its relationship to humans is old and stretches back over 9,500 years. However, a brief, very brief, look at the theme might put things into some kind of perspective. One naturally begins with ancient Egypt where, according to most accounts, the cat was first domesticated. It was the feline's predatory habit, which included hunting mice and rats, that came to the rescue of a whole generation of Egyptians who were staring at a famine because their granaries were being destroyed and emptied by attacking rodents. Once the cats took over, things changed drastically and the animal was accorded a god-like status. Killing a cat there became punishable by death, and men would shave off their eyebrows as a sign of mourning when their cat died. The cult of Bastet, the goddess with the body of a woman, and the head of a cat, was everywhere. There also grew up the cult of Mafdet who was represented as a snake-killing goddess who protected the Pharaoh in his royal palace, as also the large number of Nile-dwellers whose lives used to be lived in fear of snakes. In the average household in ancient Egypt the cat emerged as both an object of worship and an adored pet, 'frequently adorned with jewelled necklaces and gold earrings'.

Things were different in the ancient Hebrew world where the cat was as mistrusted as the Egyptians under whose rule the communities had suffered for interminably long periods of time. Occult practices followed for keeping the cat, linked as she was with 'demonism', were kept at bay. In the Bible, there is, intriguingly, no mention of cats even though later traditions speak of Christ's love of cats, or of cats being impregnated via the ear.

Domestic cats were probably first introduced to Greece in the fifth century BCE by seafaring people, as one reads, and the earliest unmistakable evidence of the Greeks having domestic cats comes from two coins which were discovered not long ago.

Housecats seem to have been extremely rare among the ancient Greeks and Romans, and, unlike in India, they are rarely mentioned in ancient Greek literature. Whatever references are found speak of them with strong reservations. Aristotle remarked somewhere that 'female cats are naturally lecherous'; Plutarch found them clean as animals; Pliny linked them with lust, and Aesop with deviousness and cunning. Hecate was a Greek goddess whose symbol was the black cat, and she was thought to be an omen of death. Some conflation took place at some point of time and the legends about the goddess Artemis, who was associated with cats, began being grafted on to the Virgin Mary. An Italian folk story asserted that the same night that Mary gave birth to Jesus, a cat in Bethlehem gave birth to a kitten.

The cat had a harrowing time in medieval France, however, the animal being cast in the satanic image. The witchcraft purges of cats in Europe wiped out vast numbers of cats even as Pope Gregory IX (1227–41) railed against people for 'kissing Lucifer in the form of a black cat', these cats being 'the colour of evil and shame'. A bishop, writing in 1233, said: 'Lucifer is permitted (by God) to appear to his worshippers and adorers in the form of a black cat or toad and to demand kisses from them: whether as a cat, abominably under the tail, or as a toad, horribly on the mouth.' It could not have been expressed more strongly and it was this view that was reflected in Germanic and Eastern European lore. Cat was Darkness and the Devil.

But things turned. The Enlightenment of the eighteenth century had much to do with the change, reason prevailing over superstition. The power of the Church over people was on the decline and, during the Victorian Age, cats were 'again elevated close to the previous high standing they had enjoyed in ancient Egypt'. Queen Victoria set a trend by adopting two Blue Persians who became 'members of the court'. Soon the trend spread to the United States, popular magazines having much to do with it, publishing stories in which cats were loved and loved people in return. There emerged legions of cat lovers and when Charles Dickens and Mark Twain, William Wordsworth and John Keats, Thomas Hardy and Lewis Carroll spoke ecstatically of their cats, everyone knew that the wind had changed. Legions of people—writers, scientists, public men—belong to the same category: from Mark Twain to Albert Schweitzer, T. S. Eliot to Ernest Hemingway, Jean Cocteau to James Mason. If one were to trust the numbers published, at last count, Japan has 7.25 million cat owners; Germany and UK about the same number, France 9.5 million, Brazil and Russia 12.5 each, USA 76.5 million, and China 53 million.

Closer to home, things never went out of hand as far as attitudes towards cats go. In Buddhism, in general, and the Buddhist countries in Southeast Asia, cats were viewed with respect, if not exactly loved in each second household. In Tibetan monasteries cats roam about freely, as noted before; in Burma there always was a temple guarded by one hundred long-haired cats with yellow eyes, for into their bodies, according to belief, passed the souls of dead priests. A Thai legend maintains that Mara, Prince of Demons, sent a plague of rats to devour the Holy Buddhist scriptures, and at that moment the Buddha created the first cat in the world which chased the rats away and saved the scriptures. About the famous Siamese cats, it is said that these cats were kept, in earlier times, to serve as repositories in which to keep the transmigrating souls of Siamese royalty. They resided only in the Royal Palace in Bangkok—hence their earlier name, the Royal Palace Cats—and it is said that they were the product of a union between an albino domestic cat belonging to the king and an Egyptian or, some say, a black temple cat.

In Islam again, the affection bordering upon reverence for cats is all too well known and it comes for the most part from the view that the great Prophet personally took of the feline. The traditions preserved in the *Hadith*—a cat saving the sleeping Prophet from a snake that was slithering up to him: the Prophet chiding a woman who did not feed her cat properly allowing it nearly to starve; his cutting off a sleeve of his great robe so as not to disturb his cat that was sleeping on it; the Prophet's wife, Aisha, speaking with great affection of her cat; and so on—have been a lesson and a model to follow in the entire Islamic world.

This is the way then it has been in our own land seen as she is almost as a human, differences of approach, seemingly irreconcilable views of the feline, notwithstanding. So much of it is reflected in our texts and our stories, but there have been no purges, no great upheavals. For most people, a cat's a cat, and that's that.

A possible source to which one can turn for getting the 'Indian view' of cats is—apart from texts of course—paintings. Interestingly—oddly perhaps—one does not even think, ordinarily, of cats as a subject for painters in India, very unlike the Western world where, the Renaissance onwards, one can be smothered by material: young girls playing with or having themselves portrayed hugging cats; cats roaming around in plush interiors, unconcerned; witnessing the *alltag* of life with curiosity; providing company to seniors; hiding, getting up on rooftops, climbing up and climbing down stairs, clambering onto shoulders. But, with effort, one can put together at least a small gallery of works in which they are there, virtually unnoticed but there. Very rarely do we see them 'in profound meditation' here, or 'engaged in rapt attention' as T. S. Eliot often thought he saw them. But they are seen, from time to time, in 'illustrations' of stories woven around their character, or in paintings in which they figure: planning, strategizing, pretending, thieving; or, at other times, keeping watch, nestling against soft bosoms, reading their masters' expressions. Of great interest in this context, and not easily explicable, is the fact that we see them often in copies of European paintings, especially of Biblical themes, that Mughal masters made in numbers. The original of which a copy, or version, was made might not have even a trace of a cat and yet, when that copy, or version, was made, a cat comes in: soft-footedly sometimes, brashly at others. The Madonna might be feeding the child Christ at her breast and a cat would be looking; David and Bathsheba might be having a conversation under a tree, and a cat could be seen brushing one person's leg or another's; preparations might be in the process of being made for taking the infant Jesus on the fortieth day to the temple at Jerusalem, and a cat might come in, becoming with perfect ease a part of the group; and so on. This leaves one a trifle puzzled for if the painters were really interested in cats per se, why would they not paint them as subjects proper, much as a deer or a sheep, a hawk or a zebra were? At the same time if cats were not ordinarily parts of royal households for which the painters often worked, where might they have seen and studied them? It has been suggested that while copying, or producing a version, of a painting with a Biblical theme, they might have thought of changing things a bit, even 'stating' that cats roaming around exalted figures would make those scenes look more natural, as if what was happening was not up in the heavens somewhere but it happened here, around ourselves. Where—another question—might the painters have had the chance to observe domestic cats? Around priests in Christian monasteries—in Agra or Lahore or Goa—to which they might have secured access through their royal patrons for going and seeing original European works? It is hard to know.

In more recent times, there is some turning to cats for 'portraying' them. The painters of Kalighat—ever keen on capturing scenes from ordinary life—apparently found them rich material:

very often rendering them as having stolen a fish or a prawn and then shown sitting boldly, wearing a sacred tilak mark on their forehead, in a veiled reference to holy men wearing pretence as a garment. Many others followed, of course.

A CLUTCH OF CAT STORIES

For some of the earliest references to cats—as far as stories featuring them are concerned—one turns to the Jatakas (literally, 'birth stories'), a voluminous body of literature which mainly concern the previous births of Gautama Buddha in both human and animal form. In these stories, the future Buddha may appear as a king, an outcast, a deva, an animal, but, in whatever form, he exhibits some virtue that the tale thereby commends. Often, the Jataka Tales include an extensive cast of characters who interact and get into various kinds of trouble—whereupon the Buddha character intervenes to resolve all the problems and bring about a happy ending. The tales are a massive collection of Buddhist folklore. Originally written in Pali, and dating to at least 380 BCE, these are stories which have travelled afar.

The Buddha tells a tale known as the 'Babbu Jataka'.

This story was told by the Master while at Jetavana, about the precept respecting Kana's mother. She was a lay-sister at Savatthi known only as Kana's mother, who had entered the Paths of Salvation and was of the Elect. Her daughter Kana was married to a husband of the same caste in another village, and some errand or other made her go to see her mother. A few days went by, and her husband sent a messenger to say he wished her to come back. The girl asked her mother whether she should go, and the mother said she could not go back empty-handed after so long an absence, and set about making a cake. Just then up came a Brother going his round for alms, and the mother sat him down to the cake she had just baked. Away he went and told another Brother, who came up just in time to get the second cake that was baked for the daughter to take home with her. He told a third, and the third told a fourth, and so each fresh cake was taken by a fresh comer. The result of this was that the daughter did not start on her way home, and the husband sent a second and a third messenger after her. And the message he sent by the third was that if his wife did not come back, he would get another wife. And each message had exactly the same result. So the husband took another wife, and at the news his former wife fell a-weeping. Knowing all this, the Master put on his robes early in the morning and went with his alms bowl to the house of Kana's mother and sat down on the seat set for him. Then he asked why the daughter was crying, and, being told, spoke words of consolation to the mother, and arose and went back to the monastery.

Now the Brethren came to know how Kana had been stopped three times from going back to her husband owing to the action of the four Brothers; and one day they met in the Hall of Truth and began to talk about the matter. The Master came into the hall and asked what they were discussing, and they told him. 'Brethren,' said he, 'think not this is the first time those four Brothers have brought sorrow on Kana's mother by eating of her store; they did the like in days gone by too.' So saying he told this story of the past.

At this point begins another story within the earlier story.

Once upon a time when Brahmadatta was reigning in Benares, the Bodhisattva was born a stonecutter, and growing up became expert in working stones. Now in the Kashi country there dwelt a very rich merchant who had amassed forty crores in gold. And when his wife died, so strong was her love of money that she was reborn a mouse and dwelt over the treasure. And one by one the whole family died, including the merchant himself. Likewise the village became deserted and forlorn. At the time of our story the Bodhisattva was quarrying and shaping stones on the site of this deserted village; and the mouse often used to see him as she ran about to find food. At last she fell in love with him; and, bethinking her how the secret of all her vast wealth would die with her, she conceived the idea of enjoying it with him. So one day she came to the Bodhisattva with a coin in her mouth. Seeing this, he spoke to her kindly, and said, 'Mother, what has brought you here with this coin?'

'It is for you to lay out for yourself, and to buy meat with for me as well, my son.'

Nowise loth, he took the money and spent a halfpenny of it on meat which he brought to the mouse, who departed and ate to her heart's content. And this went on, the mouse giving the Bodhisattva a coin every day, and he in return supplying her with meat. But it fell out one day that the mouse was caught by a cat.

'Don't kill me,' said the mouse.

'Why not?' said the cat. 'I'm as hungry as can be, and really must kill you to allay the pangs.'

'First, tell me whether you're always hungry, or only hungry today.'

'Oh, every day finds me hungry again.'

'Well then, if this be so, I will find you always meat; only let me go.'

'Mind you do then,' said the cat, and let the mouse go.

As a consequence of this the mouse had to divide the supplies of meat she got from the Bodhisattva into two portions and gave one half to the cat, keeping the other for herself.

Now, as luck would have it, the same mouse was caught another day by a second cat and had to purchase her release on the same terms. So now the daily food was divided into three portions. And when a third cat caught the mouse and a like arrangement had to be made, the supply was divided into four portions. And later a fourth cat caught her, and the food had to be divided among five, so that the mouse, reduced to such short commons, grew so thin as to be nothing but skin and bone. Remarking how emaciated his friend was getting, the Bodhisattva asked the reason. Then the mouse told him all that had befallen her.

'Why didn't you tell me all this before?' said the Bodhisattva. 'Cheer up, I'll help you out of your troubles.'

So he took a block of the purest crystal and scooped out a cavity in it and made the mouse get inside. 'Now stay here,' said he, 'and don't fail to fiercely threaten and revile all who come near.'

So the mouse crept into the crystal cell and waited. Up came one of the cats and demanded his meat. 'Away, vile grimalkin,' said the mouse, 'why should I supply you? Go home and eat your kittens!'

Infuriated at these words, and never suspecting the mouse to be inside the crystal, the cat sprang at the mouse to eat her up; and so furious was its spring that it broke the walls of its chest and its eyes stared from its head. So that cat died and its carcass tumbled down out of sight. And the like fate in turn befell all four cats. And ever after the grateful mouse brought the Bodhisattva two or three coins instead of one as before, and by degrees she thus gave him the whole of the hoard. In unbroken friendship the two lived together, till their lives ended and they passed away to fare according to their deserts.

His lesson ended, the Master identified the birth by saying, 'These four Brethren were the four cats of those days, Kana's mother was the mouse, and I the stonecutter.'

The cats do not come out too well from this story, and it is the Bodhisattva himself who has to intervene in order to restore some kind of order to things. How the story got the name 'Babbu Jataka' is not easy to understand, but this is the manner in which the Jataka Tales proceed. A situation called paccuppannavatthu, or 'story of the present', is first described and, in order to place it in perspective, the Bodhisattva tells another story, speaking of himself in a different form—animal or bird, or human being—from which a clear moral can be drawn. In this case he was the stonecutter who thought of a stratagem to save the poor mouse from predatory cats.

Another tale, named the 'Kukkuta Jataka', proceeds using much the same framework.

The Master told this tale in Jetavana, concerning a Brother who longed for the world. The Master asked him, 'Why do you long for the world?'

'Lord, through passion, for I saw a woman adorned.'

'Brother, women are like cats, deceiving and cajoling to bring to ruin one who has come into their power,' so he told an old tale.

Once upon a time when Brahmadatta was king in Benares,

Bodhisattva was born as a cock and lived in the forest with a retinue of many hundred cocks. Not far away lived a she-cat: and she deceived by devices the other cocks except the Bodhisattva and ate them: but the Bodhisattva did not fall into her power. She thought, 'This cock is very crafty, but he knows not that I am crafty and skilful in device: it is good that I cajole him, saying, "I will be your wife," and so eat him when he comes into my power.' She went to the root of the tree where he perched, and in a speech preceded by praise of his beauty, she spoke the first stanza:

Much poetry between the characters flows from this point onwards, stanza matched by stanza.

Bird with wings that flash so gaily, crest that droops so gracefully,
I will be your wife for nothing, leave the bough and come to me.

The Bodhisattva, hearing her, thought, 'She has eaten all my relatives; now she wishes to cajole me and eat me: I will get rid of her.' So he spoke the second stanza:

Lady fair and winning, you have four feet, I have only two:
Beasts and birds should never marry: for some other husband sue.

Then she thought, 'He is exceedingly crafty; by some device or other I will deceive him and eat him'; so she spoke the third stanza:

I will bring thee youth and beauty, pleasant speech and courtesy:
Honoured wife or simple slave-girl, at thy pleasure deal with me.

Then the Bodhisattva thought, 'It is best to revile her and drive her away,' so he spoke the fourth stanza:

Thou hast drunk my kindred's blood, and robbed and slain them cruelly:

'Honoured wife'! there is no honour in your heart when wooing me.

She was driven away and did not endure to look at him again.

So when they see a hero, women sly,
(Compare the cat and cock,) to tempt him try.
He that to great occasion fails to rise
'Neath foeman's feet in sorrow prostrate lies.
One prompt a crisis in his fate to see,
As cock from cat, escapes his enemy.

These are stanzas inspired by *Perfect Wisdom.*

His lesson ended, the Master declared the Truths and identified the Birth: after the Truths, the backsliding Brother was established in the fruition of the First Path: 'At that time the cock was myself.'

One can see that neither the cat nor women in general fare too well in this tale.

The Bilari—also called the 'Bilarivrata Jataka'—is told in two versions sometimes. The treacherous character in it is a jackal in one version, and a cat in another. The emphasis in the fuller name of the Jataka is on the word vrata—Pali version of Sanskrit vrata, meaning 'vow'. The reference here is to the usage of the term vidala-vrata or bilari-vrata—literally 'cat vow'—which stands essentially for 'hypocrisy', a charge often flung at the opponent in discussion or argument. A man who always displays the banner of righteousness and yet is greedy and deceitful, who deludes the world, who is given to violence, and beguiles everybody should be viewed as one who observes the 'cat-vow' is how it is defined: a charge incidentally which, in the Mahabharata, Duryodhana lays on the far more upright Yudhishthira. The story that follows—featuring a cat, not a jackal, as the treacherous character—helps explain the usage.

This story was told by the Teacher while at Jetavana, about a deceitful person. When the monk's deceit was reported to him, the Teacher said: 'This is not the first time he has shown himself a deceitful person; he was just the same in times gone by.' So saying he told this story of the past.

In the past when Brahmadatta was reigning in Benares, the Bodhisattva was born a rat, perfect in wisdom, and as big as a young boar. He had his dwelling in the forest and many hundreds of other rats owned his sway.

Now there was a roving cat who espied this troop of rats and fell to scheming how to beguile and eat them. And he took up his stand near their home with his face to the sun, snuffing up the wind, and standing on one leg. Seeing this when out on his road in quest of food, the Bodhisattva conceived the cat to be a saintly being, and went up and asked his name.

'Dhammika [Righteous] is my name,' said the cat.

'Why do you stand only on one leg?'

'Because if I stood on all four at once, the earth could not bear my weight. That is why I stand on one leg only.'

'And why do you keep your mouth open?'

'To eat the air. I live on air; it is my only food.'

'And why do you face the sun?'

'To worship him.'

'What uprightness!' thought the Bodhisattva, and thenceforward he made a point of going, attended by the other rats, to pay his respects morning and evening to the saintly cat. And when the rats were leaving, the cat seized and devoured the hindermost one of them, wiped his lips, and looked as though nothing had happened.

This is the point where the phrase equating 'cat's vow' with complete hypocrisy comes in: perhaps even originated.

In consequence of this the rats grew fewer and fewer, till they noticed the gaps in their ranks, and wondering why this was so, asked the Bodhisattva the reason. He could not make it out, but suspecting the cat, resolved to put him to the test. So next day he let the other rats go out first and himself brought up the rear. The cat made a spring on the Bodhisattva who, seeing him coming, faced round and cried, 'So this is your saintliness, you deceitful person and rascal!' And he repeated the following verse:

> *Yo ve Dhammam dhajam katva, nigulho papam-acare,*
> *Vissasayitva bhūtani, bilaram nama tam vatan-ti.*
>
> He who raises the flag of Dhamma, and conceals his wrongdoing, from beings who have confidence, that vow is known as a cat's vow.

So saying, the king of the rats sprang at the cat's throat and bit his windpipe asunder just under the jaw, so that he died. Back trooped the other rats and gobbled up the body of the cat with a 'crunch, crunch, crunch', that is to say, the foremost of them did, for they say there was none left for the last-comers. And ever after the rats lived happily in peace and quiet.

His lesson ended, the Teacher made the connection by saying: 'This hypocritical monk was the cat of those days, and I the king of the rats.'

This is not the only time that one comes upon one version or the other of the story of a cat putting on the garb of a saintly person and hiding under it her evil intent. The verse towards the end, beginning with the words 'Yo dhammam...' turns into a phrase of great use.

Similar, but not exactly alike, is the core of a folk tale told in the Buddhist community of Tibet: derived almost certainly from a Jataka tale. This is how it has been recorded.

Once upon a time there was a cat who lived in a large farmhouse in which there were a great number of mice. For many years the cat found no difficulty in catching as many mice as she wanted to eat, and she lived a very peaceful and pleasant life. But as time passed on, she found that she was growing old and infirm, and that it was becoming more and more difficult for her to catch the same number of mice as before; so after thinking very carefully about what was the best thing to do, she called all the mice together one day, and after promising not to touch them, she addressed them as follows:

'Oh, mice!' said she, 'I have called you together in order to say something to you. The fact is that I have led a very wicked life, and now, in my old age, I repent of having caused you all so much inconvenience and annoyance. So I am going to turn over a new leaf. It is my intention now to give myself up entirely to religious contemplation and no longer molest you, so henceforth you are at liberty to run about as freely as you will without fear of me. All I ask of you is that twice every day you should all file past me in procession and each one make an obeisance as you pass me by, as a token of your gratitude to me for my kindness.'

When the mice heard this they were greatly pleased, for they thought that now, at last, they would be free from all danger from their former enemy, the cat. So they very thankfully promised to fulfil the cat's conditions, and agreed that they would file past her and make a salaam twice every day.

So when evening came the cat took her seat on a cushion at one end of the room, and the mice all went by in single file, each one making a profound salaam as it passed.

One can almost predict at this point of the narrative what is going to follow. But things take a surprising turn.

Now the cunning old cat had arranged this little plan very carefully with an object of her own; for, as soon as the procession had all passed by with the exception of one little mouse, she suddenly seized the last mouse in her claws without anybody else noticing what had happened, and devoured it at her leisure. And so twice every day, she seized the last mouse of the series, and for a long time lived very comfortably without any trouble at all in catching her mice, and without any of the mice realizing what was happening.

Now it happened that amongst these mice there were two friends, whose names were Rambe and Ambe, who were very much attached to one another. Now these two were much cleverer and more cunning than most of the others, and after a few days they noticed that the number of mice in the house seemed to be decreasing, inspite of the fact that the cat had promised not to kill any more. So they put their heads together and arranged a little plan for future processions. They agreed that Rambe was always to walk at the very front of the procession of the mice, and Ambe was to bring up the rear, and that all the time the procession was passing, Rambe was to call to Ambe, and Ambe to answer Rambe at frequent intervals. So next evening, when the procession started as usual, Rambe marched along in front, and Ambe took up his position last of all.

As soon as Rambe had passed the cushion where the cat was seated and had made his salaam, he called out in a shrill voice, "Where are you, Brother Ambe?"

'Here I am, Brother Rambe,' squeaked the other from the rear of the procession.

And so they went on calling out and answering one another until they had all filed past the cat, who had not dared to touch Ambe as long as his brother kept calling to him.

The cat was naturally very much annoyed at having to go hungry that evening, and felt very cross all night. But she thought it was only an accident which had brought one of the two friends to the front and one to the rear of the procession, and she hoped to make up for her enforced abstinence by finding a particularly fat mouse at the end of the procession next morning. What, then, was her amazement and disgust when she found that on the following morning the very same arrangement had been made, and that Rambe called to Ambe, and Ambe answered Rambe until all the mice had passed her by, and so, for the second time, she was foiled of her meal. However, she disguised her feelings of anger and decided to give the mice one more trial; so in the evening she took her seat as usual on the cushion and waited for the mice to appear.

Meanwhile, Rambe and Ambe had warned the other mice to be on the lookout, and to be ready to take flight the moment the cat showed any appearance of anger. At the appointed time the procession started as usual, and as soon as Rambe had passed the cat he squeaked out, 'Where are you, Brother Ambe?'

'Here I am, Brother Rambe,' came the shrill voice from the rear.

This was more than the cat could stand. She made a fierce leap right into the middle of the mice, who, however, were thoroughly prepared for her, and in an instant, scuttled off in every direction to their holes. And before the cat had time to catch a single one, the room was empty and not a sign of a mouse was to be seen anywhere.

After this the mice were very careful not to put any further trust in the treacherous cat, who soon after died of starvation owing to her being unable to procure any of her customary food. But Rambe and Ambe lived for many years, and were held in high honour and esteem by all the other mice in the community.

When one moves into the delightful world that Pandit Vishnu Sharma conjured into being with his Panchatantra *which goes back to the early centuries of the Common Era—and bears the widely believed name of the author of that ancient classic—the flavour of the tales changes. For it is a world, as someone said, 'of philosophy and merriment and mirth' in which through five major sections, each containing sets of stories, lessons are taught and learnt, questions raised and answered. In the third section named 'Of Crows and Owls' occurs a story in which the cat is seen as an unremitting treacherous being, capable of serving only her own end at everyone else's expense. The stories, as has been remarked, travelled far and wide and went through transformations in the process. In the Eastern world alone, it moved from Sanskrit to Pehlavi and on to Arabic and Persian, and versions of the* Panchatantra *appeared, one after another, one of the most celebrated being the fifteenth-century work, the* Anwar-i Suhayli*—named both after a vizier of Sultan Husain Mirza Bayqara, Ahmed Suhaily, and after the heavenly body called Suhail or Canopus—written by the scholar Husain Waiz Kashifi. Kashifi's style followed the rich Persian tradition of flowery language—he speaks of the original text as 'an orchard, the branches of the hidden meanings of which are made bright with the flowers, and environs of rose-garden of which are aromatized and* *perfumed with gentle breezes'—and peripheral information, but it has a very distinct flavour of its own: poetic on the one hand and philosophical on the other. Without changing a word from the early English translation by the English orientalist Edward Eastwick, one story is gone into here. In the larger context of constant exchanges between an owl and the crows, one character narrates this to others in the assembly, as a cautionary tale. 'A Cat's Judgement' is how the story is generally named.*

At one time (the narrator says) I was myself living in a certain tree. And beneath the same tree dwelt another bird, a partridge. So by virtue of our near neighbourhood there sprang up between us a firm friendship. Every day after taking our meals and airings we spent the evening hours in a round of amusements, such as repeating witty sayings, telling tales from the old storybooks, solving puzzles and conundrums, or exchanging presents.

One day the partridge went foraging with other birds to a spot where the rice was ripe and abundant, and he did not return at nightfall. Of course, I missed him greatly and I thought: 'Alas! Why does not my friend the partridge come home tonight? I am much afraid he is caught in some trap, or has even been killed.' And many days passed while I grieved in this way.

Now one evening a rabbit named Speedy made himself at home in the partridge's old nest in the hole. Nor did I say him nay, for I despaired of seeing the partridge again.

However, one fine day the partridge, who had grown extremely plump from eating rice, remembered his old home and returned. This, indeed, is not to be wondered at.

No mortal has such joy, although
In heaven's fields he roam,
As in his city, in his land,
And in his humble home.

Now when he saw the rabbit in the hole, he said reproachfully: 'Come now, rabbit, you have done a shabby thing in occupying my apartment. Please begone, and lose no time about it.'

'You fool!' said the rabbit, 'don't you know that a dwelling is yours only while you occupy it?'

'Very well, then,' said the partridge, 'suppose we ask the neighbours. For, to give you a legal quotation,

For ownership of cisterns, tanks,
Wells, groves, and houses, too,
The neighbours' testimony goes
Such is the legal view.
And again:
When house or field or well or grove
Or land is in dispute,
A neighbour's testimony is
Decisive of the suit.'

Then the rabbit said: 'You fool! Are you ignorant of the consecrated tradition which says:

Suppose beside your neighbour you
For ten long years abide,
What weight have learned arguments?
Eyewitnesses decide.
Fool! Fool! Did you never hear the dictum of the sage Narada?
The title to possession is
A ten years' habitation
With men. But with the birds and beasts
Mere present occupation.

'Hence, even supposing this apartment to be yours, still it was unoccupied when I moved in, and now it is mine.'

'Well, well!' replied the partridge, 'if you appeal to consecrated tradition, come with me, and we will consult the specialists. It shall be yours or mine according to their decision.'

'Very well,' said the other, and together they started off to have their suit decided. I, too, was at their heels, out of curiosity.

'I will just see what comes of all this,' I said to myself.

Now they had not travelled far when the rabbit asked the

partridge: 'My good fellow, who is to pass judgment on our disagreement?'

And the partridge answered: 'On a sandbank by the sacred Ganga—where there is sweet music from the dancing waves that intercross and break when the water is swept by nimble breezes—there dwells a tomcat whose name is Curd-ear (Dadhikarna). He abides unshaken in his vow of penance and self-denial, and character has begotten compassion.'

But when the rabbit spied the cat, his soul staggered with terror, and he said: 'No, no! He is a seedy rascal. You must have heard the proverb:

Oh, never trust a rogue for all
His pharisaic puzzling:
At holy shrines some saints are found
Quite capable of guzzling.'

Upon hearing this, Curd-ear, whose manner of life had been assumed for the purpose of making an easy livelihood, desired to win their confidence. He therefore gazed straight at the sun, stood on his hind legs, lifted his forepaws, blinked his eyes, and in order to deceive them by pious sentiments, delivered the following moral discourse. 'Alas! Alas! All is vanity. This fragile life passes in a moment. Union with the beloved is an empty dream. Family endearments are a conjurer's trick. But for the moral law, there would be no escape. Oh, listen to the Scripture!

Each transitory day, O man,
To moral living give;
Else, like the blacksmith's bellows, you
Suck air, but do not live.

And furthermore:

Non-moral learning is a curse,
A dog's tail, nothing less,
That does not save from flies and fleas,
Nor cover nakedness.

And yet again:

A rotten ear among the wheat,
Among the birds a bat,
Is he who spurns the moral law;
The merest living gnat.
The flowers and fruit are better than the tree;
Better than curds is butter said to be;
Better than oil-cake, oil that trickles free;
Better than mortal man, morality.
The praise of constant steadfastness
Some wise professors sing;
But moral earnestness is swift,
Though many fetters cling.
Forget your prosings manifold;
The moral law is briefly told:
To help your neighbour—this is good;
To injure him is devilhood.

Having listened to this moral discourse, the rabbit said: 'Friend partridge, here on the riverbank is the saint who expounds the moral law. Let us ask him.'

But the partridge said: 'After all, he is our natural enemy. Let us ask him from a distance.'

So together they began to question him: 'O holy moralist, a dispute has arisen between us. Pray give judgment in accordance with the moral law. And whichever of us is found to speak falsely, him you may eat.'

'Dear friends,' said the cat, 'I implore you not to speak thus. My soul abhors every act of cruelty, that street-sign pointing to hell. Surely, you know the Scripture:

The holy first commandment runs
Not harsh, but kindly be—
And therefore lavish mercy on
Mosquito, louse, and flea.
Why speak of hurting innocence?
For he, with purpose fell

Who injures even noxious beasts,
Is plunged in ghastly hell.'

'Nay, even those who slay living creatures in the act of sacrifice are befuddled, and their hermeneutic theology is at fault. And if you object to me the passage, "One should sacrifice with goats", in that passage the word "goats" signifies grain that has aged seven years. "Go, oats"—such is the true exegesis. And then, consider the passage:

If he who cuts down trees or cattle,
Or makes a bloody slime in battle,
Should thereby win to heaven-well
Who (let me ask you) goes to hell?

'No, no. I shall eat nobody. However, I am somewhat old and do not readily distinguish your voices from a distance. So how am I to determine winner and loser? In view of this, pray draw near and make me acquainted with the case. Then I can pronounce a judgment that discriminates the essence of the matter, and thus causes no impediment in my march to the other world. You know the stanza:

If any man, from pride or greed,
Timidity or wrath,
Judge falsely, he has set his foot
On hell's down-sloping path.

And again:

Who wrongs a sheep, slays kinsmen five;
Who wrongs a cow, slays ten;
A hundred die for maidens wronged;
A thousand die for men.

'Therefore confide in me and speak clearly at the edge of my ear.'

Why spin it out? That seedy rogue won their trust so fully that both drew near him. Then, of course, he seized them simultaneously, one with his paw, the other with the saw of his teeth. And when they were dead, he ate them both.

And that is why I say: A seedy umpire is not very...
and the rest of it.

A surprising tale comes from the tenth century Sanskrit classic, the Kathasaritsagara*—surprising because it speaks of a small group of people (even if designated in the story itself as especially 'foolish') who did not know what a cat—marjara in Sanskrit—looked like! It is the story of the foolish teacher, the foolish pupils, and a cat.*

In Ujjayini there lived in a convent a foolish teacher. And he could not sleep, because mice troubled him at night. And wearied with this infliction, he told the whole story to a friend. The friend, who was a Brahman, said to that teacher, 'You must set up a cat, it will eat the mice.'

The teacher said, 'What sort of creature is a cat? Where can one be found? I never came across one.' When the teacher said this, the friend replied, 'Its eyes are like glass, its colour is a brownish grey, it has a hairy skin on its back, and it wanders about in roads. So, my friend, you must quickly discover a cat by these signs and have one brought.'

After his friend had said this, he went home. Then that foolish teacher said to his pupils, 'You have been present and heard all the distinguishing marks of a cat. So look about for a cat, such as you have heard described, in the roads here.' Accordingly, the pupils went and searched hither and thither, but they did not find a cat anywhere.

Then at last they saw a Brahman boy coming from the opening of a road, his eyes were like glass, his colour brownish grey, and he wore on his back a hairy antelope skin. And when they saw him they said, 'Here we have got the cat according to the description.' So they seized him, and took him to their teacher. Their teacher also observed that he had got the characteristics mentioned by his friend; so he placed him in the convent at night. And the silly boy himself believed that he was a cat, when he heard the description that those fools gave of the animal. Now it happened that the silly boy was a pupil of the Brahman, who out of friendship gave the teacher the description of the cat. And that Brahman came in the morning, and, seeing the boy in the convent, said to those fools, 'Who brought this fellow here?'

The teacher and his foolish pupils answered, 'We brought him here as a cat, according to the description which we heard from you.' Then the Brahman laughed and said, 'There is considerable difference between a stupid human being, and a cat, which is an animal with four feet and a tail.' When the foolish fellows heard this, they let the boy go and said, 'So let us go and search again for a cat such as has been now described to us.' And the people laughed at those fools.

The story ends here, but not before it promises another story about another set of fools.

'Ignorance makes everyone ridiculous. You have heard of the fools and their cat, now hear the story of another set of fools.'

Remarkable as it is, a story—long, and told in seductive detail—involving a cat and other animals or characters occurs in the Shanti Parva section of that great epic, the Mahabharata. The context? Yudhishthira, most senior among the Pandava brothers, approaches Bhishma, the grandsire, seeking counsel, for he is 'firmly wedded to the truth and having all his senses under control'. The essence of the question is: 'what does one do when one is surrounded by foes on all sides?' The old Bhishma does not address the question directly, at least to begin with, but decides to tell Yudhishthira a story from which to draw what lessons he can. On the part of the animals that feature in the story there is cogitation, nervousness, negotiation, compromise, shrewd calculation which, in the original, read like remarkable lessons in statecraft. This story travelled into other texts in a curtailed or edited version in later years, including in the eighth century Arabic classic, Kalila wa Dimna, *by Ibn-al Muqaffa. A considerably shortened version, in which the flavour of the original Sanskrit is sadly lost—one misses for instance Bhishma being addressed as 'O Bull of Bharata's race' by the deeply respectful Yudhishthira—follows.*

'...what has been laid down in the scriptures,' he asks, 'about the manner in which a king should conduct himself when he is assailed by many foes. When a king falls into distress, a large number of foes, provoked by his past acts, range themselves against him and seek to vanquish him. How may, a king, weak and alone, succeed in holding up his head when he is challenged on all sides by many powerful kings leagued together?'

Bhishma said, 'O Yudhishthira, this question is certainly worthy of thee.... In seasons of distress...a foe becomes a friend and a friend also becomes a foe. One should make peace with even one's foes, when, O Bharata, one's life cannot otherwise be saved. In this connection is cited the old story of the discourse between a cat and a mouse at the foot of a banyan.'

'There was a large banyan in the midst of an extensive forest...' *is how the long story begins.* It stood in the midst of the forest, and animals of diverse species lived on it. A mouse of great wisdom, named Palita, lived at the foot of that tree, having made a hole there with a hundred outlets. On the branches of the tree there lived a cat, of the name of Lomasa, daily devouring a large number of birds....

There was also a Chandala hunter living nearby, who used to set up traps made of net every evening. Various animals would fall into traps each night, and the Chandala would return the next morning to collect his nets and catch.

One night, the cat Lomasa 'in a moment of heedlessness got caught' in one of the traps. Seeing this agreeable sight—his natural enemy caught in a trap—the mouse, Palita, 'aided by proper means and intelligence', came out of his hole and started feasting on a piece of meat left behind by the hunter. The mouse even got upon the trapped cat that lay helpless. Suddenly, the mouse Palita observed two threats—a mongoose by the name Harita which had arrived there attracted by the mouse's scent, and an owl Chandraka of sharp beaks that lay perched on one of the tree's branches.

The mouse here is guided by the principle that 'it is better to have a learned person for an enemy than a fool for a foe'. The cogitation, the reasoning, on the part of the mouse, is quite remarkable and is put in the original text in these words.

Warding off even innumerable dangers by hundreds of means, one should always save one's life. Danger, at the present moment, encompasses me on every side. If I were to descend from this trap on the ground, without adequate precautions, the mongoose will surely seize and devour me. If I remain on this trap, the owl will surely seize me. If, again, that cat succeeds in disentangling himself from the net, he also is certain to devour me. It is not proper, however, that a person of our intelligence should lose his wits. I shall, therefore, strive my best to save my life, aided by proper means and intelligence. A person possessed of intelligence and wisdom and conversant with the science of policy never sinks, however great and terrible the danger that threatens him. At present, however, I do not behold any other refuge than this cat. He is an enemy. But he is in distress. The service that I can do him is very great. Sought to be made a prey by three foes, how should I now act for saving my life? I should now seek the protection of one of those foes, viz., the cat. Taking the aid of the science of policy, let me counsel the cat for his good, so that I may, with my intelligence, escape from all the three. The cat is my great foe, but the distress into which he has fallen is very great. Let me try whether I can succeed in making this foolish creature understand his own interests. Having fallen into such distress, he may make peace with me. A person when afflicted by a stronger one should make peace with even an enemy. Professors of the science of policy say that even this should be the conduct of one who having fallen into distress seeks the safety of his life. It is better to have a learned person for an enemy than a fool for a friend.

Having weighed all his considerations, the mouse Palita said to Lomasa. 'O cat, are you alive? I wish to make peace with you as both the owl and the mongoose are intent upon feasting on me. I shall rescue you if you agree not to kill me. Without my help, you cannot escape. A wood that supports a man to cross a river also crosses the river with the help of the man. Let us escape from this unfavourable situation by helping each other. Let our love for each other increase and let there be union among us two.'

The cat Lomasa 'possessed of sharp front teeth and having eyes that resembled the stone called lapis lazuli' eyed the mouse gently and pleaded with the mouse to release him from the trap in which she had been caught. 'I swear by Truth, O friend,' she said, 'I shall do you no harm.' She asked the mouse to come and hide under her; and this did happen. Palita soon crouched beneath the cat's body as if the cat were its parent. Seeing no chances of seizing the prey, the disappointed owl and mongoose soon left that place.

The mouse then started cutting the ropes of the snare, but at a slow pace. The cat soon became impatient, and said, 'Have you forgotten your words now that you are out of the reach of danger? Expedite your work, for the hunter will soon be here.'

Palita replied, 'Expedition is not necessary. When I see the hunter approach, I will free you and you go to that tree and I will enter my hole. As they say, "that friendship in which there is fear should be maintained with great caution like the hand of the snake charmer from the snake's fangs". If I release you now, you are sure to eat me. I shall free you at the time when the hunter is in sight. At that moment, your heart will not be set upon eating me, as your focus will be on escaping from the hunter. I too shall use that moment to save my life.'

The cat was getting edgy but the mouse said: 'Be assured that I will cut the last string at a time expedient to both of us.'

As the mouse and the cat were thus talking with each other, the night gradually wore away. Soon the Chandala, whose name was Parigha, appeared on the scene. The mouse very quickly cut the remaining string that held the cat. Freed from the noose, the cat ran with speed and got upon the tree. Palita also quickly fled and entered his hole. The hunter, seeing everything, was frustrated and he quickly left that spot.

The cat Lomasa, from the branches of that tree, then

addressed the mouse Palita inside the hole, 'You suddenly ran away without conversing with me. I hope you do not suspect my intentions, as I am certainly grateful to you. Why should we not enjoy the sweets of friendship?' and spoke other words to that same effect. The mouse however knew what he was doing and said to the cat: 'I have heard all that you have said. Friends should be well examined. Foes should also be well studied. The affection between us arose from a sufficient cause. That cause exists no longer. Each of us has served the other. You have now no use for me except to make me your meal. I am your food. You are the eater. I am weak. You are strong.' Thus, rebuked soundly by Palita, Lomasa the cat blushed with shame.... Saying this, the wise mouse Palita, having completed its conversation, entered another hole.

The cat and the mouse survive; the mongoose and the owl, even the hunter, are denied their prey; life gets on an even keel for everyone.

So, Bhishma said: 'There son, you have an example of what should be done and when. Also of what should not be done, and why.'

The story in the Mahabharata *keeps appearing—at least its plot does—in many later texts. In the* Kathasaritsagara, *for instance, under a slightly changed form but clearly in a different context than in the* Mahabharata. *It is of interest all the same, because the changes bring to it a different flavour. It bears the title, 'The tale of the mongoose, the owl, the cat, and the mouse'.*

Once upon a time there was a large banyan tree outside the city of Vidisa. In that vast tree dwelt four creatures, a mongoose, an owl, a cat, and a mouse, and their habitations were apart. The mongoose and the mouse dwelt in separate holes in the root, the cat in a great hollow in the middle of the tree: but the owl dwelt in a bower of creepers on the top of it, which was inaccessible to the others. Among these the mouse was the natural prey of all three, three out of the four of the cat. The mouse, the mongoose, and the owl ranged for food during the night, the two first through fear of the cat only, the owl partly because it was his nature to do so. But the cat fearlessly wandered night and day through the neighbouring barley field, in order to catch the mouse, while the others went there by stealth at a suitable time out of desire for food. One day a certain hunter of the Chandala caste came there. He saw the track of the cat entering that field, and having set nooses all around the field in order to compass its death, departed. So the cat came there at night to slay the mouse, and entering the field was caught in one of the hunter's nooses. The mouse, for his part, came there secretly in search of food, and seeing the cat caught in the noose, danced for joy. While it was entering the field, the owl and mongoose came from afar by the same path, and seeing the cat fast in the noose, desired to capture the mouse. And the mouse, beholding them afar off, was terrified and reflected: 'If I fly to the cat, which the owl and the mongoose are afraid of, that enemy, though fast in the noose, may slay me with one blow, but if I keep at a distance from the cat, the owl and the mongoose will be the death of me. So being compassed about with enemies, where shall I go, what shall I do? Ah! I will take refuge with the cat here, for it is in trouble, and may save me to preserve its own life, as I shall be of use to gnaw through the noose.' Thus reflecting the mouse slowly approached the cat, and said to him, 'I am exceedingly grieved at your being caught, so I will gnaw through your noose; the upright come to love even their enemies by dwelling in their neighbourhood. But I do not feel confidence in you, as I do not know your intentions.' When the cat heard that, he said, 'Worthy mouse, be at rest, from this day forth you are my friend as giving me life.' The moment he heard this from the cat, he crept into his bosom; when the owl and mongoose saw that, they went away hopeless. Then the cat, galled with the noose, said to the mouse, 'My friend, the night is almost gone, so quickly gnaw through my bonds.' The mouse for its part, waiting for the arrival of the hunter, slowly nibbled the noose, and protracted the business, making a continual munching with its teeth, which was all pretence. Soon the night came to an end, and the hunter came near; then the mouse, at the request of the cat, quickly gnawed through the noose which held it. So the cat's noose was severed, and it ran away, afraid of the hunter; and the mouse, delivered from death, fled into its hole. But when called again by the cat, it reposed no confidence in him, but remarked, 'The truth is, an enemy is occasionally made a friend by circumstances, but does not remain such forever.'

Thus the mouse, though an animal, saved its life from many foes, much more ought the same thing to take place among men.

Possessed of a very different flavour is an almost contemporary folk tale involving a cat from Madhya Pradesh.

There once lived four traders, who jointly owned a big shop of grains. Year after year, their business flourished and they made quite a profit. Until one season, some rats took refuge in the shop. They rampaged the storeroom, destroying almost a quarter of the grains.

The four traders were worried. 'This is a calamity!' said one of them.

'We must do something about these rats.'

'Let's buy a cat and keep it here in our shop,' suggested the other.

'Good idea!' agreed the other three partners. So, they bought a cat.

They fed the cat milk and fish, and gave her all the attention and care she needed. The cat felt proud and roamed about the shop freely. At night, the traders left the cat in the storeroom of their shop and went home. Soon, the cat began her work. In just a short span, she caught and ate up all the rats. The next day when the four traders arrived at their shop, they found the storeroom neat and tidy, with all the sacks intact. 'Ah, it seems the cat has done her job,' said the traders, happily. They decided to take good care of the cat and keep her as a guard in their shop.

After long consultations among themselves, the traders decided to look after her. But who was to take care of her?

The consensus that emerged was: the cat has four legs, each of us should look after a leg. That will ensure we all look after the cat equally.' Everyone liked the idea; so, each of the partners took charge of one leg of the cat.

One day, the cat hurt one of its legs. Instantly, the trader who was supposed to look after the leg cleansed the wound and bandaged the leg. 'You will be all right soon, dear!' he said, patting the cat, lovingly. Slowly, the cat recovered. One night, as she was roaming about in the storeroom, she went too close to a lamp and knocked it down by mistake. The glass cover of the lamp broke and the cat's bandage caught fire. 'Meaaaaaoooow!' cried the cat, running around panic stricken.

To put off the fire, she began to rub her bandaged leg against a sack. Now the sack caught fire too. The cat jumped onto another sack and began to rub the bandage on that sack, setting it on fire as well. One by one all the sacks caught fire and soon the entire shop was in flames. In the morning, the four traders were in for a shock. 'We are ruined!' they cried. 'What shall we do now?'

When they figured out the reason for the fire, they began to blame the partner who took care of the bandaged leg. 'It was all because of you!' they shouted at him. 'You bandaged the leg that belonged to you; the bandage caught fire and spread all over, destroying the entire shop. You must compensate us for it!'

They took the partner to the magistrate. The magistrate, a wise old man, listened to the whole story, then said, 'It is true that the bandage caught fire. But how did the fire spread? Certainly not because of the bandaged leg. But, because of the three sound legs that carried the cat from one sack to another, setting the entire shop on fire. So, not the fourth partner but the other three are to blame. You three, who own the three sound legs of the cat, must compensate your fourth partner for his loss.'

Now the three partners began to beg for mercy. The fourth partner, who was kind-hearted, requested the magistrate to forgive the other partners. The magistrate advised them, 'If you trust an animal to guard your place, this will be the consequence.' The four partners thanked the magistrate and went home wiser.

From the Anwar-i Suhayli *which relies so heavily upon the much older* Panchatantra*, there is another story that draws attention to the greed of the cat rather than on its cleverness. Greed meets a truly sorry end, in this tale. The usual poetic flourishes abound. The story is being told by a kite to an assembly of birds.*

The kite said, 'In former times there was an old woman in a state of extreme debility. She possessed a cot more narrow than the heart of the ignorant, and darker than the miser's grave: and a cat was her companion, which had never seen even in the mirror of imagination, the face of a loaf, nor had heard from friend or stranger the name of meat. It was content if occasionally it smelt the odour of a mouse from its hole, or saw the print of the foot of one on the surface of a board, and if, on some rare occasion, by the aid of good fortune and the assistance of happy destiny, one fell into its claws,

HEMISTICH

Like a poor wretch who finds out buried gold, its cheek lighted up with joy, and it consumed its past sorrow with the flame of its natural heat, and a whole week, more or less, it subsisted on that amount of food, and used to say,

COUPLET

In slumber see I this, my God, or with my waking eyes?
Myself in plenty such as this, after such agonies?

And inasmuch as the house of the old woman was also the house of that cat, it was always miserable and thin, and from a distance appeared like an idea. One day, through excessive weakness, it had, with the utmost difficulty, mounted on the top of the roof; thence it beheld a cat which walked proudly on the wall of a neighbouring house, and after the fashion of a destroying lion, advanced with measured steps, and from excessive fat, lifted its feet slowly. When the cat of the old woman saw one of its own species in that state of freshness and fat, it was astonished, and cried out, saying,

HEMISTICH

'Truly with pride thou advancest,
then wilt thou not tell me from whence?

Thou, whose state is thus pleasant, whence art thou? And since it appears that thou comest from the banquet chamber of the Khan of Khata, whence is this sleekness of thine, and from what cause this thy grandeur and strength?' The neighbour cat replied, 'I am the crumb eater of the tray of the sultan. Every morning I attend on the court of the king, and when they spread the tray of invitation, I display boldness and daring, and in general I snatch off some morsels of fat meats, and of loaves made of the finest flour; and I pass my time happy and satisfied till the next day.' The cat of the old woman, enquired 'What sort of a thing may fat meat be? And what kind of relish had bread made of fine flour? I, during my whole life, have never seen nor tasted aught save the old woman's broths, and mouse's flesh.' The neighbour cat laughed, and said, 'Therefore it is, that one cannot distinguish thee from a spider and this form and appearance that thou hast, is a reproach to our whole race; and the shape and character which thou hast brought the house to the desert, is an eternal disgrace.

COUPLET

Cat, by thy tail and ears, one might thee deem,
Yet, in all else, a spider thou wouldst seem.

And if thou shouldst see the court of the sultan, and smell the odour of those delicious viands and agreeable meats, it is probable that the mystery, "Who shall restore bones to life when they are rotten," may come forth from the curtain of what is hidden, to the plain of manifestation, and thou mayst acquire a fresh form.'

COUPLET

The scent of the beloved one passed o'er the lovers' grave,
What marvel if to those dry bones the breath of life it gave.

The cat of the old woman, said, most beseechingly, 'O brother! thou art bound to me by the rights of neighbourship and the link of homogeneousness, why not perform what is due to courtesy and fraternity, and this time, when thou goest, take me with thee; perchance by thy good fortune, I may obtain food, and by the blessing of thy society, I may acquire a place.

COUPLET

From pious company withdraw thou not,
Nor those unclasp who share a prosperous lot.'

The heart of the neighbour-cat melted at his lamentable position, and he resolved that he would not attend the feast without him. The cat of the old woman, from the happy tidings of this promise, felt new life, and descending from the roof, stated the case to her. The old dame began to advise the cat, saying, 'O kind companion, be not deceived by the words of worldly people, and abandon not the corner of content, for the vessel of covetousness is not filled save with the dust of the grave; and the eye of lust is not stitched but with the needle of annihilation and the thread of death.'

VERSE

Contentment makes man wealthy
Tell it then To the unsatisfied and world-o'er-wandering men,
They ne'er knew God, nor paid Him worship due,
Since with their lot they no contentment knew.

The cat had not taken into its head a longing for the table of the delicacies of the sultan, to such an extent only as that the medicine of advice could be profitable to it.

COUPLET

'Tis but to cage the wind advice to give
To lovers, 'tis but water in a sieve.

In short the next day, along with its neighbour, the old woman's cat, with tottering steps conveyed itself to the court of the sultan, and before that helpless one could arrive there, ill-fortune had poured the water of disappointment on the fire of its crude wish, and the reason was as follows: the day before, the cats had made a general onslaught on the table, and raised a clamour and uproar beyond bounds, all had annoyed, to the last degree, the guests and their host. Wherefore, on this day, the sultan had commanded that a band of archers, with swiftly impelling notches, standing in ambush, should watch, so that for every cat, who holding before its face the buckler of impudence, should enter the plain of audacity the very first morsel that it ate, should be a liver-piercing shaft. The old woman's cat, ignorant of this circumstance, as soon as it smelt the odour of the viands, without the power of checking itself, turned its face like a falcon, to the hunting ground of the table, and the scale of the appetite had not been weighted by heavy mouthfuls, when the heart-piercing arrow quivered in its breast.

VERSE

From the bone trickling flowed the sanguine tide,
In terror of its life it fled and cried:
'Could I escape this archer's hand
I'd dwell Content with mice and the old woman's cell.
Dear friend the honey pays not for the sting, Content with
syrup is a better thing.'

'And I have introduced this apologue, that thou, too, mayest regard the secluded corner of my nest as a blessing, and mayest understand the value of the food and morsels, which reach thee, untoiled for by thee; and showing thyself contented with a little, mayest not seek for more, lest, God forbid! thou arrive not at the condition thou seekest, and this place, too, depart from thy hand.' The hawk said, 'What thou hast been pleased to say, is the essence of good advice and kindness, nevertheless, to stoop to trifles is the business of the mean, and to show content with mere eating and drinking, is the disposition of brutes. Everyone who would sit on the throne of greatness must rise up in pursuit of high things, and he who wishes to put on his head the crown of exaltation, must belt himself with the girdle of search. A lofty spirit is not satisfied with low things, and a noble intellect approves not of base positions.

VERSE

None ever found the way on high to rise,
Till he obtained the step of high empire.
Seek rank, that to the moon thou mayest mount,
None drink cloud-water from a well's low fount.

In Maharashtra, the Warlis, with the extraordinary repertoire of animals which people their paintings, the cat comes in frequently. When a tale involving a cat gains currency in their tribe, therefore, it does not come as a surprise. The story is simple, and it is told in a quiet but clever manner.

Walking through a forest in search of fruits and berries, a poor man chanced upon a pig being attacked by a tiger. The man helped the pig escape by driving the tiger away. Filled with gratitude, the pig said, 'I am very grateful—you have saved my life today. I must repay my debt to you. Please follow me.'

The man followed the pig who led him to a cave, from which the animal brought out a ring and said, 'Take this ring and tie it to the top of your house and good fortune will follow you.' The man accepted the gift, thanked the pig, and made his way home.

As night fell, the man and his wife went to sleep. The next morning, their once empty house had grown in prosperity with sacks of pulses and spices in the attic, and vegetables in the kitchen. They could finally eat their fill and feed their pets. With the family's good fortune, the couple and their pets lived comfortably.

As weeks passed, onlookers became curious and neighbours wondered at the unexpected good fortune of the household. A crafty villager spied on them and found out about the magic ring. That night, he snuck into the house and stole the ring.

The fate of the house quickly reversed back to its impoverished state. The woman was upset as she couldn't feed her cat and dog any more. She said to them, 'Please go away, there's nothing for you here. Find another home!'

The dog asked the cat, 'How did our fate change? What do we do?' The cat recalled, 'There used to be a ring tied to the roof, but it isn't there any more. I think we should find it.'

The duo set out in search of the ring. They searched their village and the surrounding villages, even crossing a trickle of a stream. They were determined to find the ring and take it back to the kind couple.

Soon they came upon a prosperous house. The dog guessed that the house was newly prosperous, because there was a wedding of rats right next to it, and it was an odd season for weddings. This was surely the thief's house, they concluded.

As they stood wondering what to do, the cat had an idea. She caught the rat bridegroom from next door. The other rats panicked and pleaded with the cat, 'Please, please let the groom go! Please do not harm him.'

The dog replied, 'We mean him no harm. The cat will let him go in return for a favour. We need the ring that is tied to the roof of the rich man's house.'

The rats scampered onto the thief's roof, detached the ring from there and brought it to the dog. The cat kept her word and let go of the groom. The wedding celebrations continued with merriment.

As the cat and the dog made their way back with the ring, it began to rain heavily and frogs croaked joyfully all around them. Water levels at the trickle of a stream they had crossed earlier had risen, and it had become a torrent. They had no choice but to brave the current. The cat jumped in first and the dog followed. As they were crossing the gushing waters, the ring slipped out of his mouth. Once they reached the shore, they had to think quickly about how they would retrieve the ring from the depths of the stream.

Soon the rain stopped, and they spotted a wedding ceremony of river frogs nearby—a common occurrence during the rains. They repeated their trick, catching hold of the bridegroom. The other frogs begged, 'Please let our groom go, please do not hurt him!' Now it was the frogs' turn to fetch the ring from the depths of the stream in return for an unhurt groom. They dived into the stream and brought the ring out. Once the dog had the ring in his mouth again, the groom frog was released, and the wedding party resumed.

Without any more untoward incidents, the cat and dog reached their home. The cat climbed to the roof and tied the ring where it used to be. The woman was happy to see her pets again. This is how the cat and the dog returned the ring to their house, and brought prosperity back to the family.

In the Tuti Nama*—the Persian version of the twelfth century Sanskrit classic,* Shuka Saptati*—there is tale after absorbing tale, and it needs to be told in the engaging, poetic manner that the translator, fourteenth century physician and Sufi, Zia-ud Din Nakhshabi, who had settled in northern India and observed the tenor of Indian life, did. He changed many things in the original story—for one thing all names of characters so as to fit them into an Islamic milieu (the name, for instance, of the lady for whom her pet parrot had been commissioned by her husband to direct her interest towards a luscious story rather than head for her secret lover at night, from Padmavati to Khojasteh)—and imparted to it a poetic flavour with his entertaining and often philosophic verses. This story was told by the parrot on the fifteenth night to his wayward mistress.*

When like a golden fawn the Sun entered his retreat in the west and like a swift moving deer the moon emerged from the meadows in the east, Khojasteh, whose beauty outshone that of the moon, went to Tuti to ask permission to leave and said, 'Oh Tuti, the throbbing pain of separation and the radiant fire of yearning have exhausted me. Will this dark night ever be followed by the dawn; and will a key ever be found to this padlock [on my heart]?

'Wise men say that people can be divided into two kinds: the first one, those who are so engrossed with earning their livelihood that they have no time to go on their pilgrimage—they are the lost souls. The second, those who are preoccupied with the duties of their pilgrimages that they are unable to earn their living—they are the extremists. I do not know from whence this third concern [my love] came to me. But both my thoughts about a pilgrimage and my interest in my daily responsibilities have been forgotten.'

Oh Nakshabi, romance is delightful recreation,
Fair play is never a serious consideration;
Whenever one becomes enraptured with a love idol
He will have no time for any other occupation.

Tuti had feigned indisposition during this [monologue] by making himself appear perplexed, morose, and pensive. Later he changed his bearing and observed the amenities by casting down his eyes in respect and assuming a polite manner. Like perpetrators of evil deeds and those suffering from afflictions, he put on a submissive attitude and was going to speak gently when Khojasteh interrupted by saying, 'Oh Tuti, what is the cause of this lassitude and the reason for this languor?'

Tuti said, 'I have neither ulterior motives nor physical infirmities, but your troubles have caused me anxieties and your worries have bought me unhappiness. You are diverted by the extent of my knowledge and my ability as a storyteller. You are intrigued by the sound of my voice and my fables, but you are losing your opportunity. How long will you keep your poor lover in suspense? Should your husband return, you will regret not having gone [to see him] just as the cat repented having killed the mice.'

Khojasteh was surprised at these words and said, 'Oh Tuti, your amazing statement is more extraordinary than the philosopher's stone, and your amusing stories are more astonishing than an antidote of poison. The mouse is the natural food of the cat. How can he feel guilty for having killed it? How can he repent having destroyed it? If it is not too much trouble, could you possibly tell me the story?'

Tuti replied: 'It is said that in the remote regions of China there was a field abounding in fresh green grass. In that region a ferocious lion with a majesty of a king was the ruler of the wild beasts. He had brought all the animals under his domination and control. As time went by, the evening of the lion's youth turned into the dawn of old age and the spring of his manhood into the autumn of his declining years. Because of advanced age and lack of vigour, the lion was ailing and had spells of weeping. Yes, although old age commands respect, youth is a time of joy.

O Nakhshabi, an old man may be likened to a child
Who is easily frightened because of dependency;
Even if the old one is an angry roaring lion,
To kill a tiny mouse may be beyond his potency.

With the advance of old age and aggravation of infirmities, his teeth became defective and cavities developed. Many morsels of meat which he chewed remained caught between his teeth. In that green valley there were many mice. While the lion was sleeping the mice came, pulled the shreds of meat from his teeth and ate them, thus disturbing the lion's sleep.

The lion with all its might was at the mercy of the mice. This courageous animal was in despair because of their encroachments. Oh, how many dignified persons have been powerless in the hands of their inferiors! Situations have left them confused and alarmed, and they have been unable to protect themselves from the long arm of adversity. Indeed, the ocean with all its strength and power is the playground of the dolphin, and the mountain with all its magnitude is the trampling ground of the leopard!

It is said that at the time of birth when the lion cub is separated from its mother, the ants infest it. Most of the deaths of baby lions are caused by ants. The lions see this, but they are helpless and cannot save their little ones from their assault. Why should this be? The purpose is to show that those with power should understand their weaknesses and not depend entirely on their strength.

Listen! Imam Shafi'i—may God's mercy be upon him—was seated next to one of the caliphs. A fly was annoying the caliph who said, 'I do not understand the wisdom of the Lord in creating the fly.'

Imam Shafi'i replied, 'In my humble opinion the purpose is to show to those with power their own helplessness.'

O Nakhshabi, everyone is worried and defenseless;
Who is not astonished by this sad fact so true and real?
Even though the mighty lion is brave and courageous,
He can suffer from fever and headaches as an ordeal.

In short, the king of the wild beasts was in despair because of the mice. One day he consulted the wolf about his problem. The wolf, who was experienced and had great knowledge about situations of this kind, said, 'For every ailment there is a remedy and for every poison an antidote. If the trouble cannot be solved by use of force, it can be overcome by trickery! A problem which can be settled by consultation cannot be handled by the use of power. The task of ridding the house of litter can be performed with a broom—not with a stick, and the chore of taking rubbish out of the home can be accomplished by means of a basket—not with a sword or an arrow. Moreover, the cat is a subject of the king and a native of the realm. The responsibility of eliminating the mice should be entrusted to him.'

This speech pleased the lion. He ordered that the cat be summoned. When the cat arrived and kissed the ground as a token of respect, the lion explained to him that the mice had become a nuisance and were beyond control.

The cat replied, 'Although the king of wild beasts does not deal directly with your servant and does not consider him as one of the nobles of the court and the kingdom, there is a real kinship between the fur of the cat and the ermine of the majestic lion. The king must have heard the story of the mice in the ark of Noah, may peace be upon him, which caused so much damage that the wooden supports of the ship were weakened. Confronted with this problem Noah was helpless. He was directed [by God] to take some action which would cause the lion irritation. Noah acted accordingly. The lion sneezed and immediately a cat dropped from each of the two openings of his nostrils. When the mice heard the cat's meows, they fled, and the passengers on the ship were saved from the harassment of the mice. If the king of the wild beasts will entrust the Office of the Magistrate of the Court and the Guardianship of the Palace to his servant, I, too, will handle this emergency for Your Majesty just as my forebears served the ancestors of the king.'

The lion appointed him to the position of the Magistrate of the Court, and the cat with a clear conscience devoted his time to his duties. When the mice observed the cat, they all loathed him and dispersed. The lion was relieved of his irritation, showed great favour and kindness to the cat, kept him under his custody, and gave him protection.

O Nakhshabi, always value the good work of others
And so avoid bringing on yourself humiliation;
When workers perform their services with devotion and skill,
Nobles should also bestow their own appreciation.

Although the cat had opened the door of fear and terror to the mice, he also treated them with consideration, showed them politeness and did not try to exterminate them completely. He thought to himself, 'If they are all destroyed, the lion will not have any need for me and will not honour me with his favour and approbation.'

It is well known that even an ignorant person is familiar with his own trade.

O Nakhshabi, the people are concerned about their own trade.
There is no one as depressed as you by disillusion.
Of all you see whether an infant or an honoured chief,
None is unaware of his own gain or resolution.

Time passed and one day the cat brought one of his younger cats to the lion and said, 'This is my son. Among his friends and companions, he is known for his veracity, religious devotion, and ability. He is well versed in the manners of the court. If you will give the order, I will have him take my place from time to time so that I can go and visit my other children.' The lion gave his permission.

That night the cat left his son in his place. Unaware of his father's strategy and ignorant of the fact that the mice were being treated with consideration, the young cat killed every mouse which appeared so that during the night all the mice were exterminated. Not a single one of their species survived.

The next day he found that fortune had something else in store for him. When the east wind laden with the odour of musk blew open the door of the day, the cat returned from his home. When he saw what had happened to the mice, he exploded in anger and reprimanded his son saying, 'The very calamity which I have long feared has come about. The great misfortune which I have always dreaded has taken place. It would not be surprising if from now on the King's favour and bounty for us would diminish, because a person's liberality is affected by his own desires and an individual's benevolence is linked to his own purposes. When his objectives are achieved and his purposes are realized, then his kindliness disappears and his generosity vanishes.'

O Nakhshabi, no one is free from his selfish motives,
Although a paragon of virtue, each knows what he intends;
Whether a rich man or a dervish, everyone you see
Leaves his home in order to pursue his own worldly ends.

Some time elapsed and the lion was freed of the vexation of the mice. Many anxieties which were troubling the heart of the cat began to develop in the breast of the lion who said to himself, 'Having the cat in my household was for the purpose of getting rid of the mice. Now that the plague of the mice no longer exists, it is time to dispense with his services. Besides, the cat by nature is a predatory animal and can subsist on what he catches. Why should I for his sake have the blood of other animals on my hands?' Later he relieved the cat of the position of the Magistrate of the Court.

The cat said to his son, 'The spark of this calamity was set by you and the robe of this disaster was tailored by you. If you had not annihilated the mice and had not entirely relieved the lion's heart of his grief, he would not have dismissed me.' The young cat was filled with remorse for having killed the mice.

When Tuti brought his story to this point, he said to Khojasteh, 'Oh Mistress, I find you very negligent in the affairs of love and very tardy in going to your rendezvous. I feel your husband will soon return, and you will be just as repentant as the young cat was for having slain the mice.'

Khojasteh's heart was deeply moved by these words. She wanted to go at once to the house of her lover, but at that moment the sun's fiery rays emerged and the radiant light of day burst forth. The dawn unveiled its brilliant face, and her departure was delayed.

O Nakhshabi, today a fair lady longed to accept
The invitation of the one who was her temptation,
But the early light of dawn prevented her departure.
The cock's call is the foe of lover's infatuation.

Spectacular success for the cat on the one hand, but one slip, one miscalculation, and it was all gone: the power, the riches, the insolence of office.

The cat plays virtually no real role in this passage—it is just that among the greatest of gods, Indra, has to assume the form of a cat in fear of a misdeed of his being exposed—but one is tempted to draw attention to it because it occurs in that other great epic of India, the Ramayana. *The excerpt below is from the* Kathasaritsagara *the author of which condensed the* Ramayana *story befitting another context. The whole episode of the great sage, Gautama's wife, Ahalya, turning into a rock due to a curse pronounced upon her by her irate husband who accused her of adulterous conduct is not part of general awareness. The story, generally but widely told as an episode of the* Ramayana, *emphasizes the greatness of Rama at whose mere touch Ahalya recovered her original form, changing from a rock into the beauteous lady she was. But hardly, if ever, the details of the story are known, or pointed out. Those details, it might be added, are the subject of much discussion and difference among scholars.*

Once upon a time there was a great hermit named Gautama, who knew the past, the present, and the future. And he had a wife named Ahalya, who in beauty surpassed the nymphs of heaven. One day Indra, in love with her beauty, tempted her in secret, for the minds of rulers, blinded with power, run towards unlawful objects.

And she in her folly encouraged that husband of Sachi, being the slave of her passions; but the hermit Gautama found out the intrigue by his superhuman power, and arrived upon the scene. And Indra immediately assumed, out of fear, the form of a cat. Then Gautama said to Ahalya, 'Who is here?' She answered her husband ambiguously in the Prakrit dialect (the Sanskrit word for cat is *marjara*, but Ahalya, instead of using that word in response to her husband's angry question, said '*majjara*' which is Prakrit for 'lover').

'Here forsooth is a cat,' so managing to preserve verbal truth.

Then Gautama said, laughing, 'It is quite true that your lover is here,' and he inflicted on her a curse, but ordained that it should terminate because she had showed some regard for truth.

The curse ran as follows: 'Woman of bad character, take for a long time the nature of a stone, until thou behold Rama wandering in the forest.' And Gautama at the same time inflicted on the god Indra the following curse: 'A thousand pictures of that which thou hast desired shall be upon thy body, but when thou shalt behold Tilottama, a heavenly nymph, whom Visvakarma shall make, they shall turn into a thousand eyes.' When he had pronounced this curse, the hermit returned to his austerities according to his desire, but Ahalya for her part assumed the awful condition of a stone. And Indra immediately had his body covered with repulsive marks; for to whom is not immorality a cause of humiliation?

In the Hitopadesha*—the Book of Good Counsels—another classic of Sanskrit literature, the core of which goes back to the eighth–ninth century and which leans from time to time upon the* Panchatantra, *there are moral stories in which birds, beasts, and humans interact. Among them is this instructive story of the Vulture, the Cat, and the Birds, as rendered by Edwin Arnold in 1861.*

On the banks of the Ganges there is a cliff called Vulture-crag, and thereupon grew a great fig tree. It was hollow, and within its shelter lived an old Vulture, named Grey-pate, whose hard fortune it was to have lost both eyes and talons. The birds that roosted in the tree made subscriptions from their own store, out of sheer pity for the poor fellow, and by that means he managed to live. One day, when the old birds were gone, Long-ear, the Cat, came there to make a meal of the nestlings; and they, alarmed at perceiving him, set up a chirruping that roused Grey-pate.

'Who comes there?' croaked Grey-pate.

Now Long-ear, on espying the Vulture, thought himself undone; but as flight was impossible, he resolved to trust his destiny and approach.

'My lord,' said he, 'I have the honour to salute thee.'

'Who is it?' said the Vulture.

'I am a Cat.'

'Be off, Cat, or I shall slay thee,' said the Vulture.

'I am ready to die if I deserve death,' answered the Cat; 'but let what I have to say be heard.'

'Wherefore, then, comest thou?' said the Vulture.

'I live,' began Long-ear, 'on the Ganges, bathing, and eating no flesh, practising the moon-penance, like a Brahmacharya. The birds that resort thither constantly praise your worship to me as one wholly given to the study of morality, and worthy of all trust; and so I came here to learn law from thee, sir, who art so deep gone in learning and in years. Dost thou, then, so read the law of strangers as to be ready to slay a guest? What say the books about the householder?

Bar thy door not to the stranger, be he friend or be he foe,
For the tree will shade the woodman while his axe doth lay it low.

And if means fail, what there is should be given with kind words, as—

Greeting fair, and room to rest in; fire, and water from the well—
Simple gifts—are given freely in the house where good men dwell—

and without respect of person—

Young, or bent with many winters; rich, or poor, whate'er thy guest,
Honour him for thine own honour—better is he than the best,

Else comes the rebuke—

Pity them that ask thy pity: who art thou to stint thy hoard,
When the holy moon shines equal on the leper and the lord!

And that other, too,

When thy gate is roughly fastened, and the asker turns away,
Thence he bears thy good deeds with him, and his sins on thee doth lay.

For verily,

In the house the husband ruleth, men the Brahmans "master" call;
Agni is the Twice-born Master; but the guest is lord of all.'

To these weighty words Grey-pate answered, 'Yes! But cats like meat, and there are young birds here, and therefore I said, go.'

'Sir,' said the Cat (and as he spoke he touched the ground,

and then his two ears, and called on Krishna to witness to his words), 'I that have overcome passion, and practised the moon-penance, know the Scriptures; and howsoever they contend, in this primal duty of abstaining from injury they are unanimous. Which of them sayeth not—

He who does and thinks no wrong—He who suffers, being strong—
He whose harmlessness men know—
Unto Swarga such doth go.'

And so, winning the old Vulture's confidence, Long-ear, the Cat, entered the hollow tree and lived there. And day after day he stole away some of the nestlings, and brought them down to the hollow to devour. Meantime the parent birds, whose little ones were being eaten, made an inquiry after them in all quarters; and the Cat, discovering this fact, slipped out from the hollow, and made his escape. Afterwards, when the birds came to look closely, they found the bones of their young ones in the hollow of the tree where Grey-pate lived; and the birds at once concluded that their nestlings had been killed and eaten by the old Vulture, whom they accordingly executed. That is my story, and why I warned you against unknown acquaintances.

In the Karnataka region a cycle of stories is told with relish, lauding the young Tenali Rama who lived in the times of the great king of the Vijayanagara empire, Krishnadeva Raya, and with whom he had many encounters. Almost always, young Tenali had something to say to his monarch or solve for him a situation which others at the court could not. As in this story involving a cat.

One day, when King Sri Krishnadeva Raya was sitting in his court, he heard a commotion outside the palace gates. He commanded the guards to find out what it was. A guard came with a man who identified himself as the village head. The king asked him what the matter was. The man replied, 'Your majesty, our village is infested by rats. The rats are destroying our food grains and creating chaos in the village. Please save us.'

The king assured the village head by saying, 'Fear not, my good man. I will consult with my courtiers and find a solution to your problem.'

King Sri Krishnadeva Raya ordered his ministers to arrive at a solution. One of the ministers stood up and said, 'Your majesty, since cats eat rats, we can solve this rat menace by giving one cat to each household in the village.'

'But how would the poor villagers feed the cats?' asked another minister.

The minister suggested that they could give a cow along with a cat so that the cats can feed on milk.

The king agreed to this solution. All the villagers began feeding the cats with milk. And as days passed by, the cats became healthy and lazy.

Tenali Rama observed this and thought, 'There is something wrong with this solution.'

The next day, Rama placed a hot bowl of milk in front of one of the cats. As soon as the cat spotted the milk, it rushed to drink it and burned its tongue. The cat ran away and never touched milk again.

That cat began to hunt, and the owner's house was clean of rats.

One day, the king wanted to review the situation and ordered the villagers to get the cats to the court. The villages complained that their cats haven't been hunting rats, except the one owner whose cat stopped drinking milk thanks to Rama.

The king asked the cat's owner, 'Why is only your cat hunting rats? Haven't you been feeding it with milk?'

Rama stepped up and said, 'Your majesty, it is not the owner's fault. This cat refuses to drink milk.'

'A cat that doesn't drink milk? How is that possible, Rama?' asked the king.

'Let me show it to you, your majesty,' said Rama and asked the guards to get a bowl of milk. As soon as the cat saw the bowl of milk, it ran away. The surprised king asked for the reason behind it. Then, Rama said, 'Your majesty, I had given the cat a bowl of hot milk which burnt its tongue. From that day onwards, this cat never drank milk.'

'But, why did you do so?' enquired the king.

Rama replied, 'Your majesty, cats would hunt the rats only when they are hungry. By drinking milk every day, the cats have become healthy and lazy and do not hunt for the rats. To show you this, I gave hot milk to one of the cats.'

The king understood the flaw in the solution. He asked the ministers to find another solution to help solve the problem. He also rewarded Rama handsomely.

An oft-told tale in India speaks of two cats who found a loaf of bread while hunting together and went in search of a judge who would divide it between them equitably. The story ends however with both the cats getting cheated out of the bread completely: a rather rare occurrence because both the cats emerge from it as naïve and trusting creatures. The origins of this story are generally believed to have been in India, somewhere, in some text or the other, but it is not easy to track the source down. Meanwhile, it figures in one of La Fontaine's fables; where La Fontaine got it from is also not recorded even if one knows that, in general, he leaned heavily upon ancient Indian sources. In any case this is how the story runs.

Once upon a time, two cats, named Sehri and Mehri, were passing through a street. Suddenly, they spotted a loaf of bread lying beneath a tree. Both the cats pounced and caught the loaf at the same time. 'It is mine! I saw it first,' claimed Sehri. The other, Mehri, shouted, 'I pounced on it first. It belongs to me.'

Finally, Sehri said, 'I'm hungry! Let us divide it in half and take one piece each.'

'Good idea!' said Mehri. 'But which of us will divide it?'

A monkey sitting on the branch of the tree had been watching this all along. 'That loaf of bread looks good. I would like it for myself,' he thought. He worked up to the fighting cats. 'My dear friends! Can I help you?' said the monkey.

The cats told the monkey the story and asked. 'Could you be the judge between us? Please divide this loaf for us?' The monkey quickly agreed to be the judge. He took a scale, broke the bread making one piece bigger than the other, and put them in opposite pans of the scale.

'Oh no! So sorry! I will take a little bite of the bigger piece to make both equal,' said the monkey slyly, as he weighed. He took a bite from the bigger piece. But, he took a big bite.

'Oh! Now it has become too small! I will just have to take a little bite from this piece now,' said the clever monkey. So the judge monkey took another bite and then, another!

Sehri and Mehri sat confused, as their bread got smaller and smaller. In minutes, the whole loaf was gone! Judge monkey said, 'Wow! It was really difficult to divide that loaf! But, I must be going now.'

Then he took his scale, jumped up the tree, and was gone.

'If only we had not quarrelled among ourselves, we would not be hungry now,' moaned the cats, sadly.

Although not strictly of Indian origin, there are some very early references in Islam—going back to the times of the great Prophet himself—which deeply influenced the attitude of Muslims living in India, towards cats. In general, one is aware that as a domestic animal, cats were looked at with affection, often with reverence, in Islam because of the view that the great Prophet took of cats, starting with his own pet cat, Muezza. His attitude was taken as a model which was widely followed in the Islamic world, including in India. There are no connected accounts of cats from those early times, but much can be learnt about attitudes from what is recorded in the Hadith*—a collection of traditions containing sayings of the prophet Muhammad which, with accounts of his daily practice (the Sunna), constitute the major source of guidance for Muslims apart from the Quran. [Reference to both stories connected with the Prophet and to Abu Hurairah have been made earlier in this work, but it is of special interest to see them in the context of the* Hadith.*] It is of interest to go back to recalling what was recommended in Islam from the very beginnings of its foundation as a faith.*

Two different stories are told of how a cat saved the Prophet's life. One legend has it that the reason the Prophet loved cats so much was that his life had been saved by one. A snake had crawled into his sleeve and refused to leave. A cat was called and asked the snake to show its head, in order to discuss its departure. When the snake finally appeared, the cat pounced on it and carried it off.

About the other this is what Annemarie Schimmel has noted:

> *There are variants of the story of how the cat of Abu Huraira (a close companion of the Prophet) which he always carried in his bag, saved the Prophet from an obnoxious snake, whereupon the Prophet petted her. It is believed that the mark of his fingers is still visible in the four dark lines on most cats' foreheads, and, because the Prophet's hand had stroked her back, cats never fall on their backs.*

Regarding the Prophet's personal pet, Muezza, it is recorded that Muhammad awoke one day to the sounds of the *adhan* prayer. Preparing to attend prayer, he began to dress himself; however, he soon discovered his cat Muezza sleeping on the sleeve of his prayer robe. Rather than wake her, he used a pair of scissors to cut the sleeve off, leaving the cat undisturbed. Another story is that, upon returning from the mosque, the Prophet received a bow from Muezza. He then smiled and gently stroked his beloved cat three times, giving all cats the ability to land squarely on their feet. In Islam, the punishment for troubling or torturing cats is severe, according to the traditions associated with the Prophet who advocated kindness to creatures. In the faith a special place is held for cats as lovable and cherished creatures, and mistreating a cat is seen as a serious sin. Al-Bukhari reported a *Hadith* regarding a woman who locked up a cat, refusing to feed it and not releasing it so that it could feed itself. The Prophet Muhammad said that her punishment on the Day of Judgment will be torture and Hell.

It is believed that you will suffer no harm if you drink from the cat's water provided no impurities are seen in the cat's mouth. In another story from the *Hadith*, it is stated that when a cat ate a pudding put down during prayers, the person who was in charge of the pudding ate from the same plate as the cat and the Prophet said this was all right as the cat is not unclean and is 'one of those who go around amongst us'.The Prophet of Islam was once performing ablution (*wudhu*) for prayers from a pot of water. A cat passed there and turned its eyes at the pot of water with a thirsty look. The Prophet realized at once that the cat was very thirsty, so he stopped the ablution and placed the pot before the cat. Only after the cat had fully quenched its thirst, did the Prophet resume the ablution. Dawud ibn Salih ibn Dinar at-Tammar quoted his mother as saying that her mistress sent her with some pudding (harissa) to Aisha (one of the Prophet's wives) who was offering prayer. She made a sign to her to place it down. A cat came and ate some of it, but when Aisha finished her prayer, she ate from the place where the cat had eaten. She stated: 'The Messenger of Allah said it is not unclean: it is one of those who go round among you.' She added, 'I saw the Messenger of Allah performing ablution from the water left over by the cat.'

These references apart, there is a moving story about a cat feeding a blind cat which is often repeated for emphasizing the kind nature of cats. The story involves Ibn Babshad, a grammarian, and was recorded thus at the end of the fourteenth century by the Egyptian theologist and zoologist Damiri: 'The grammarian Ibn Babshad and his friends once sat on the roof of a mosque in Cairo. My friends ate something. When the cat passed by, they gave her some pieces of food. She took the food and ran away, but then came back again and again. Scientists followed the cat. They saw her running away to a nearby house with a blind cat sitting on the roof. Next to her, our cat left the brought pieces of food. Ibn Babshad saw this as a concern for the blind animal on the part of Allah, and this shocked the scientist so much that he left all his possessions and began to live in poverty, relying entirely on Allah until his death in 1067.'

To sum it up, an essay on cats in Islam notes: 'Islam teaches Muslims that, in relation to a cat:

- the cat should not be sold for money or other traded goods.
- cat's saliva is harmless unless the cat has 'visible impurities' in the mouth.
- that Muslims are free to live with cats but they must treat cats well, providing the cat with enough water and food and giving 'roaming time' (a degree of freedom of movement).

The life of Abu Huraira is often cited as an example to follow among Muslims. As a native of Yemen, he came to the Prophet the fame of whose piety was spreading fast and developed great respect for him and his beliefs. He soon became famous as a companion of the Prophet and a major narrator of his sayings. Many parts of the *Hadith* come from him, since he is believed to have had phenomenal memory and could recall conversations of long ago exactly as they took place years ago. Abu Huraira was not his real name, but a nickname which was given to him—it literally means 'father of kittens'—because he used to care for a small male cat. Since the word cat 'comes from Arabic *qit/Hirra*, but a tiny male is called *hurayrah*: the name stuck'. On account of his love of cats which he imbibed from the example of the Prophet himself, he started looking after hosts of cats, and always carried a small one in his bag.

Much of his life, Abu Huraira lived as a destitute but slowly he rose greatly in stature and was even appointed governor of a region by the Caliph Omar, a position he voluntarily left later because he did not want to live in luxury which early Islam did not approve of. He died at the age of seventy-eight, having led an exemplary life as a devotee of the Prophet and of the faith. It is for his kindness to animals in general but to cats in particular that he is remembered with respect and his name has survived for centuries.

CATS
IN PAINTINGS
Past & Present

• 1 •

PALACE LADIES CELEBRATING SHAB-E BARAT

Bikaner, late eighteenth century
Attributed to the painter Mola Bagas

[from Francesca Galloway sales catalogue: Asia Week, 2014]

While a group of finely clad ladies in a palace celebrate the sacred festival of the Night of Forgiveness and Atonement in Islam—lighting beautiful sparklers—a pair of palace cats, equally finely adorned, sporting beaded golden collars, are helping themselves to a repast. One of them, clearly satiated, looks the viewer boldly in the face, almost telling the viewer: 'you know, of course, that dogs eat, cats dine.'

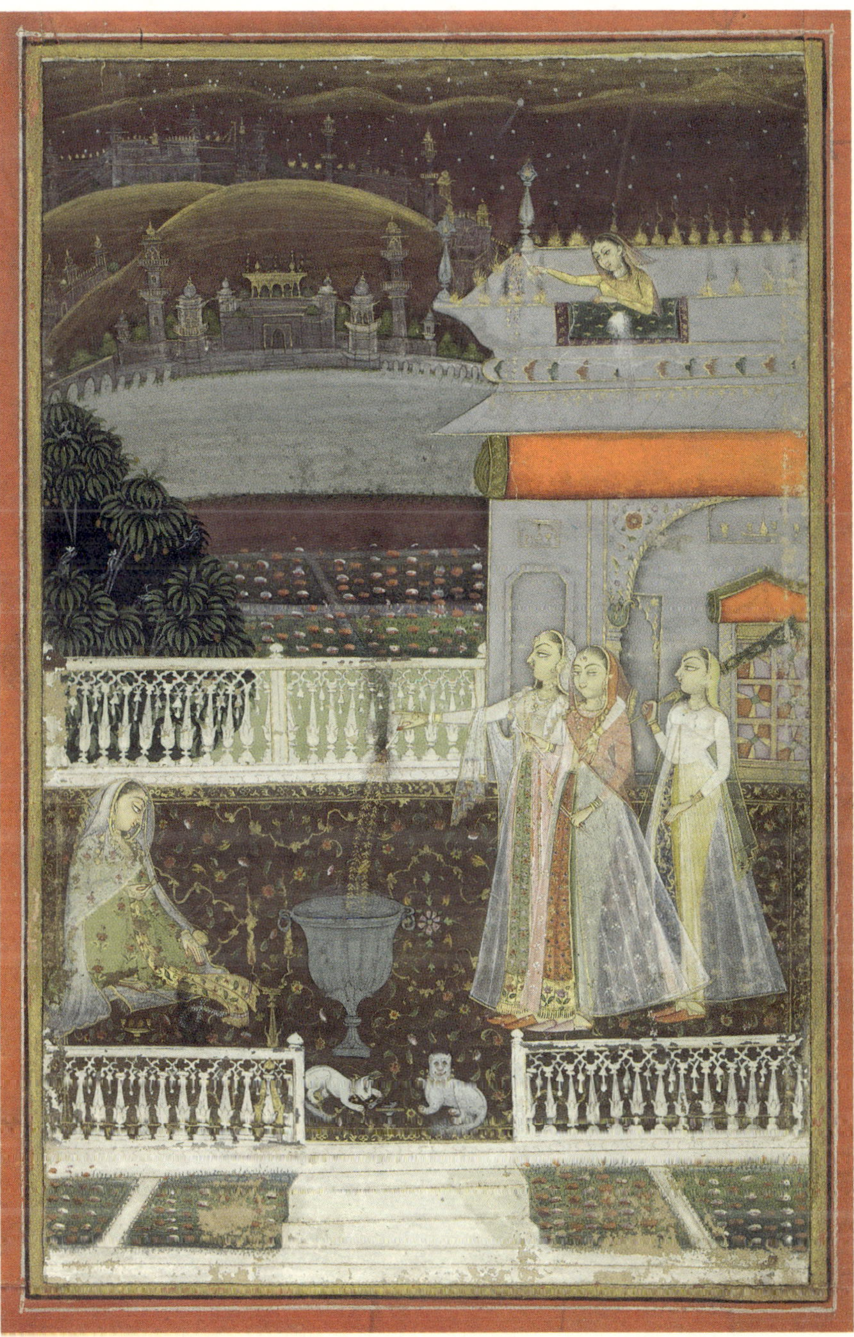

• 2 •

LOVERS ON A TERRACE

Awadh, late eighteenth century
Attributed to Faizullah

[from Sotheby's auction catalogue, Indian and Southeast Asian Works of Art, 2012, lot 223]

The night is long gone. Nearly everyone—all the palace ladies, barring three who stand solicitously next to the lovers' bed, and the princely lover himself—has gone to sleep on this magnificent terrace. Even the candles inside their elegant but now darkened glass covers, have gone out. But the palace cat is wide awake, crouched like a heraldic lion, keeping guard. 'No entry please; no disturbance', is the clear message being sent out.

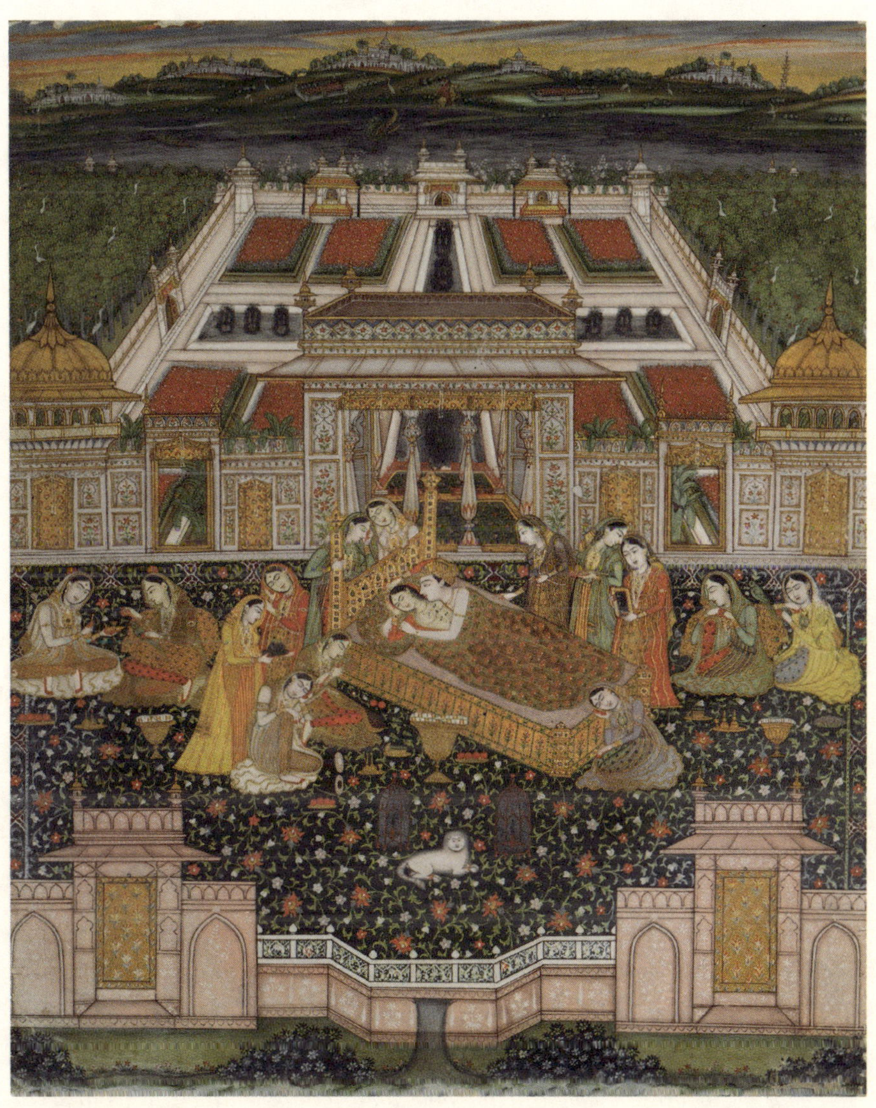

• 3 •

PRINCESS ON A TERRACE, LOST IN THOUGHT

Deccan, possibly Hyderabad, late eighteenth century
On verso, a folio containing a quatrain in the hand of a calligrapher bearing the title *Raushan Raqam*

[Chhatrapati Shivaji Maharaj Vastu Sangrahalaya, Mumbai; acc. no. 22.3438]

The verse calligraphed at the back, even though not directly related to the painting, captures, while describing the beauty of the princess, the mood of quiet contemplation tinged by melancholy. Companionably the snow-white cat sits at her feet, matching her mistress's elegance, wearing as she does a splendid gold collar herself. Absorbed in herself or the state of her mistress at this moment, she pays no attention to the bird perched on a sill behind her. But for how long, one is entitled to wonder?

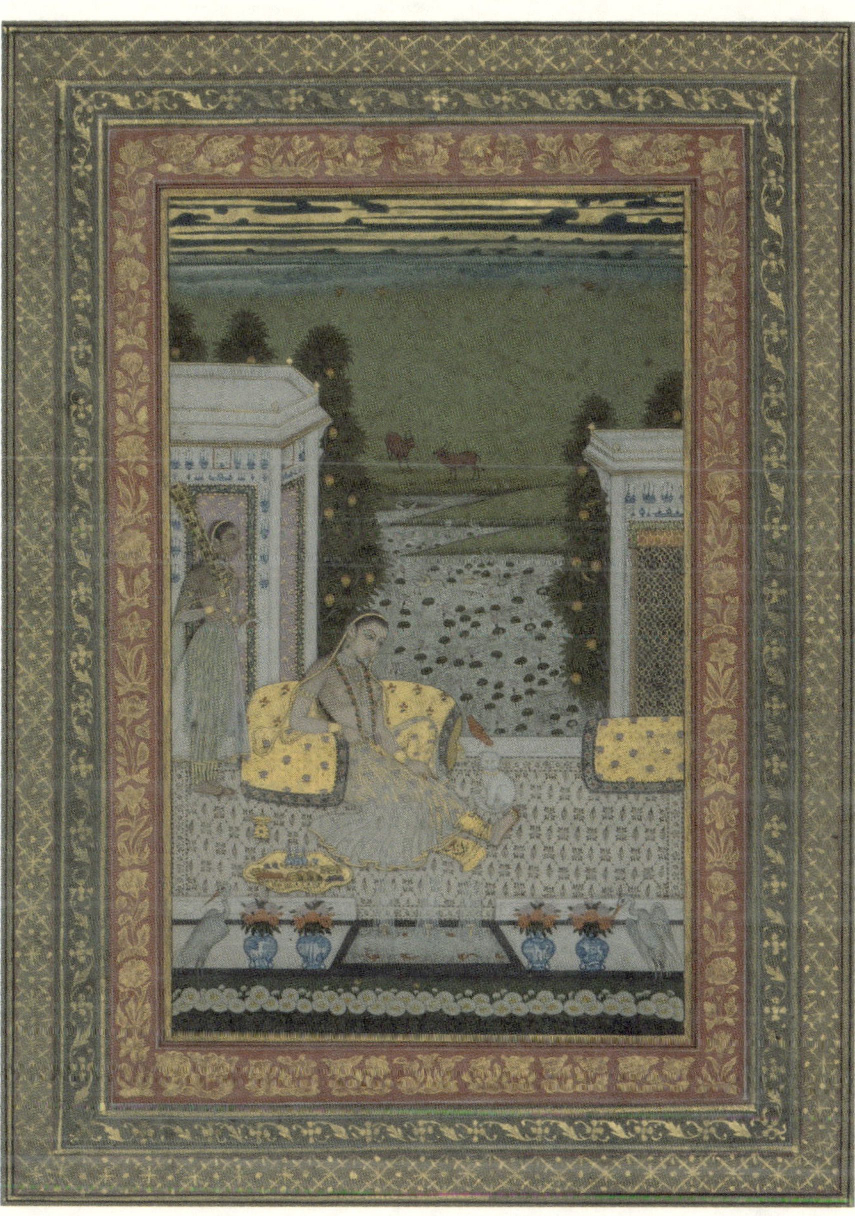

• 4 •

PRINCESS WATCHING A MAID KILLING A SNAKE

By Mir Kalan Khan
Lucknow; c. 1770

[Collection: British Library; Johnson Album 15, no. 8]

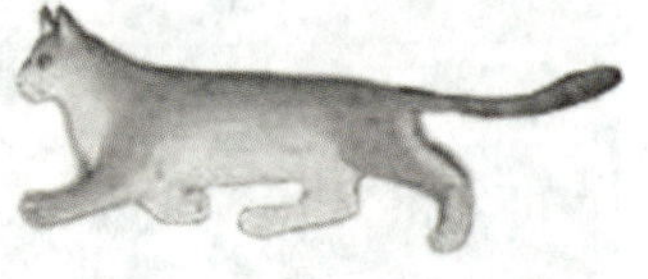

In an opulent, peaceful quarter of a palace—one notices a bird perched quietly on a balustrade at the back while a cat roams about in the same courtyard—there is sudden commotion, for a snake has sneaked in from somewhere. Quickly, however, an alert maid skewers the snake with an iron rod as her mistress, wearing a remarkably ample but elegant skirt, looks on, not half as agitated as the duenna behind her. Majestically, the palace cat walks towards the scene, thinking perhaps that even I could have done that. No?

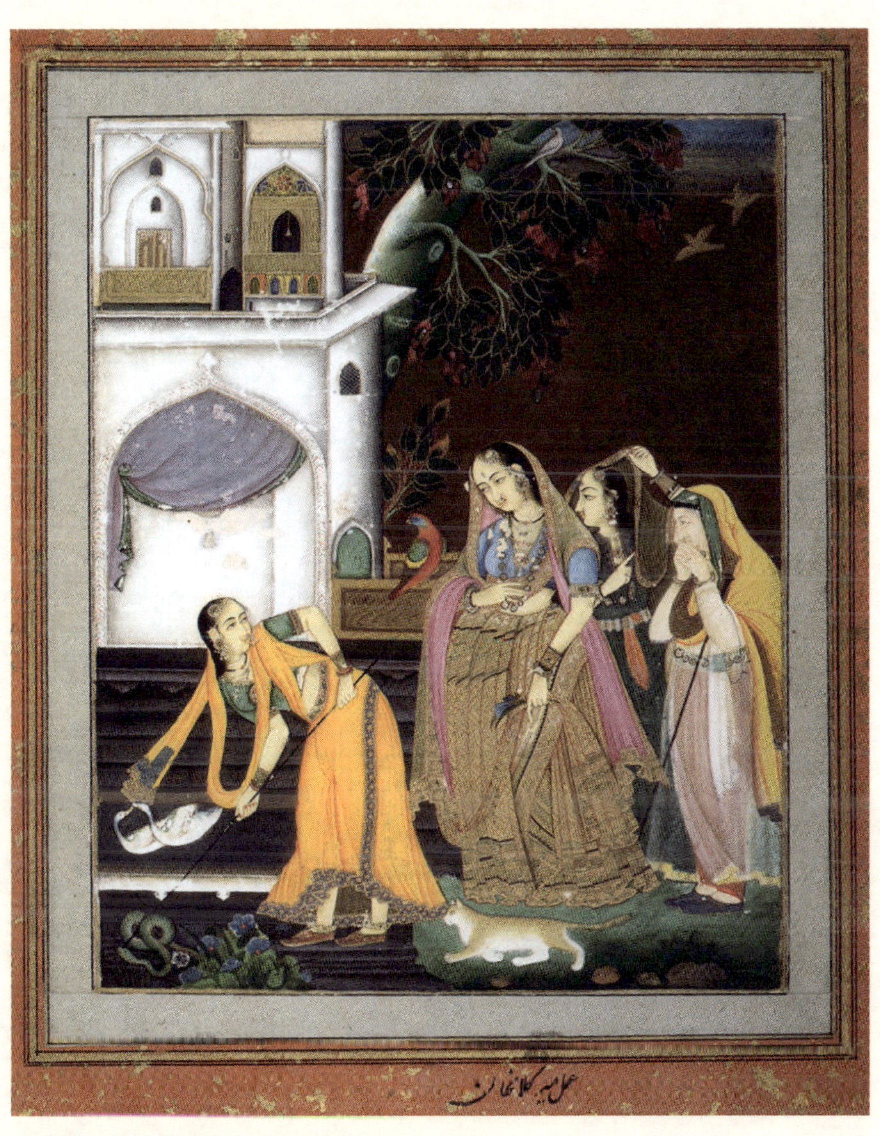

• 5 •

A GATHERING OF COURT WOMEN

From a folio of the *Davis Album*
Mughal; late seventeenth to early eighteenth century
[Metropolitan Museum of Art, New York; acc. no. 30.95.174.27]
[Bequest of Theodore M. Davis, 1915]

Women's Hour is what we have here, it seems. Carefree duennas, companions, maids of the palace, are all gathered in a courtyard, cushions lying around, a cistern with an elegant fountain spraying water. Drinks are at hand; a small child sits next to his mother sprawling on a beautiful carpet while someone plays on a drum for her.

Clearly, palace gossip is the theme at this leisured hour, but no one is paying much attention to a cat half hidden under the knee of one of the women. Is her owner going to spring a surprise—some news, some new scandal—much as the cat who could slink out and suddenly leap, taking everyone by surprise?

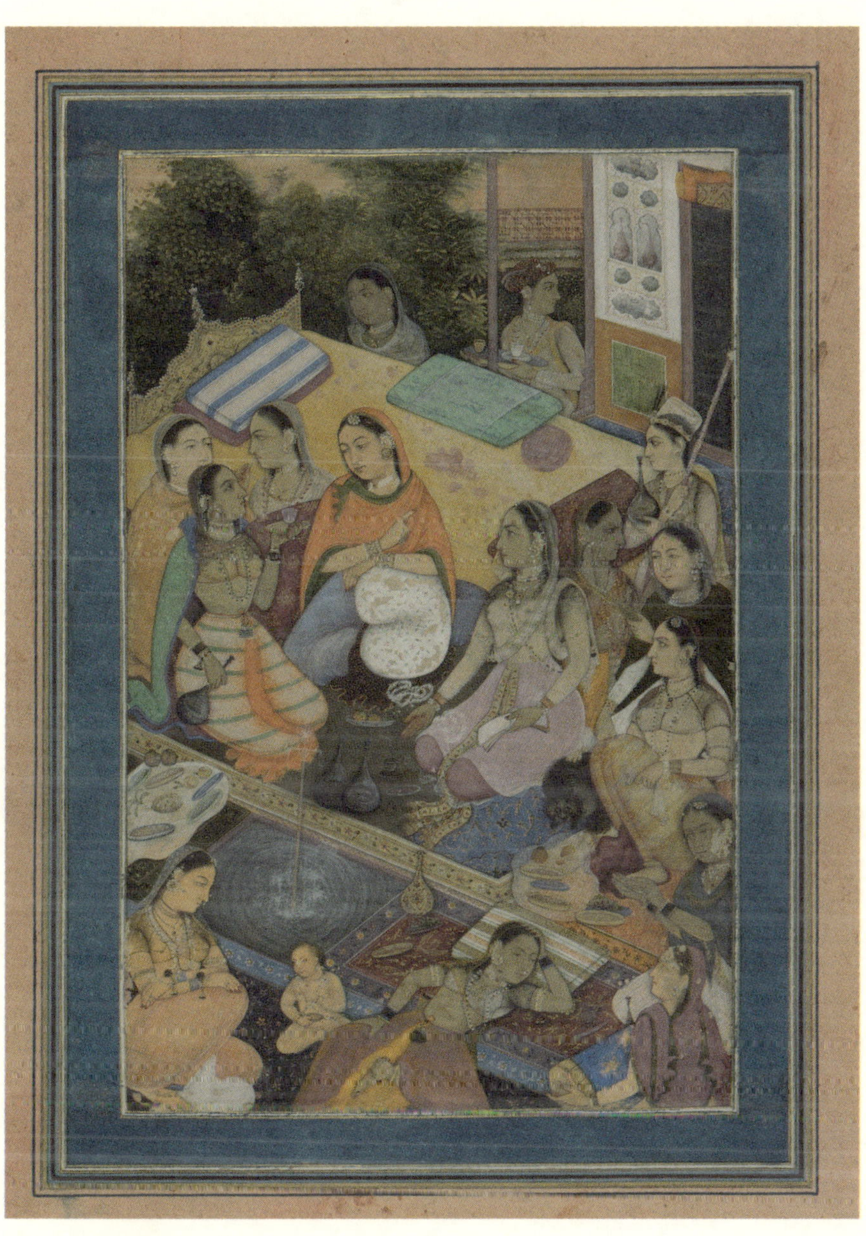

• 6 •

RULER IN THE ZENANA

Kotah; early eighteenth century

[National Museum, New Delhi; acc. no. 56.48/19]

Some celebration is in progress, but within the walled precincts one sees, apart from the prince who is smoking a huqqa, only women: some dancing; others singing; still others attending to little tasks. Outside, of course, there are men and tethered animals and guards. A cat has also, however, sneaked in, barely noticeably, a tiny figure just outside the tented pavilion. Claiming to be part of the group, pleading her gender, perhaps?

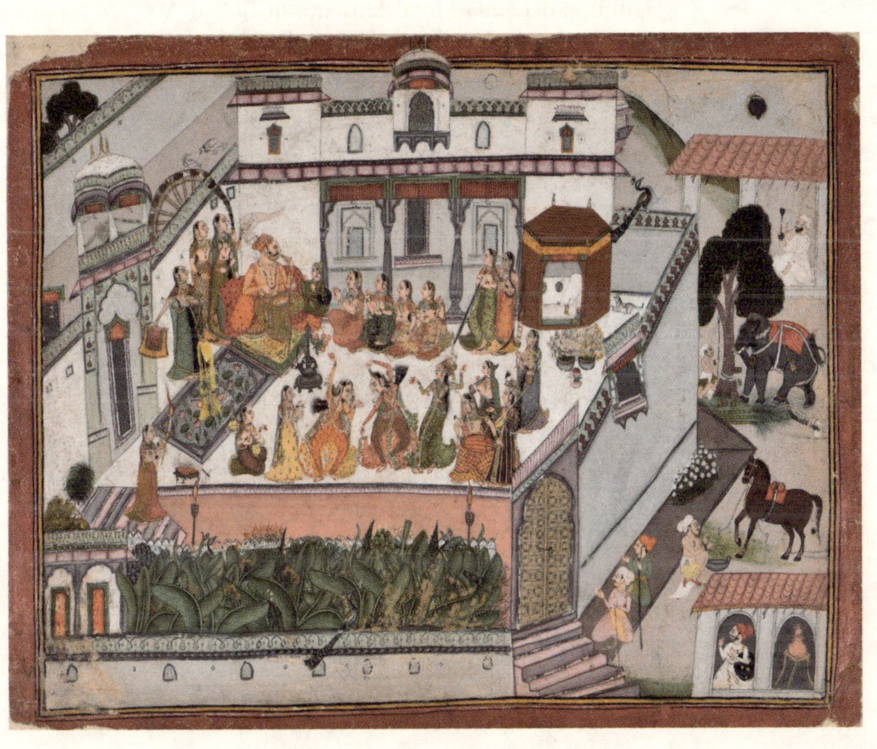

• 7 •

A GOVERNESS INSTRUCTING A PRINCESS

Chamba, ca. 1710–20

[Jagdish and Kamla Mittal Museum of Indian Art, Hyderabad; acc. no. 76.796 dr. 231]

A scene that is at once formal and informal: on the one hand one sees instruction being imparted to a Mughalized princess by a stern-looking governess; on the other the surroundings are bare, with no trappings of a palace. But there is no mistaking the context: the princess is extending a finger to touch some letters or numbers on the tablet placed on the floor. One imagines that the princess is a bit overwhelmed by the learning in front of her: so is the little, shrunken cat that looks on, muttering to herself. 'Tough, isn't it?'

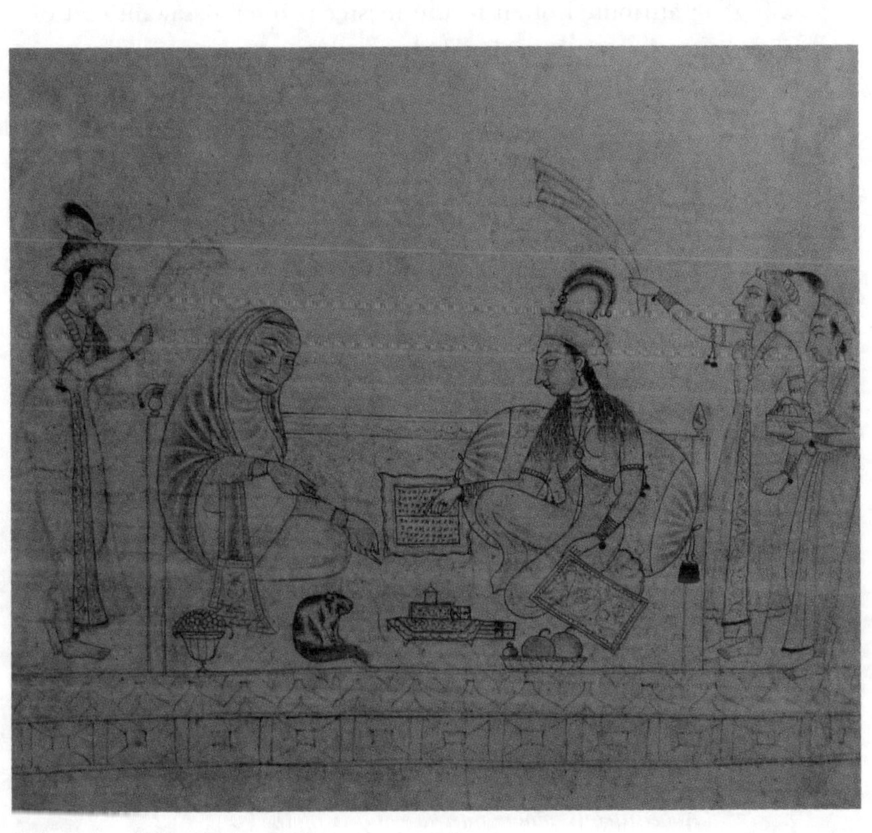

•8•

MOTHER AND CHILD

Folio from the *Muraqqa-e Gulshan*
Mughal; attributed often to the master painter Basawan; end of sixteenth century

[Edwin Binney 3rd collection; San Diego Museum of Art; acc. no. 1990–293]

With the emperor Akbar taking keen interest in Christian themes, a whole body of works centred upon and inspired by European works with Christian themes, was produced, including this, one of the most elegant in that group. The central figure reclines while nursing the child, surrounded by symbols of fertility, and her presence is celebrated in the verse on the margins:

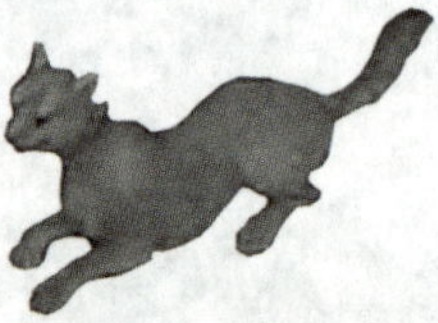

A beauteous moon has been born of the sun
And feeds upon the milk of its breast.

What, however, is the cat doing here, one wonders: just telling us by being there that this is a scene from the world we live in, and not of the heavens; or is she, seeing the child feeding himself, also eyeing something?

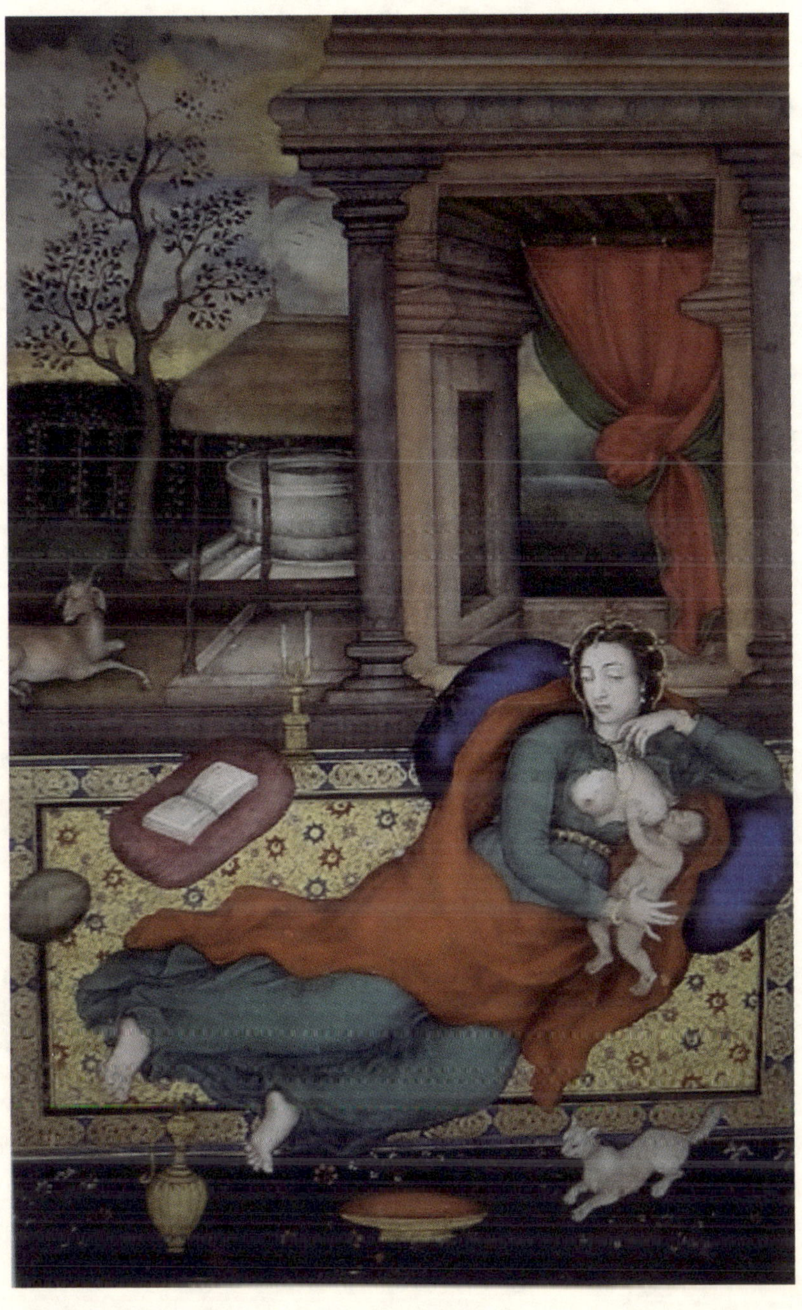

•9•

MADONNA AND CHILD IN A DOMESTIC SETTING

Folio from an album
Attributed to the artist Manohar; Mughal, ca. 1600

[The Metropolitan Museum of Art, New York, Rogers Fund; acc. no. 1970.217]

Manohar's work is evidently based on some European original, although some changes must have been made by him, as was the wont of Mughal painters who drew inspiration from, or copied, Christian themes. In a stark and simple chamber, here the Madonna looks with affection and reverence, hands folded, at her son, the Child Christ. While she does this, a cat, sitting very close to the bed, seems to be keeping guard, as it were. One is reminded somehow of the episode of the cat belonging to the great Prophet of Islam, Muhammad, having saved him by killing a snake which appeared from nowhere and was about to bite him as he slept.

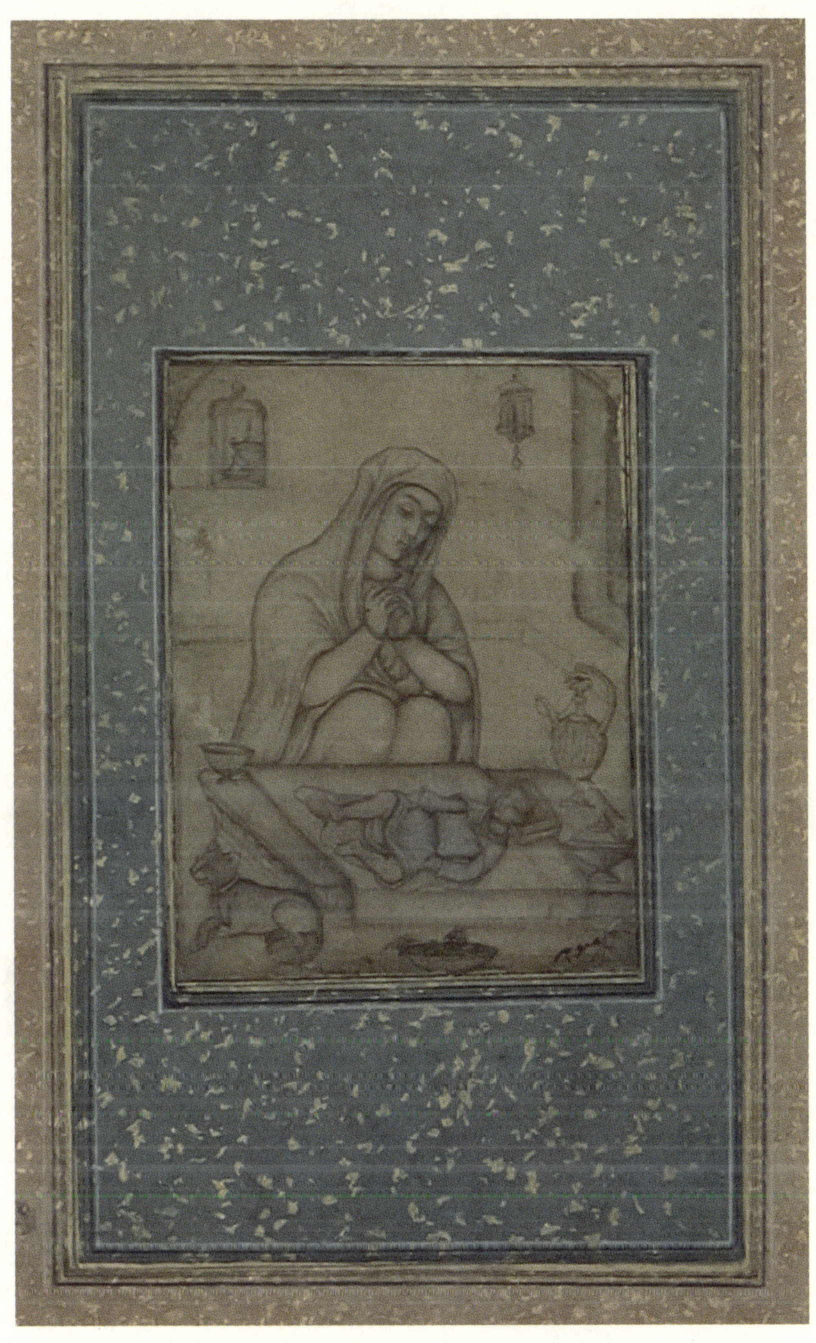

• 10 •

THE PRESENTATION OF THE INFANT JESUS IN THE TEMPLE OF JERUSALEM, FORTY DAYS AFTER HIS BIRTH

Possibly Deccan; ca. 1610–20

[Victoria & Albert Museum, London; acc. no. I.M. 14a–1913]

Evidently based on some European work, which is likely to have come through the Jesuit mission/embassy in Goa, and structured by an Indian painter in his own fashion, the painting represents—or so it seems—the occasion when the infant Jesus was presented in the temple at Jerusalem, forty days after his birth. As a part of the somewhat Indianized look of the work, the painter has brought a cat in even though it is highly unlikely that in the European original there was any. In any case she is not concerned here either with the occasion or with the exalted personages. Fun is all she is looking for.

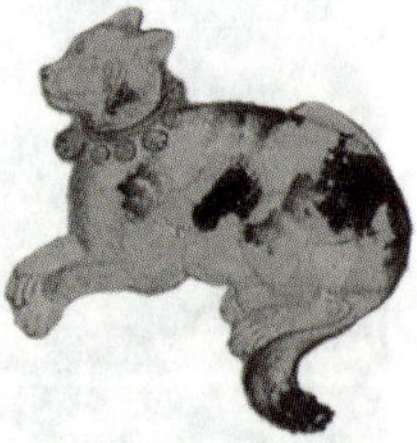

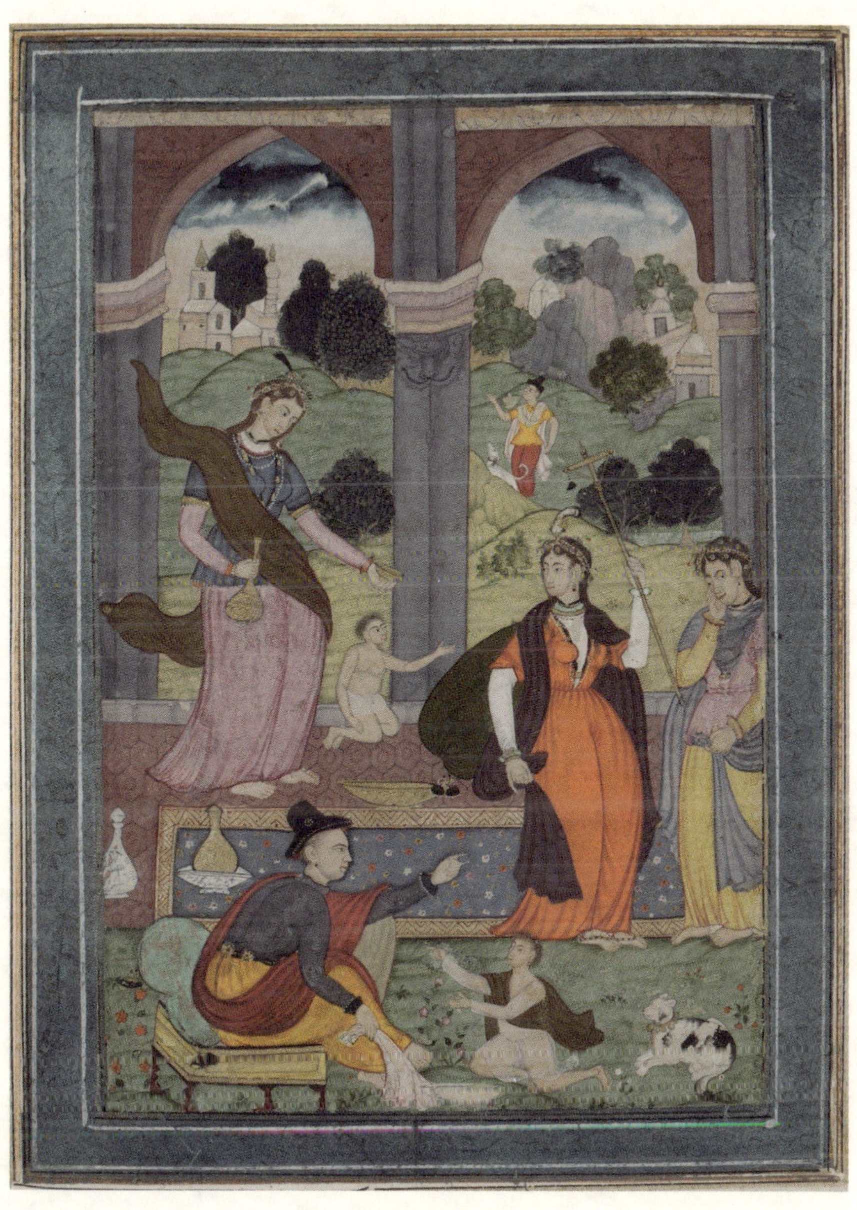

• 11 •

MELANCHOLIC WOMAN AND ATTENDANT

Mughal; attributed often to the painter Basawan, or to Keshavadas; ca. 1600
Museum of Fine Arts, Boston
[The Bartlett Collection; acc. no. 14.688]

One does not know the European original from which this elegant work draws or is inspired by. But it certainly is arresting. 'Drowned in thought'—the verses in Persian above and below in the little cartouches say—'this beauty, foremost among the beauties of China', sits here, her eye on a book next to her and her hand brushing her brow. Despite all the melancholy, however, she can still 'ensnare everyone and incarcerate them in the elegant curls of her hair'. The white cat which sits quietly next to her mistress's throne, and looks up, is certainly in thrall.

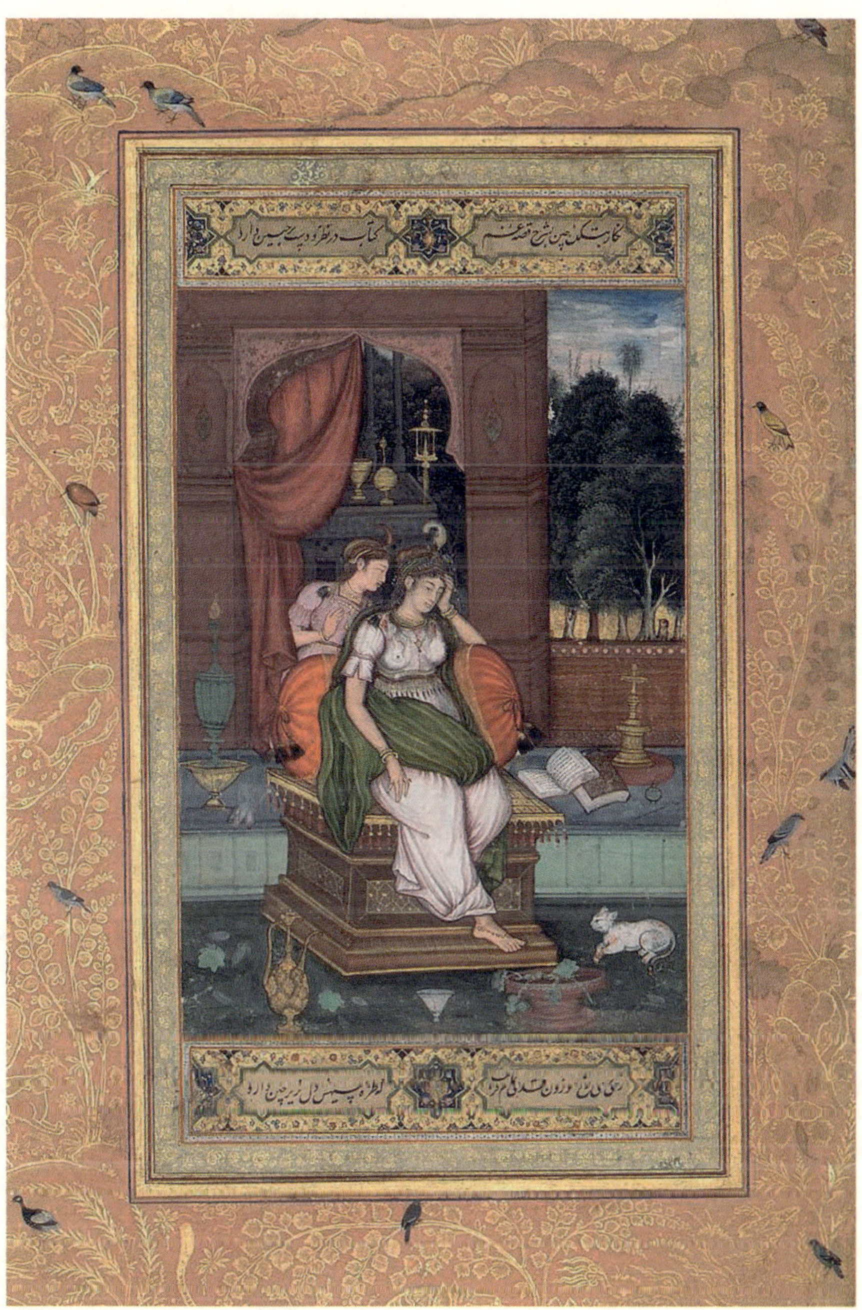

• 12 •

DAVID AND BATHSHEBA

Mughal; late eighteenth century
Collection: Franz-Josef and Birgit Vollmer
[Gundelfingen, Germany]

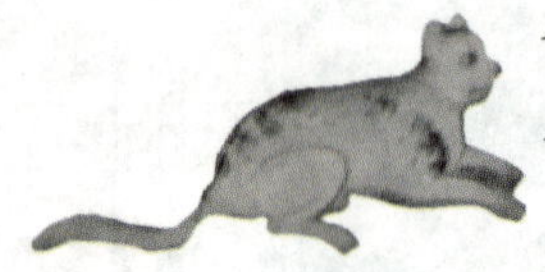

Inspired by some unidentified European painting but amended and in a manner Indianized by an unknown painter, the work depicts the twosome—the biblical King David and the beauteous Bathsheba whom he saw bathing and fell in love with only to marry her later—in an Indian-looking setting. With the cloud of scandal of adultery and a killing hovering above them, is it a bond that they are signing now? At least the cat—the only witness here—thinks so.

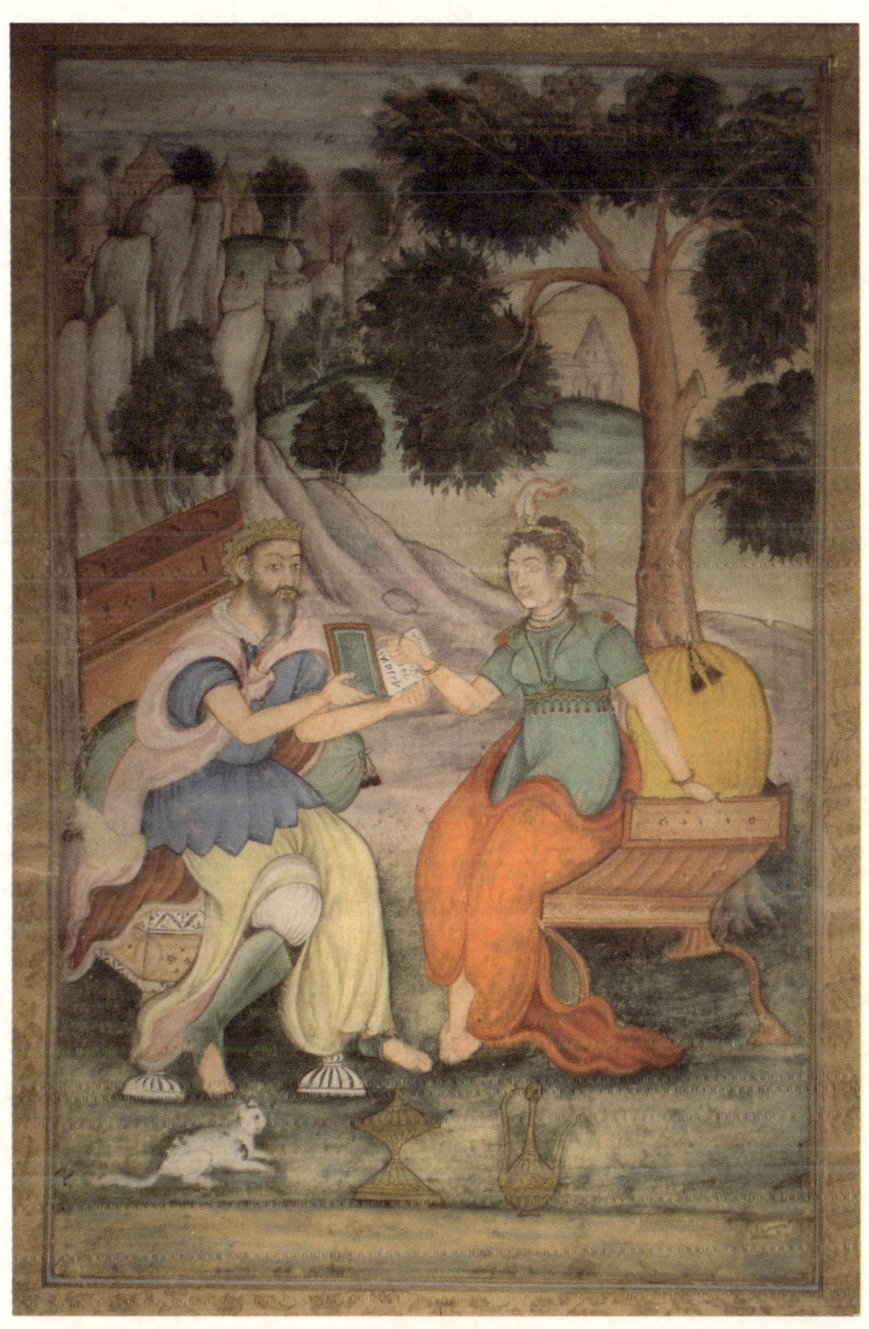

• 13 •

ST. JEROME

Mughal; ca. 1600–20
Brendan Lynch/Oliver Forge auction catalogue, 2014
[Now in the collection of Franz-Josef and Birgit Vollmer, Gundelfingen]

The great scholar that he was, St. Jerome is generally represented in European works sitting in his study stacked with books, working. Around him sits a lion, guard and companion. While drawing upon his figure from one of those works, the Mughal painter simplifies and compresses the scene. There are no shelves of books around. The saint's surroundings are simple and stark. Head resting on a hand, he is absorbed in writing, a book by his side, an ink pot in front. But in this lonesome task, who keeps him company? A cat, who has apparently edged the lion out and chosen to sit by the side of the master: wearing an expression of grave intensity on her face.

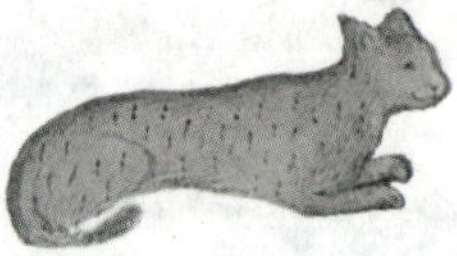

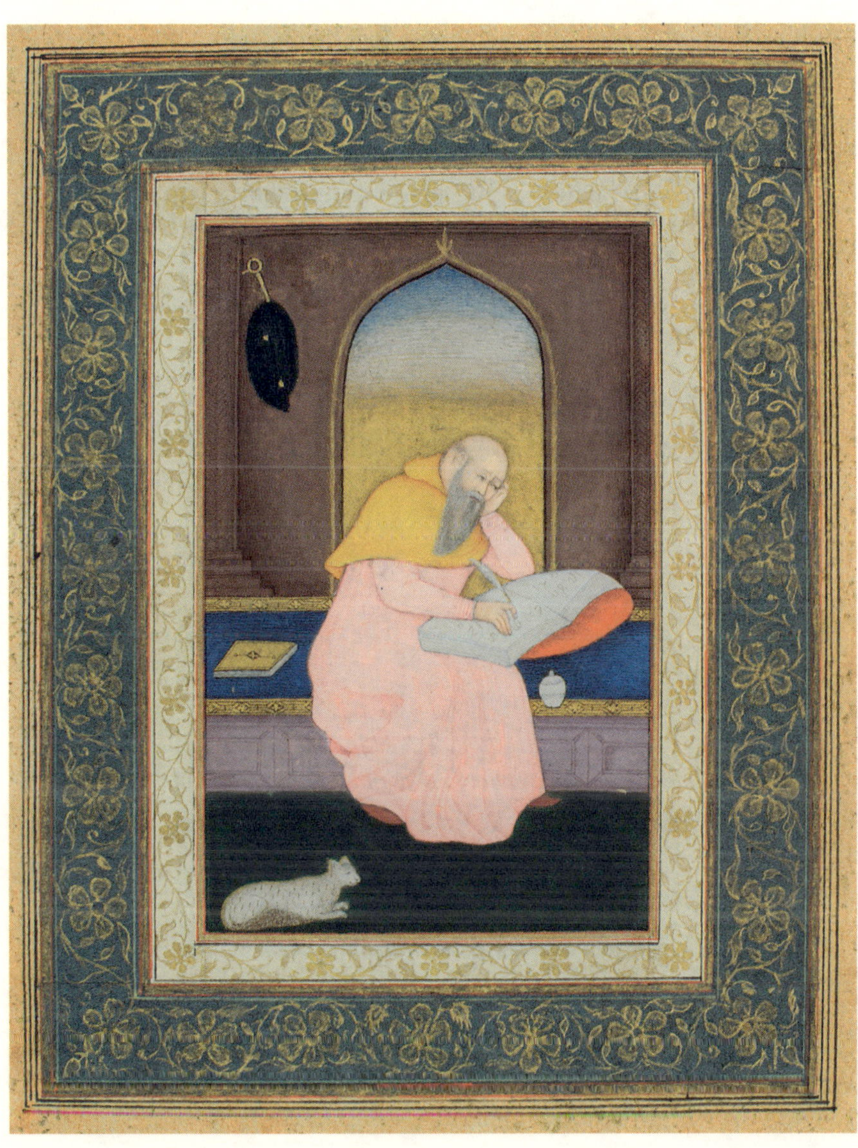

• 14 •

REPRESENTATION OF MELANCHOLY

Folio from a Royal Album of Shah Jahan
Signed by the artist Farrukh Beg; Mughal or Deccani, seventeenth century
[Museum of Islamic Art, Doha, Qatar, MS.44.2007]

Farrukh Beg, taking off from a well-known Dutch print captioned 'Dolor', meaning melancholy or depression, took that study of a bearded, old saint, and transformed it. The background changed; colour was added; the animals around the doleful man grew: but the mood was retained in its entirety. Here the man sits in his garden, staring vacantly at a large desk/cupboard where a cat is lapping up milk pouring out of a vessel that she has succeeded in upturning. He is either incapable of stirring into action, or does not care if this is happening. In keeping with the mood, a dog sleeps and two goats stand around. The only cheer in this superbly painted work belongs to the cat.

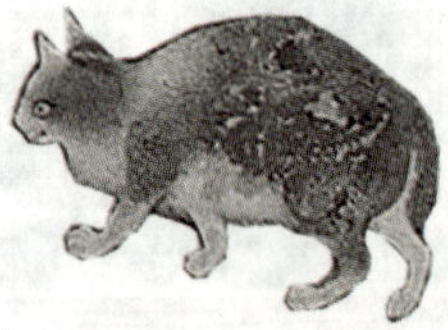

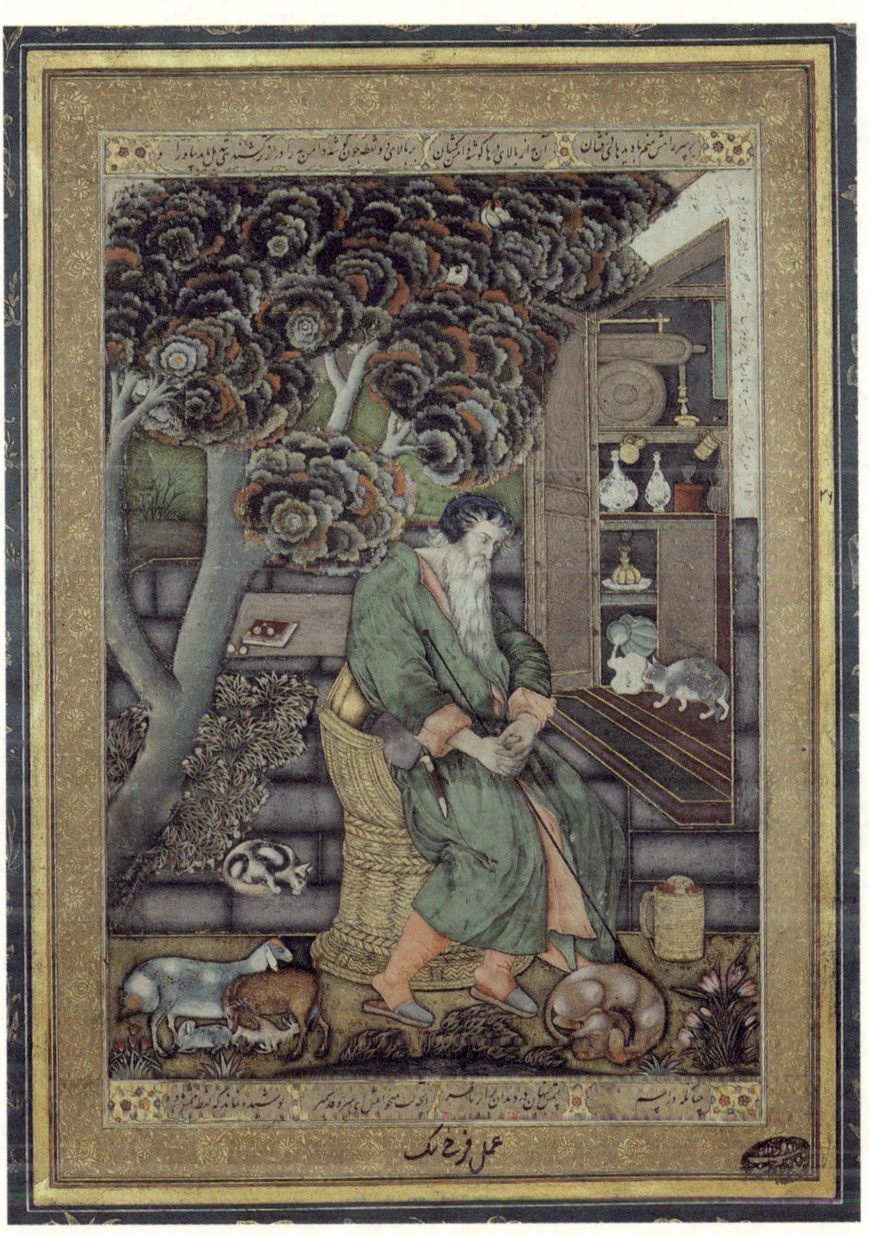

• 15 •

EUROPEAN YOUTH WITH FLASK SITTING IN A CHAIR

Folio from an album
Mughal, ca. 1700
Bharat Kala Bhawan, Varanasi; acc. no. 672

[Courtesy: Regents of the University of Michigan, Department of History of Art]

The relatively small image, framed within a broad border (now rubbed) filled with floral sprigs, shows a foppish young man, evidently a 'foreigner', seated on an elaborately crafted chair, a large bolster behind, flask in hand. The curved, cornered hat with fancy feathers stuck in it, the decorative white ruff around the neck, the elegantly designed jacket, all support the dandy-like look in the eyes of the young man. Obviously, his pet spotted cat, craning her neck and looking up at him, is expecting either to talk to him, or to be petted.

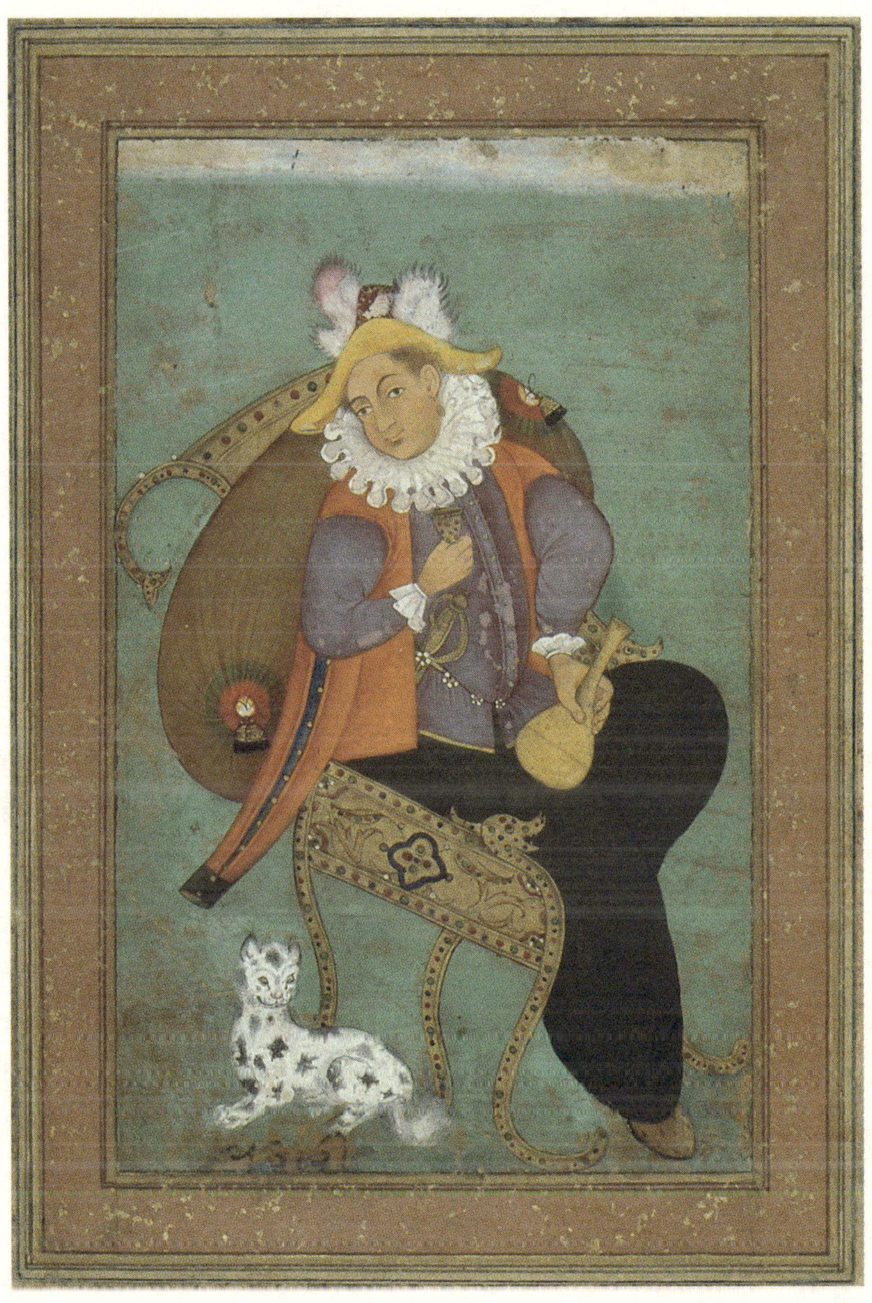

• 16 •

THE PANCAKE MAKER

Mughal (after a European original); end of seventeenth century

[From Sotheby's auction catalogue, the Art of Imperial India, 2014, lot 245]

Picking on a theme that was a favourite of Dutch and Flemish painters in the seventeenth century—a woman baking pancakes—and in this case basing himself on an etching by F. de Wit, after a work by Adriaen Brouwer, the Mughal painter shows baking in progress. While the ample-bodied woman attends to her task, two boys look expectantly on, hungry looks in their eyes. But equally interested in the delicacy—when it is ready of course—is the cat who looks slyly on from a distance, biding her time. Undoubtedly.

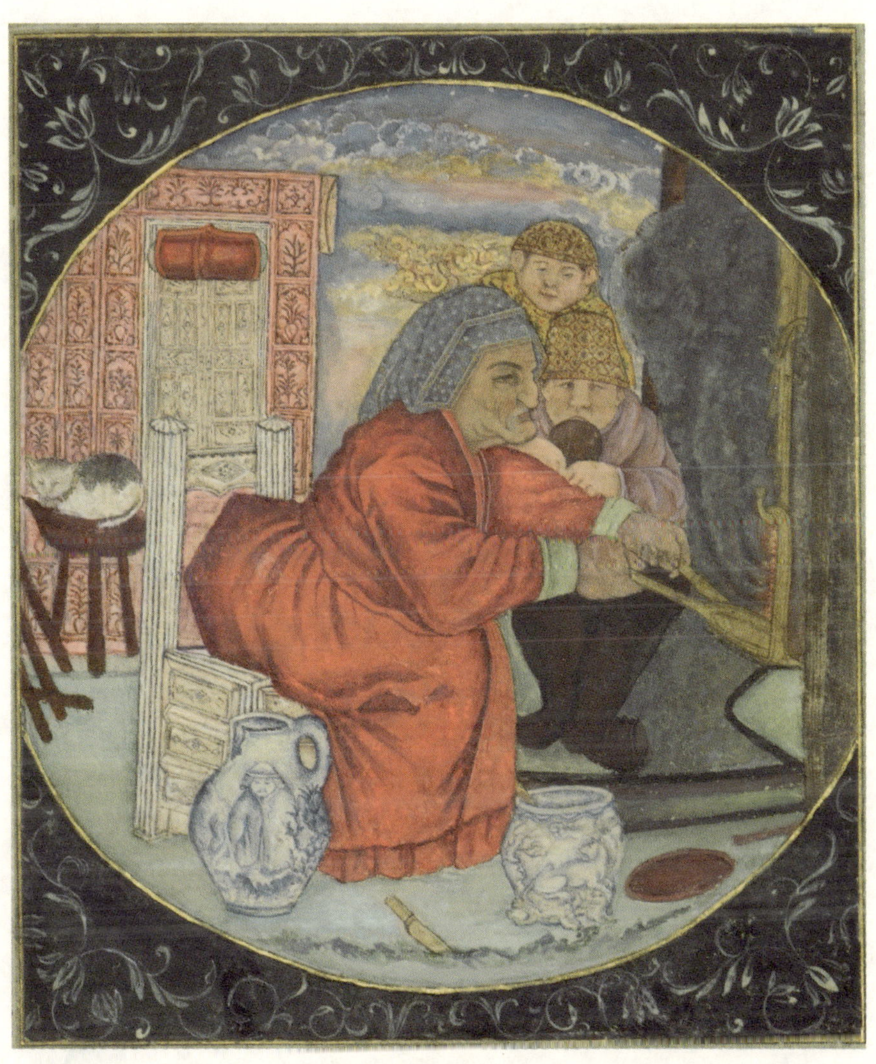

• 17 •

CAT IN THE AYODHYA PALACE

Folio from the *Freer Ramayana*
Mughal, ca. 1600

[Freer–Sackler Gallery, Washington, DC; 1907.272.102, vol. I, folio 102]

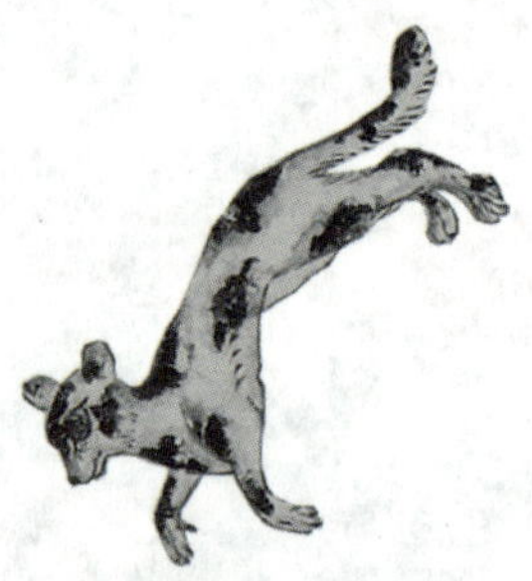

The scene is from a folio of the great epic, the Ramayana, *translated into Persian and now known as the* Freer Ramayana. *What we see here however is something that takes one by surprise, two cats (or is it one seen twice?) in the middle distance, animals hardly ever associated with the great text. Bharata and Shatrughna, Rama's brothers, have arrived and learn of Rama having been exiled in their absence. They break down and cry piteously, as do the three 'mothers', and the women of the royal household. But the cat/s jumping about in the background? Agitated by a recollection of the event, perhaps? Or stirred by the deep emotions they are witnessing?*

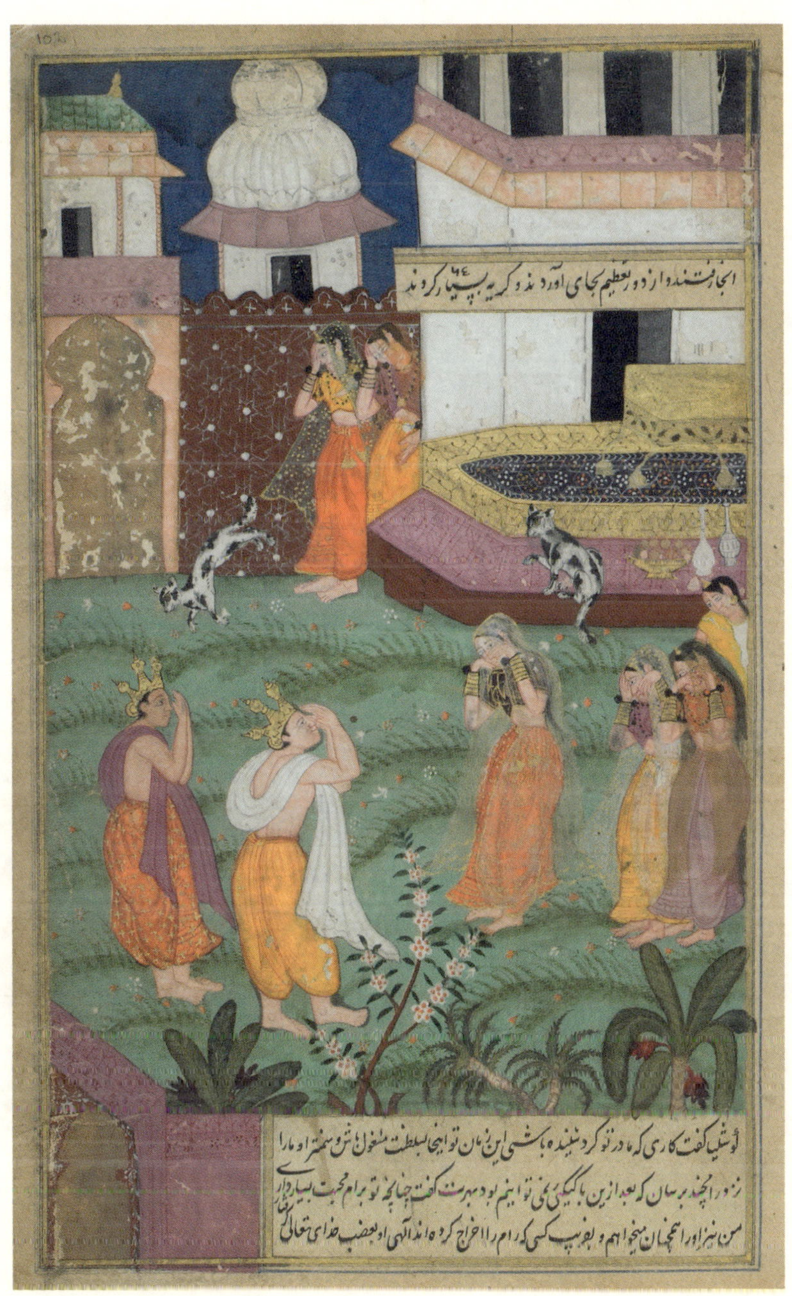
انجا رفتند و از دور تعظیم بجای آوردند و گریه بسیار کردند
کوشلیا گفت کاری که مادر تو کرد نشنیده باشی این زمان تو اینجا بسلطنت مشغول باش و سمترا و مارا
نزد رامچند برسان که بعد ازین با کیکی نمی توانیم بود بهرت گفت چنانچه تو رام محبت بسیار داری
من نیز او را همچنان میخواهم و بعضب کسی که رام را اخراج کرده اند الهی او بغضب خدای تعالی گرفتار

• 18 •

CAT IN THE *ASHOKA VATIKA*

Folio from a *Ramayana* manuscript
Mewar; mid-seventeenth century

[British Library; acc.no. Add MS 15297 (1-20; IO. SAN 3621, f. 3)]

Scripted by one scribe but painted by many hands, the Jagat Singh Ramayana *(1648–53), remains one of the most extensively illustrated manuscripts of the great epic. It is full of scenes or episodes not often seen in other versions. The surprise that lurks in this folio is of a different order, however. While Ravana comes to the Ashoka Vatika to see the captive Sita, Rama's spouse, the scene is witnessed by many as he alternately woos and threatens her. A cat seems to be a witness too till one realizes that she is not real: she is a painted image on the front wall of a large parapet, sharing space with a bouquet of flowers and a framed window.*

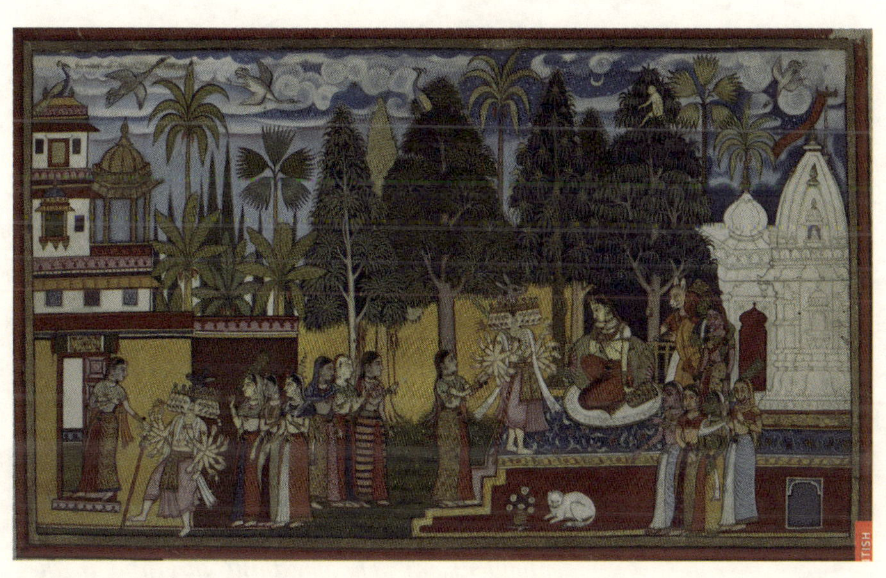

• 19 •

A RISHI'S PEACEFUL ASHRAMA

Leaf from a *Ramayana* series
Pahari; early nineteenth century
[Private Collection]

While in exile, Rama, with his wife Sita and brother Lakshmana, keep moving from place to place: encountering and eliminating evil rakshasas, paying homage to sacred sites and places, visiting the hermitages of great sages, seeking solace and enlightenment. The one thing they find in the ashramas is peace; a feeling of serenity. Here, in this ashrama, as they sit conversing with a sage, they see perfect harmony in place. Even natural enmities disappear: cats and mice live peacefully together; there is no hostility between the elephant and the tiger; none between the snake and the mongoose. That is how we see the black cat at the bottom left conversing with the mouse who is looking up at her, unafraid!

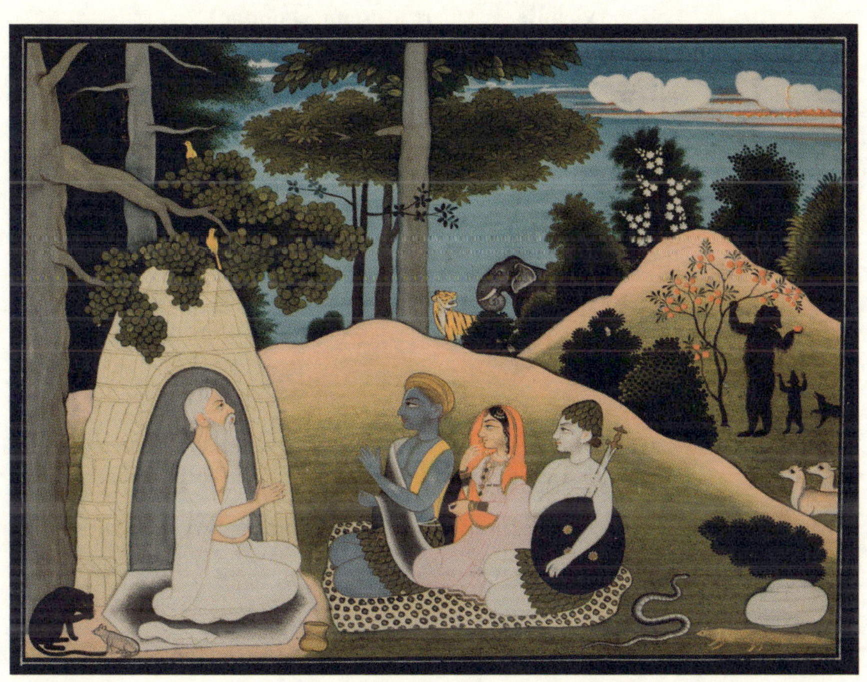

• 20 •

THE GODDESS SHASHTHI, PROTECTRESS OF CHILDREN

A popular printed poster
Bengal; twentieth century

[Victoria & Albert Museum, London]

A folk goddess, most popular in Bengal, Shashthi is widely worshipped: mostly by women, especially those with small children, and those who are pregnant. Several stories are current about her, some drawn from old texts, others newly woven. What emerges from them is the belief that she is the great, infallible protectress of children. Like Bastet, the Egyptian goddess, she is revered for this and related reasons. She is represented as having children either in her lap or playing with her while a cat is shown as her vahana or vehicle. The cat receives therefore as much reverence as, for instance, the bull Nandi does in association with Shiva, or the sunbird Garuda who is the vahana of Vishnu.

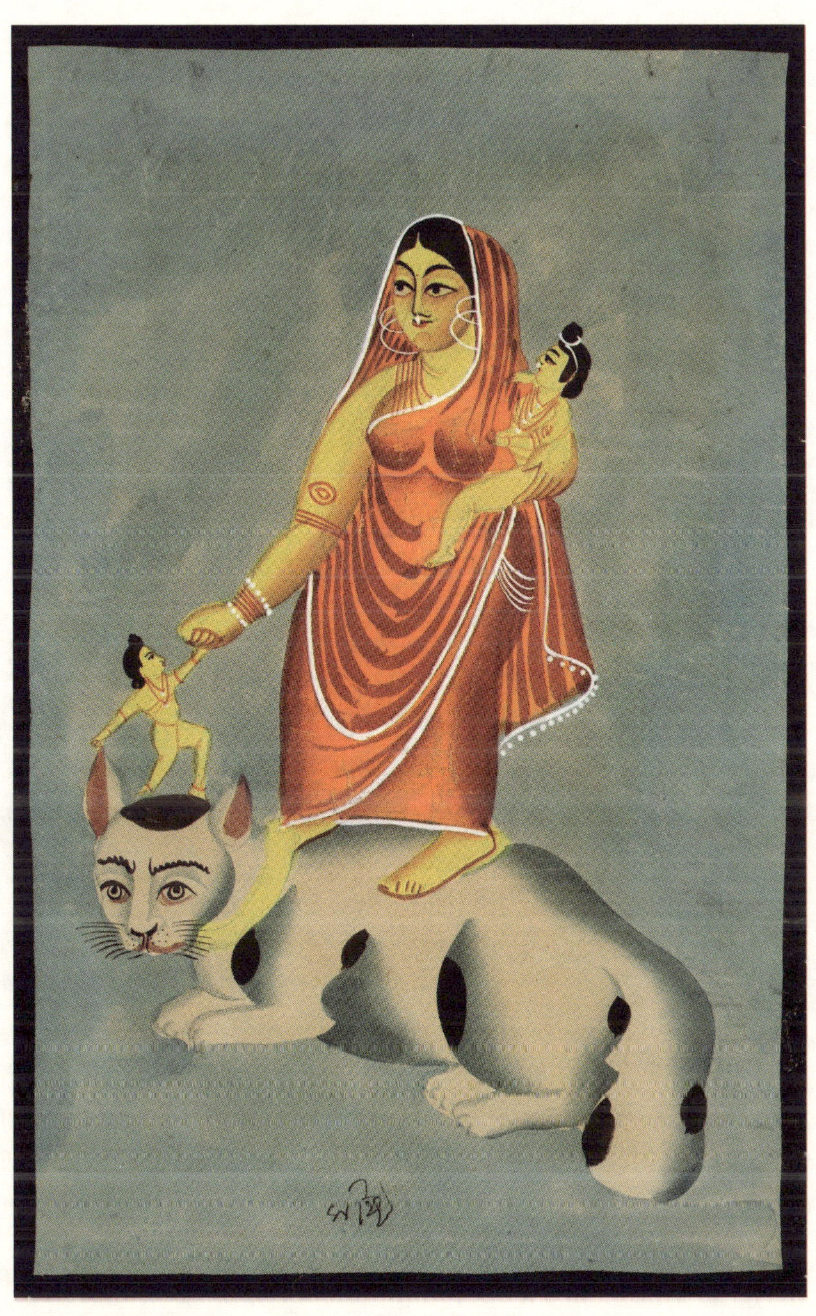

• 21 •

THE TRAPPED CAT AND THE FRIGHTENED MOUSE

Folio from a manuscript of the *Kalila wa Dimna*
Possibly from Sultanate Gujarat; second quarter of the sixteenth century

[The Metropolitan Museum of Art, New York; Gift of Alice and Nasli Heeramaneck, acc. no. 1981.373.81]

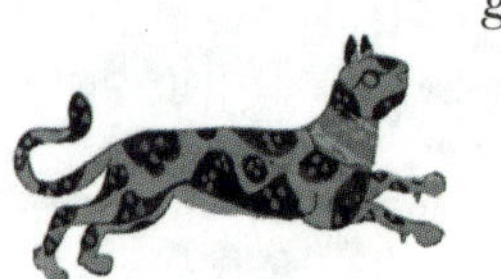

Classics like the Panchatantra *and the Buddhist* Jataka tales, *going long back in time, lived lives of their own not only in India but in different versions in different lands. They were modified, shortened or lengthened, even recast, and appeared under different names. Based broadly on the* Panchatantra, *there appeared one in Arabic entitled* Kalila wa Dimna. *In India, probably in some corner of Gujarat, a copy was made, bearing seventy-eight paintings. Here, in a folio, a cat is shown with other animals who feature in the story 'A Mouse, a Fox or Jackal, and an owl'. What exact roles do they play in the complicated story? For that one will have to go to the text.*

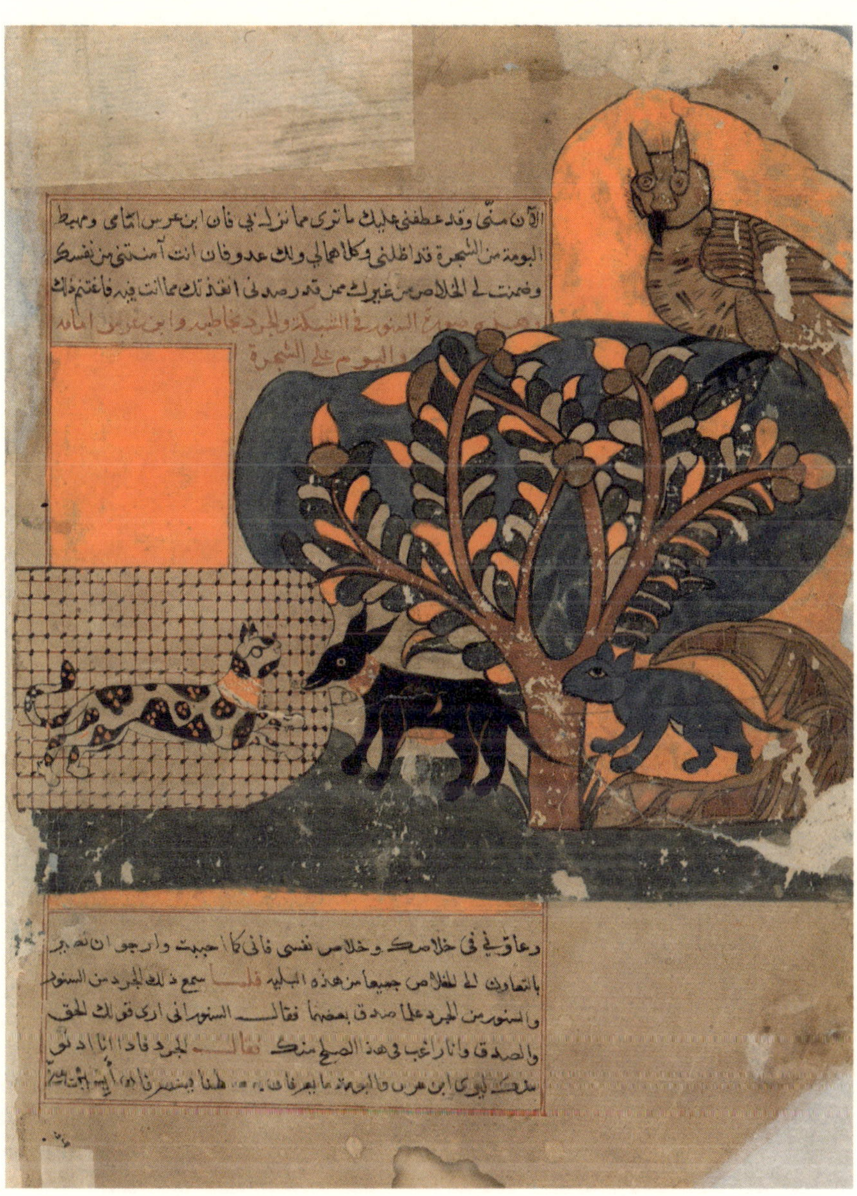

• 22 •

THE TREACHEROUS CAT

Folio from a manuscript of the *Anwar-i Suhayli*
Mughal; 1604–10

[British Library, Add Ms. 18579]

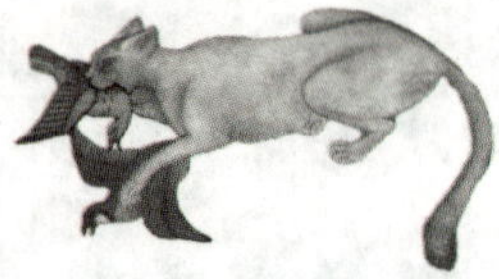

When the Indian classic, the Panchatantra, *was translated into Persian by the scholar Husayn Vai'z Kashifi, changes—in context, names, settings—were naturally made, and it is with these changes that it arrived in India, catching the fancy of emperors. The copy prepared for Jahangir had a large number of stories including one in which a treacherous cat entered. In that, projecting herself as having turned pious and neutral, the cat sat in judgement in a dispute between a partridge and a quail, and helped herself by eating up both of them, one after the other. The moral of the story? Never, but never, trust a cat.*

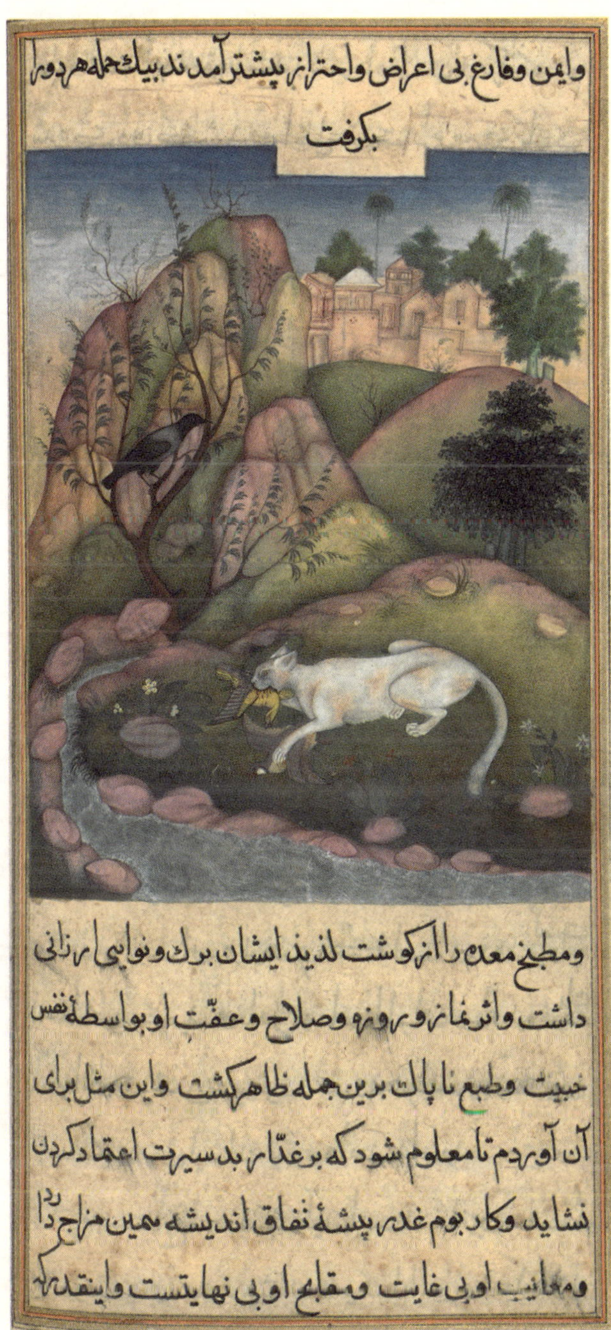

وایمن وفارغ بی اعراض واحتراز پیشتر آمدند بیک حمله هر دو را
بگرفت

ومطبخ معده را از گوشت لذیذ ایشان برگ ونوایی ارزانی
داشت واثر نماز وروزه وصلاح وعفت او بواسطهٔ نفس
خبیث وطبع ناپاک برین جمله ظاهر گشت واین مثل برای
آن آوردم تا معلوم شود که بر غدار بدسیرت اعتماد کردن
نشاید وکار بوم غدر پیشهٔ نفاق اندیشه همین مزاج دارد
ومعایب او بی غایت ومقابح او بی نهایتست واینقدر که

• 23 •

A CAT'S OPPORTUNITY

Folio from a *Tuti Nama* manuscript
Mughal; third quarter of the sixteenth century
[Cleveland Museum of Art; gift of Mrs A. Dean Perry 1962.279]

The Shuka Saptati, *a Sanskrit classic, translated into Persian by a Sufi poet, is filled with stories that form a cycle in which, night after night, tales—salacious but moral—are told by a pet parrot to its young mistress to distract her from going to her lover in her husband's absence. In one story figure a kingly but now enfeebled tiger and a cat who was appointed to save the tiger from mice who pestered him by reaching into his hapless mouth for nibbling at pieces of meat. The cat takes the command up but while scaring the mice away, she also helps herself by eating one mouse at a time. Till she overreaches herself, of course!*

وکفت این فرزند منست و میان اقران و خوان خویش بصحبت دین وصدق

یقین و فور علم و مزید حلم مشهور و معروف است و ادب مجلس ملوک نیکو

میداند اکر فرمان باشد وقت ازو قت او را جای خود بنشانم و خود بدیدن

فرزندان دیکر روم شیر کفت نیکو باشد کربه ان شب او را جای خود بنشاند

وخود در وثاق خود رفت بعد او از فقه کو بزرکی علم بود و بیدانست کر او با بکلی کشتن شدند

موشان مدار میکند هر موشی کر بیرون می امد او را میدرید بجانکر از شب موشا

• 24 •

A MONKEY'S TRICKY JUSTICE

Folio from a manuscript of moral tales
Rajasthan; early nineteenth century

[Government Museum and Art Gallery, Chandigarh; acc. no. 2523]

The fable is about two hungry cats who, moving about together, found a chapatti and decided to split it, turning it into two exact halves. But a quarrel arose when each claimed that the other had a greater share than her. Unable to agree, they decided to go to a neutral judge. A clever monkey offered his services and said he will take a balance and weigh the two halves for them. Each time, however, he would tilt the balance a bit and take a bite himself. This went on for so long that the entire chapatti was gone with the two cats left with nothing.

Seldom are cats outdone or outsmarted. But in this fable, they are: two of them.

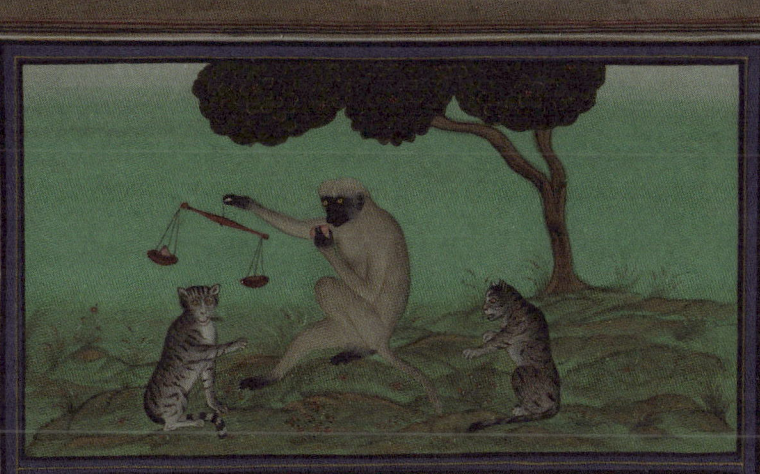

पंद्रवांपाठ

दोमुखीबिल्लियोंकोवडेश्रमसेंएकरोटीमिलीपरआपसमेंदोभाग।
करबांटनेमेंक्लेशकरनेलगीनिदानयहठहराकिसीन्यायीकेपासजा
यदोभागठीककरवालें इतनेमेंउनकोएकबंदरमिला उसनेकहा।
आवोमैंतुम्हारान्यावकरदूं बंदरनेंरोटीकेदोटूकछोटेबडेकरतखडी
केपलडेमेंधरे धरतेंहीएकपलडाऊपरऔरएकनीचेहोगयातबबडे-
टूकमेंसेंएकऐसाटूकडातोडअपनेंमुहमेंरखाजोभारीपलडाहलका।
औरहलकाभारीहोगयाफिरउसभारीटूकमेंसेंऔरटूकतोडलियाइ
सीभांतिसबरोटीखागया केवलएकछोटाटूकबचरहाथा तबबि-
ल्लियांयोंचिल्लाऊठी हमतेरान्यावनहींचाहतें हमेंयहीटूककृपाकर
फेरदे बंदरबोलामैंनेंतेरेलियेंइतनाकष्टकियाहै मुझेभीतोकुछदे
नाउचितहै यहकहवहबचाटूकभीमुहमेंरखलिया औरबिल्लियांअ
पनीरोटीसेंरोती आपसमेंफटकरज्योंन्याईकेपासन्यावकरानेजाताहै व
हअपनीनिजवस्तुकोभीखोताहै

सिक्षा

• 25 •

A NAYIKA'S CLEVER RUSE: THE *GUPTA PARAKIYA*

Folio from a *Rasamanjari* series
Pahari; attributed to the painter Kripal of Nurpur; ca. 1670
[Victoria & Albert Museum; acc. no. IS 20-1958]

The day has dawned, and a friend comes visiting the nayika—one of the heroines, in other words: women in love and placed in different categories according to age, nature, and experience—who has a secret lover. Seeing her friend staring at the light scratches on her face and shoulders—marks of passionate love made in the night just passed—the nayika quickly says to her friend. 'That chamber is not good for me! There is a cat there who leapt up on me last night and scratched me all over.' Her friend simply smiles. Up there the painter brings in a cat while a mouse—the lover of course—quietly sneaks away. Clever?

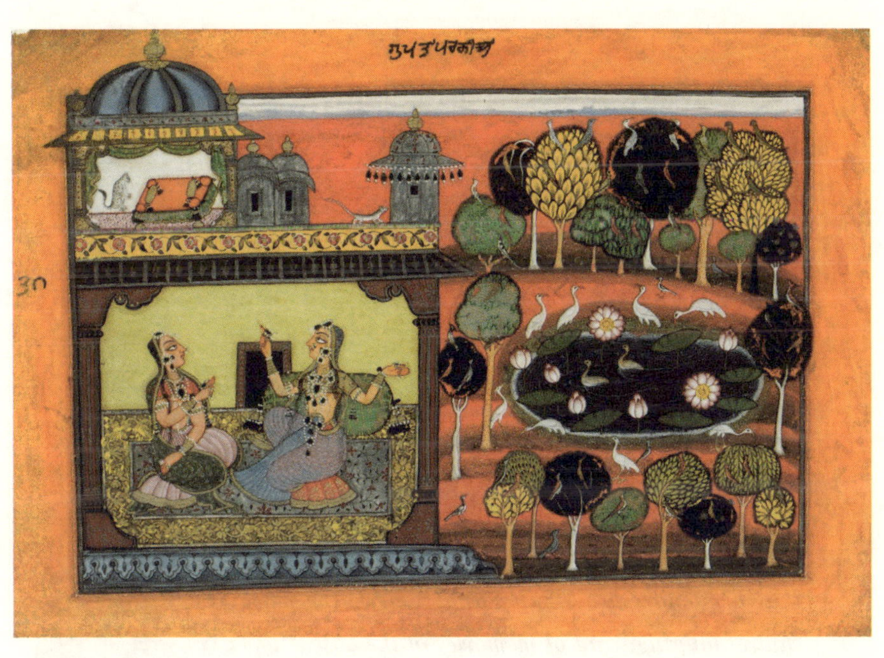

• 26 •

RAGINI PATAMANJARI

Folio from a *Ragamala* series
Mewar, Rajasthan; first half of the seventeenth century
[Museum Rietberg, Zurich, acc. no. RVI 1937]

In a text of the Ragamala*—in other words, 'A Garland of Musical Modes'—the ragini is described as a virahini—separated from her lover—suffering deeply on that account, and of a sakhi or friend sharing her grief. Anguish is the recurring, dominant theme, incessant tears 'the sole consolation that her tender heart will admit'. Here, the mood is that of longing, and of memories of the absent lover. The ragini shares her feelings with her friend who tries—vainly—to console her. So, the text above says. But, without knowing the text, the cat gazing anxiously at the ragini, seems to be keen to play the role of a friend, too.*

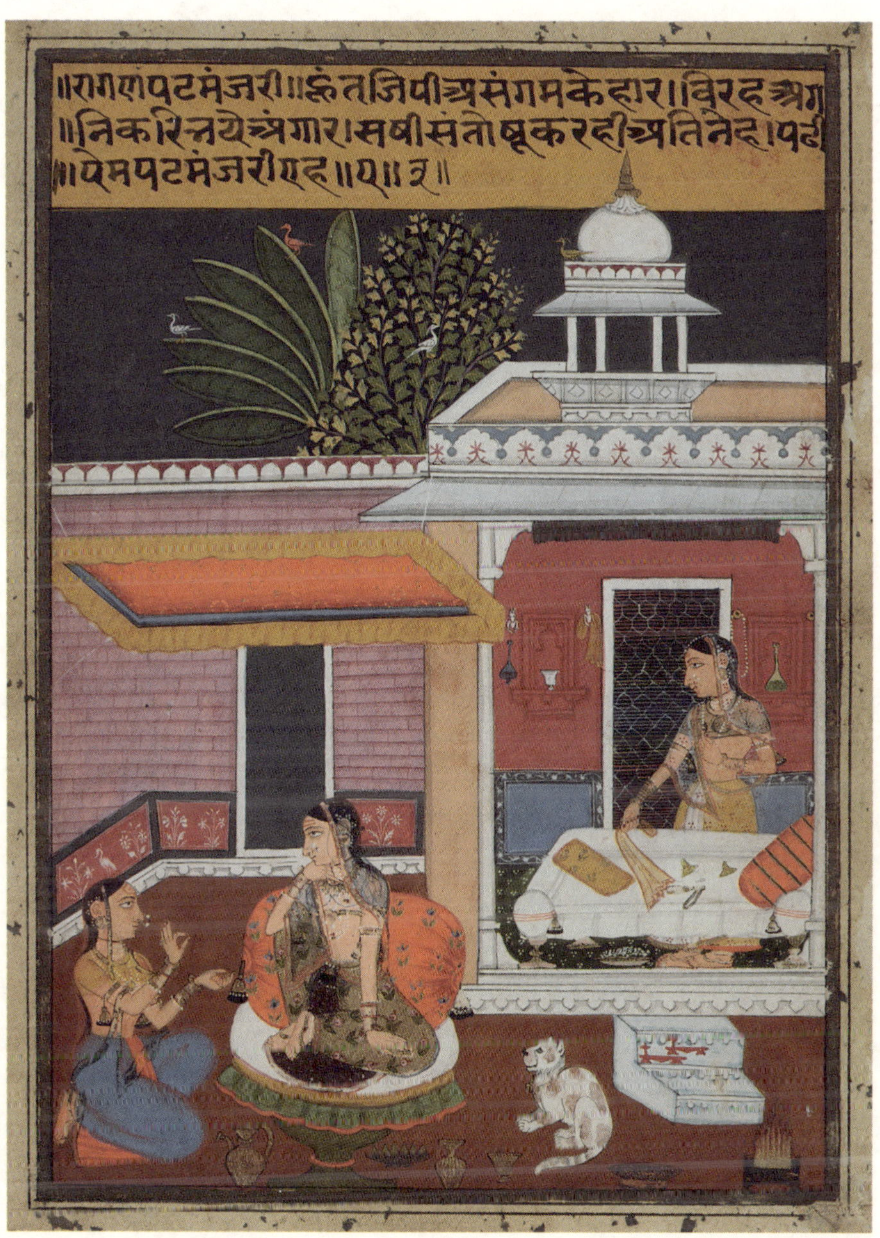

• 27 •

RAGINI ASAVARI

Folio from a *Ragamala* series
Malwa; mid-seventeenth century
[Museum Rietberg, Zurich, acc. no. RVI 955]

In the midst of a forest landscape—Shiva in the far distance being worshipped, tigers and monkeys and deer and peacocks abounding—the ragini, rendered as a dark-bodied tribal woman, perched on a parapet, dressed in leafy garments, and playing on a double-gourded string instrument, is seen luring snakes with her music so that she can catch them. She is obviously succeeding, for at this moment one snake coiled around a tree trunk has appeared, and she has caught it by its tail. Much like the cat in the distance, inside a chamber, who has lured a rat and got firm hold of it?

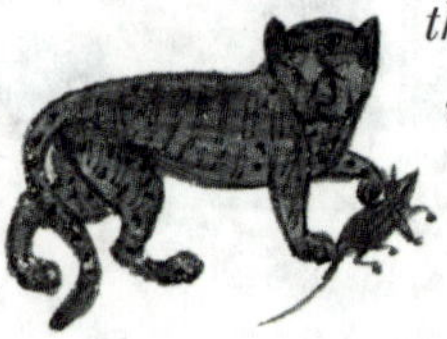

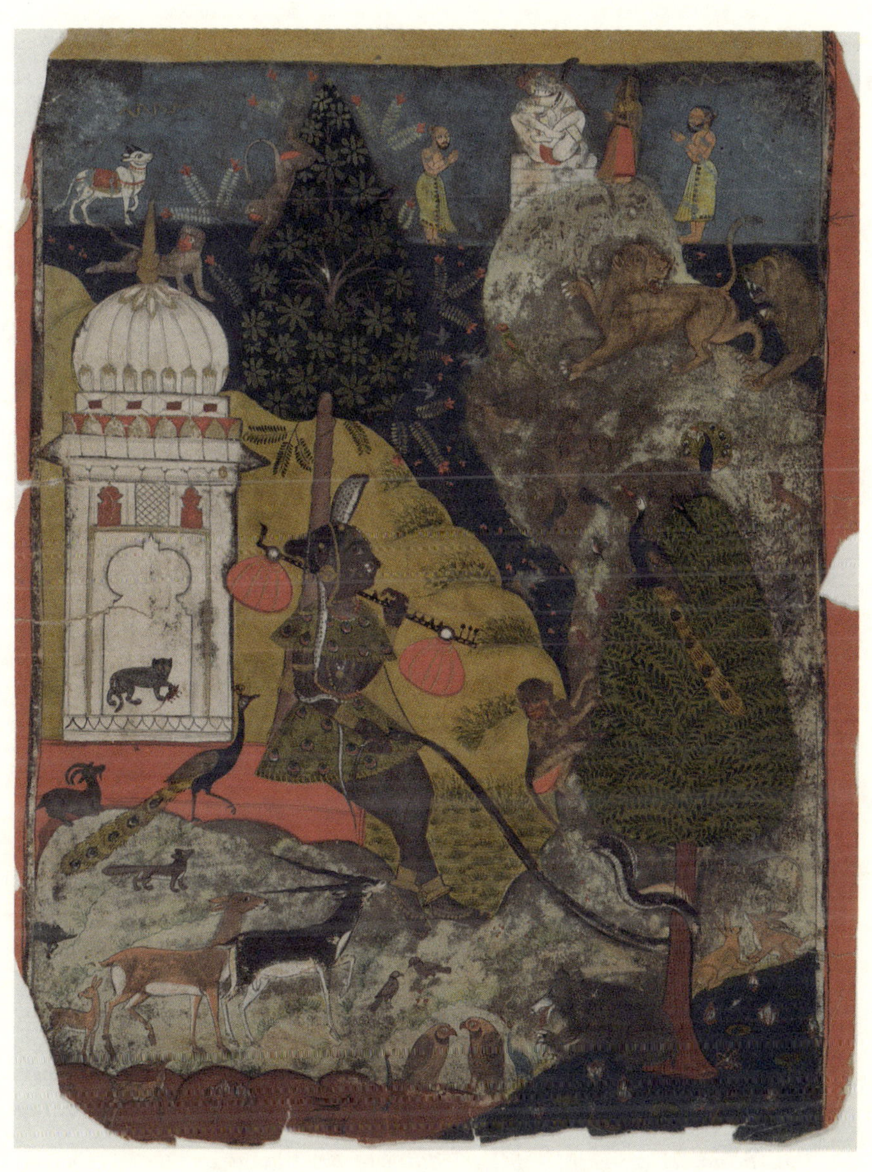

• 28 •

THE PATAMANJARI RAGINI

Folio from a *Ragamala* series
Pahari, from a Bilaspur workshop;
end of the seventeenth century

[From Rosebery's auction catalogue, Arts of India, 2020]

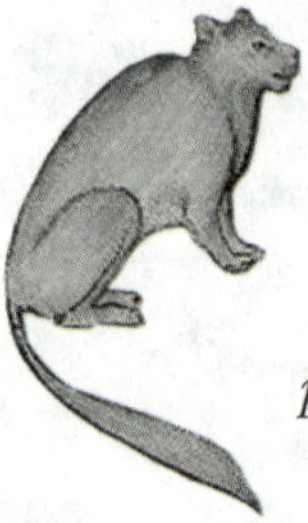

The ragini is Patamanjari, and the mood of this musical mode, at least here, is of lonesomeness and longing. The ragini, sitting cross-legged at the edge of the parapet of her chamber, extends her hand as if to pat the cat that has come up to her and is gazing at her, gentleness in the eyes. There is not only sympathy in the air but also companionship. The ragini is not exactly looking at the cat, however: she is gazing towards the distance where her lover might be at this time, having left her alone at home. The maid, standing at the back, platter (of food?) in hand, is also, perhaps, thinking of her absent master.

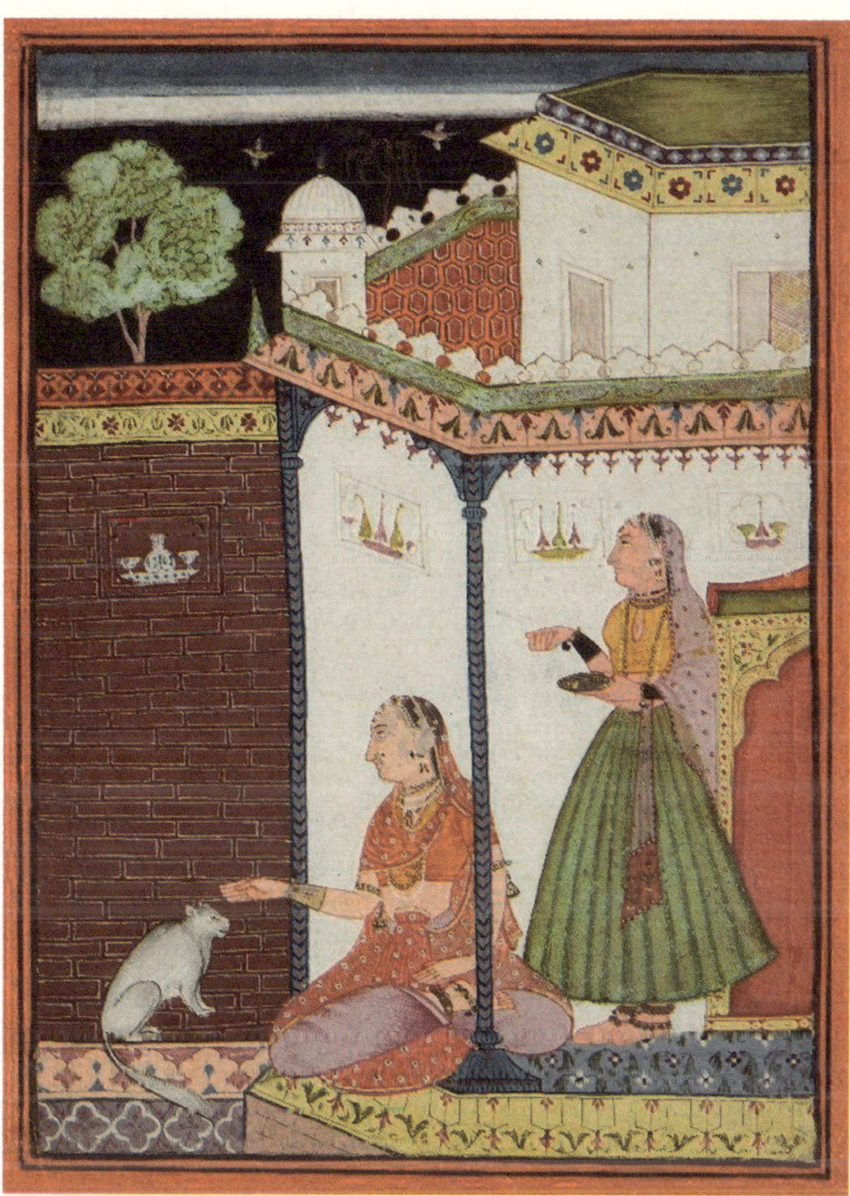

• 29 •

RAGA KEDARA

Folio from a *Ragamala* series
Pahari; by Nainsukh of Guler; ca. 1765–75

[Sarabhai Foundation, Ahmedabad; acc. no. SFPL-12]

'Raga Kedara is (a man) of dark complexion, young and handsome in all his limbs, but pained by the separation from his beloved....' so runs the text of the Raga. Here he sits, hands folded, listening to music played by a young man who is his mentor; who, at any rate, or whose divine-sounding notes will take his pain away.

Nainsukh creates an image of quiet contemplation induced by great music. Silence reigns in the atmosphere; complete detachment from the world outside. The little furry cat—evidently a pet, wearing as she does a gold collar—sitting all curled up, completely still at this hour of the night, seems also to be entranced by the music. An aficionada?

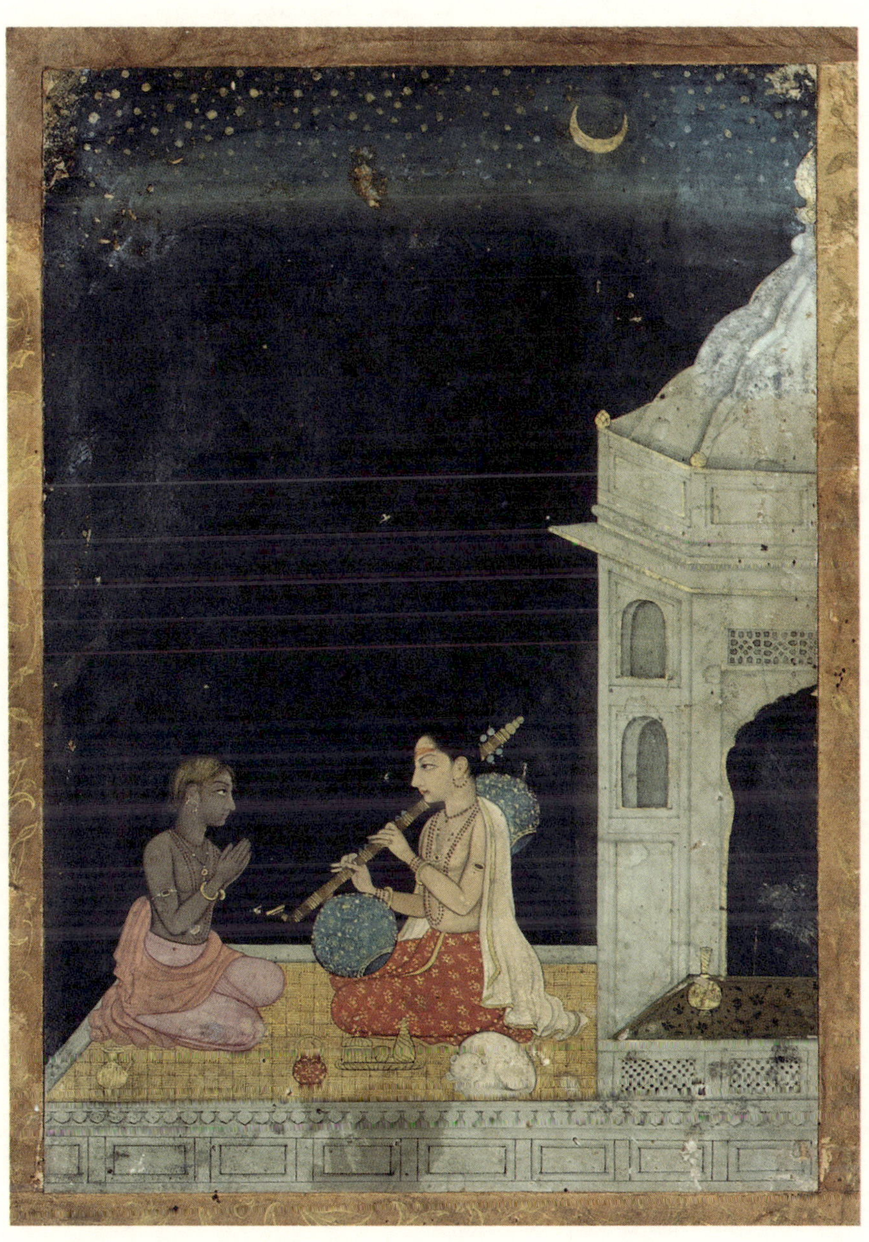

• 30 •

AS TWO CHILDREN FIGHT OVER A CAT, A SUFI LOOKS ON

Late Mughal; eighteenth century

[Collection: Eberhard Rist]

The strangeness in this painting—theme, atmosphere, location—is not easy to put out of one's mind. Two small boys, princes perhaps—one notices the string with gold pieces on one, and gold wristlets and necklace on the other—are struggling over a cat while an old man—a Sufi perhaps, living away from habitation—looks on with amusement. Is this a visualization of some Sufi saying or poem about possession? Or a genre scene of princes sent by a king to a trusted old mystic for educating them? None of this, however, is of concern to the cat: all she wants obviously is to be freed. Why me, she must be saying?

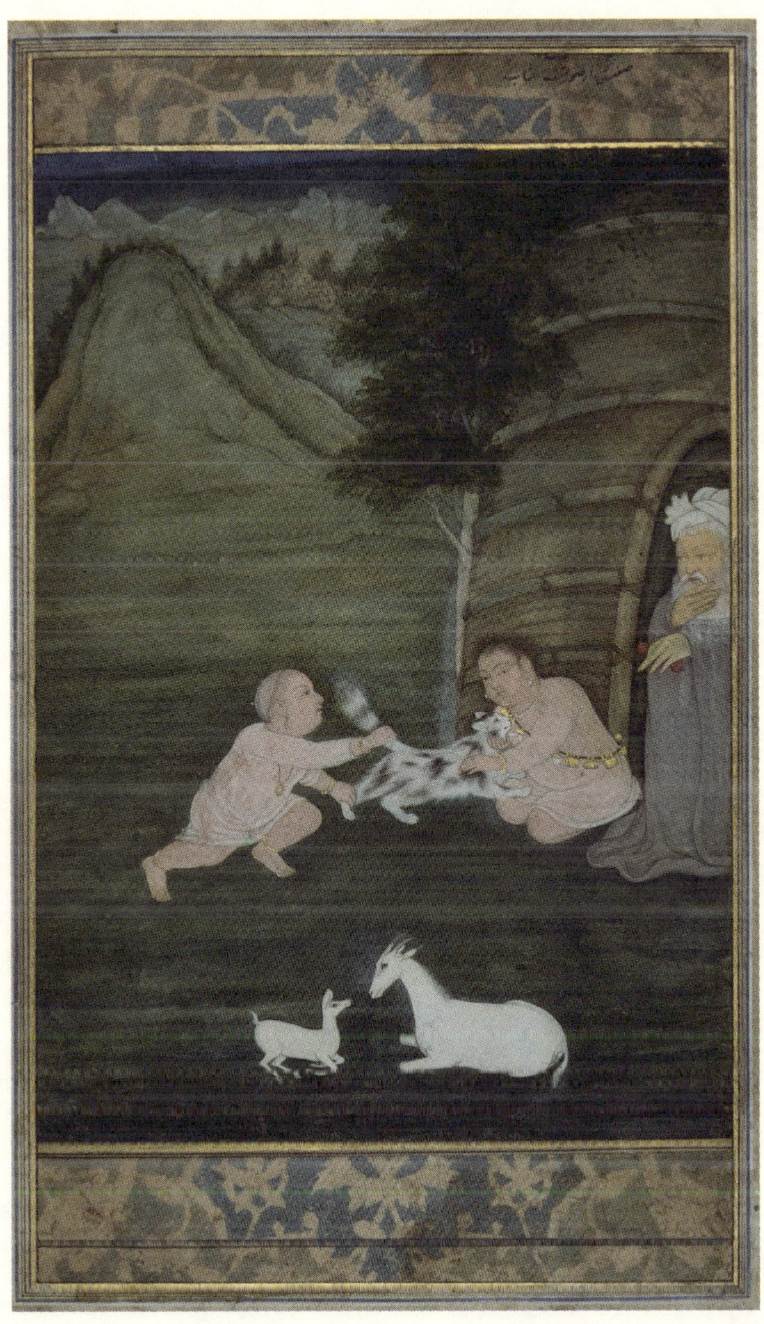

• 31 •

PALACE LADY IN THOUGHTFUL MOOD

Rajasthan, from a Kotah workshop; early eighteenth century

[Francesca Galloway sales catalogue]

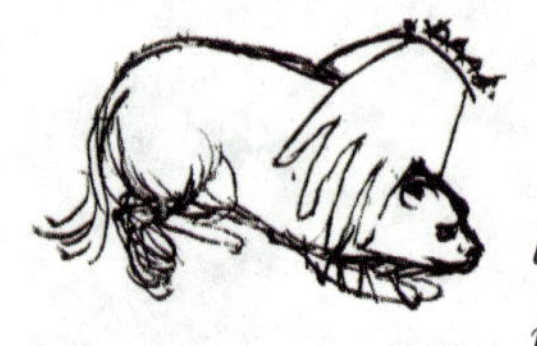

Is this lady—evidently of some rank judging by the jewellery she wears and the comfortable looking bolster behind her—scheming or planning something, unbeknown to others in the palace? The look in the eyes—sly and thoughtful at the same time—certainly seems so. The hesitation and the repeated working over of lines in the drawing is of a piece with the complexity of her stance and her mood. Is the insignificant and unadorned looking cat that she pets, almost absent-mindedly, brought in to stand possibly for cleverness here? Or, seen more plainly, simply for companionability? In any case, something is about to break, it seems.

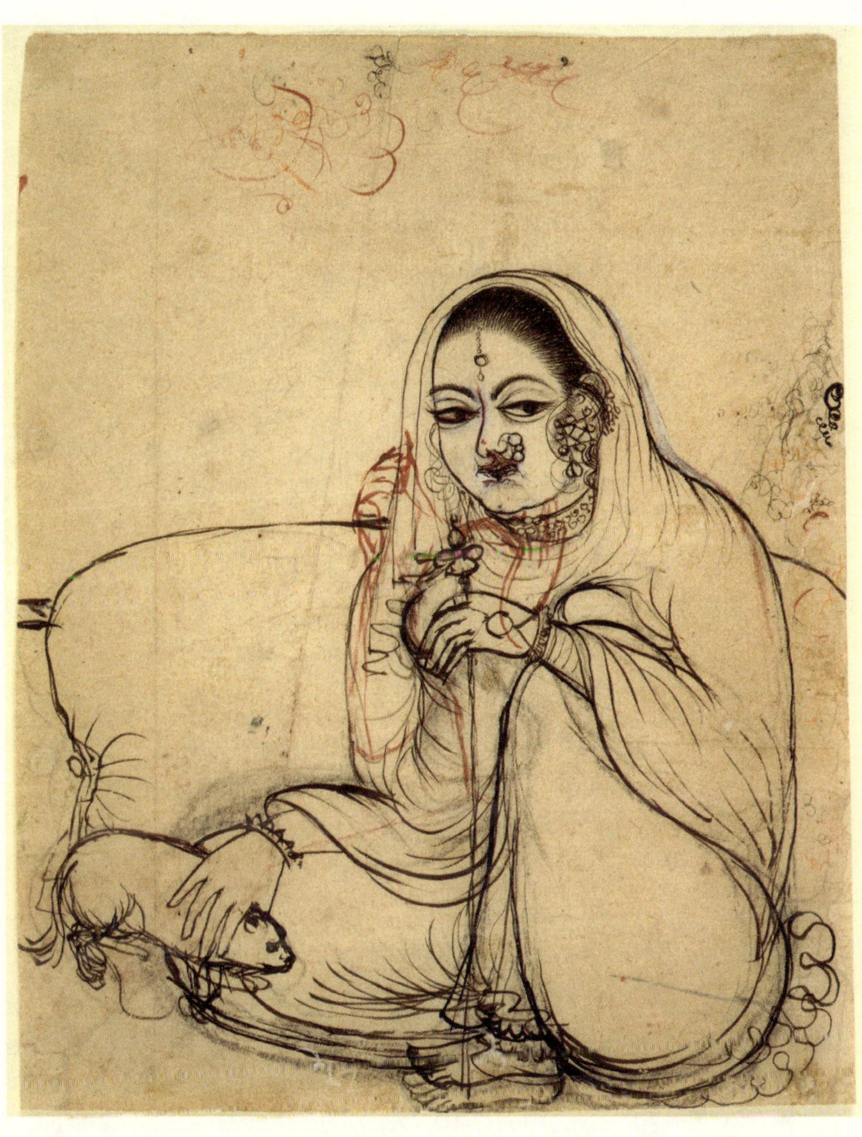

• 32 •

STRANGE HAPPENINGS IN A SPRAWLING HOUSEHOLD

Company style, possibly Calcutta; ca. 1850

[Francesca Galloway sales catalogue]

Bizarre things happen here. Inside a home, a middle-aged man is seen twice: once down below and again on the roof with his barber; a couple make an accusatory gesture at a gardener thumbing his nose at them; a clownish figure bends in a strange stance. In the courtyard next door some Muslims pray; a dark-skinned man massages his body; and two 'Chinese-looking' men and two donkeys stand. In this mayhem a cat appears twice: once on the roof with a mouse she has just hunted, and, again, when one of the Chinese men offers her to the other. What all this amounts to—unless it is a visual nonsense rhyme—is hard to fathom. The cat must be wondering too.

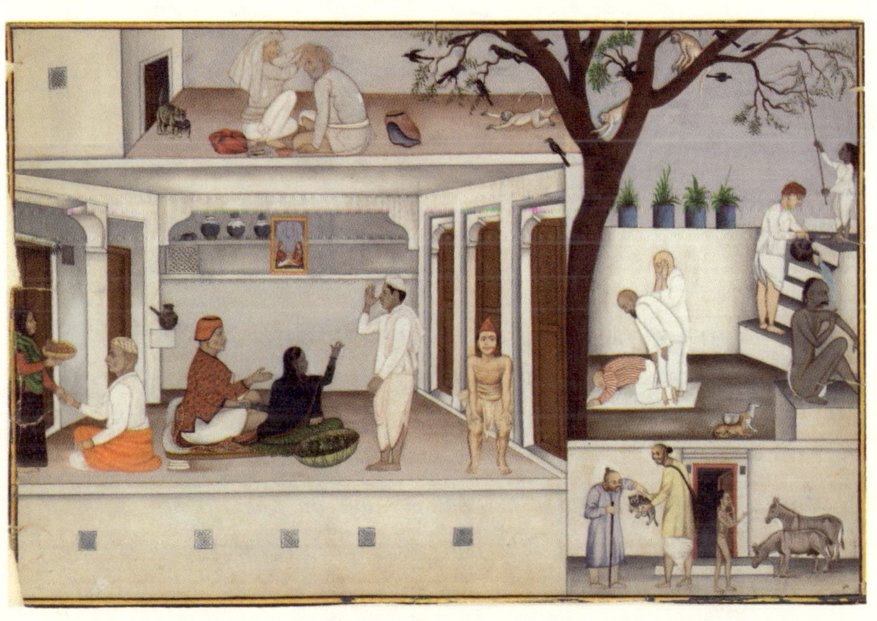

• 33 •

A PALACE LADY CHASES A CAT AWAY

Rajasthan, from a Bundi workshop; early eighteenth century

[Museum Rietberg, Zurich; acc. no. RVI 2032]

The parrot was a pet, and the cat an intruder. Purely inadvertently, the 'gate' of the parrot's cage swung open and an intruder cat was about to pounce on the bird, when the lady sprang into action. Here she holds her parrot aloft on one raised hand, while with the other she shoos the cat away with a cane. It was a matter of seconds, the painter seems to tell us. There is however a poetic slant to all this. 'My heart was my own,' the poet says, using the nayika's voice, 'till he came and tried to steal it. I resisted.'

Even while running away, the cat looks back lingeringly. At the parrot, or is it at the nayika?

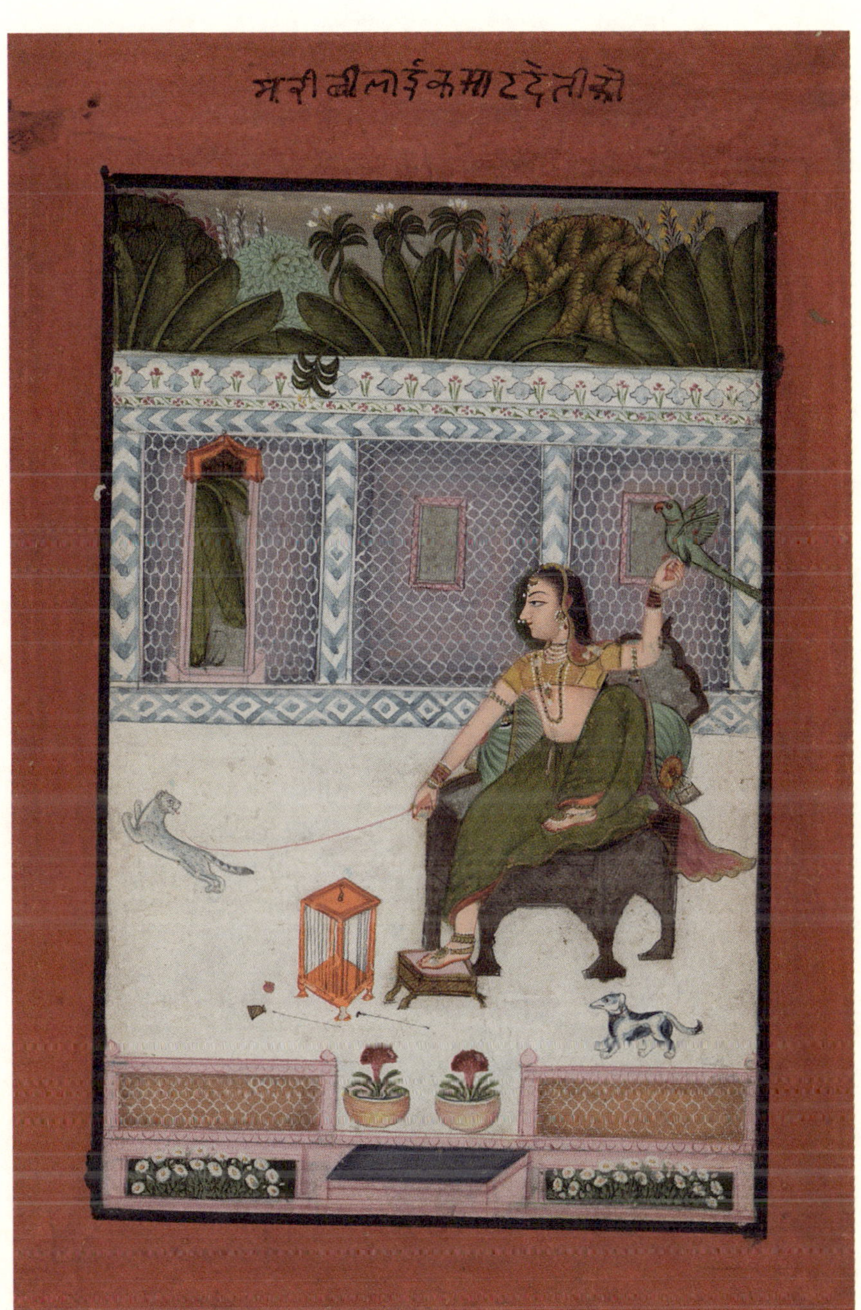

• 34 •

THE *NAYIKA* SPRINGS INTO ACTION

Pahari; from a Guler workshop; ca. 1810

[Victoria & Albert Museum; acc. no. IS.140–1955]

Was I lost in my thoughts when all this happened, the nayika seems to say to herself, one hand raised towards her chin in the familiar gesture of wonder? The cage with my beloved bird must have swung open by mistake, and this thieving creature, attractive though she is, sneaked in, reached into the cage, and seized the bird in her mouth. It was, in the poet's words, about time to wake up from my reverie. Compositions of this nature abound in Hindi literature: the cat is the eager lover, the parrot the heart of the nayika. It is all elegantly said and here, in this delicate work, the painter matches the elegance of the words.

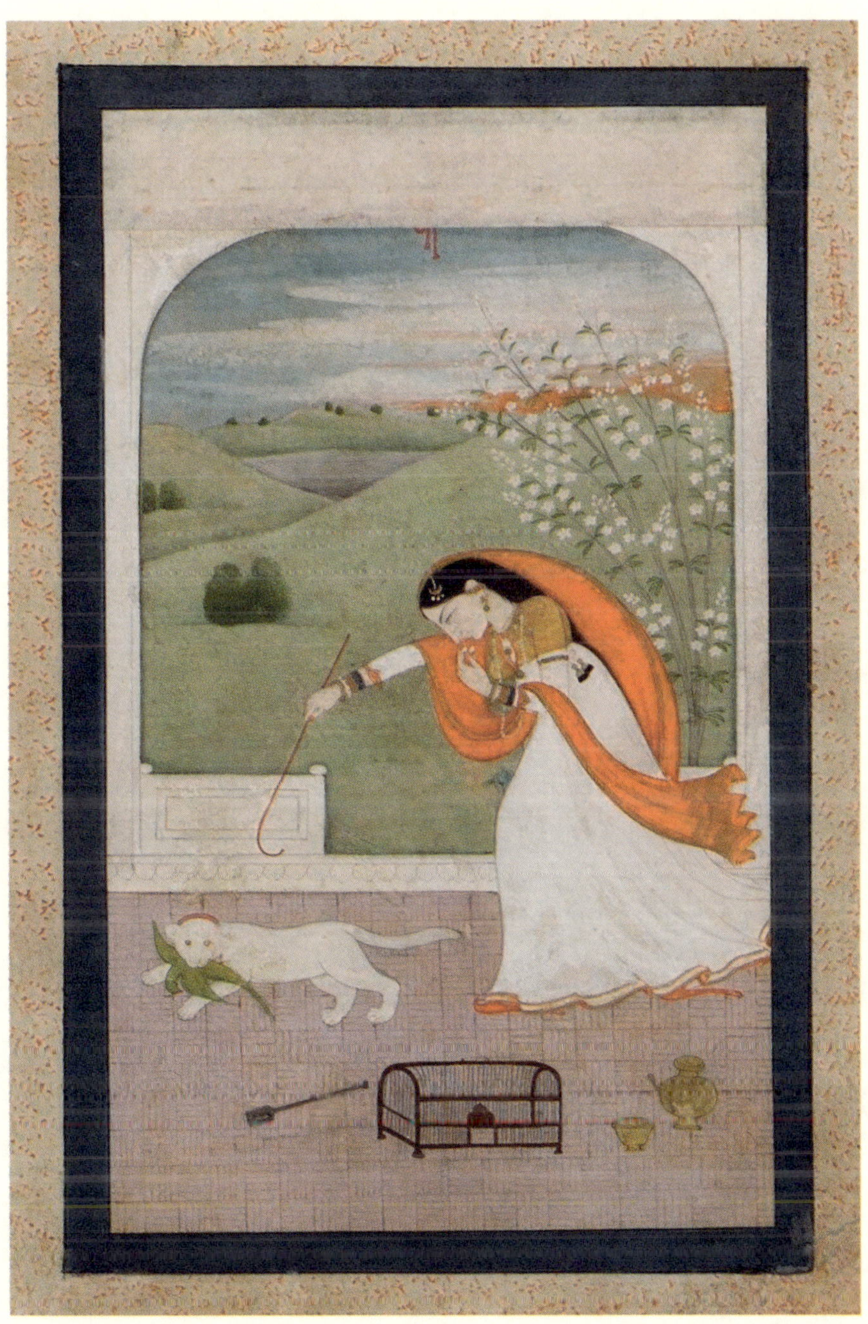

• 35 •

TWO LADIES, A CAT, AND A PARROT IN A PALACE

Rajasthan; from a Bundi workshop; mid-eighteenth century

[The British Museum; acc. no. 1999-1202-0-4-19]

The scene—cat pouncing on a pet bird, mistress running, cane in hand, the bird saved in the nick of time—is all too familiar. But in this painting the air is almost that of a rehearsed mime. The princess, wearing a crown-like Mughalized headgear, wields a cane but seems to be posing rather than intending to attack the cat; her maid catches hold of the cat by her leg but looks at the poaching animal with tenderness. Meanwhile, however, the parrot shrieks setting off a flutter in the sky where pigeons begin to fear for their lives also. The glistening white walls illumine the scene. Everything is rendered with great elegance but the action remains unconvincing.

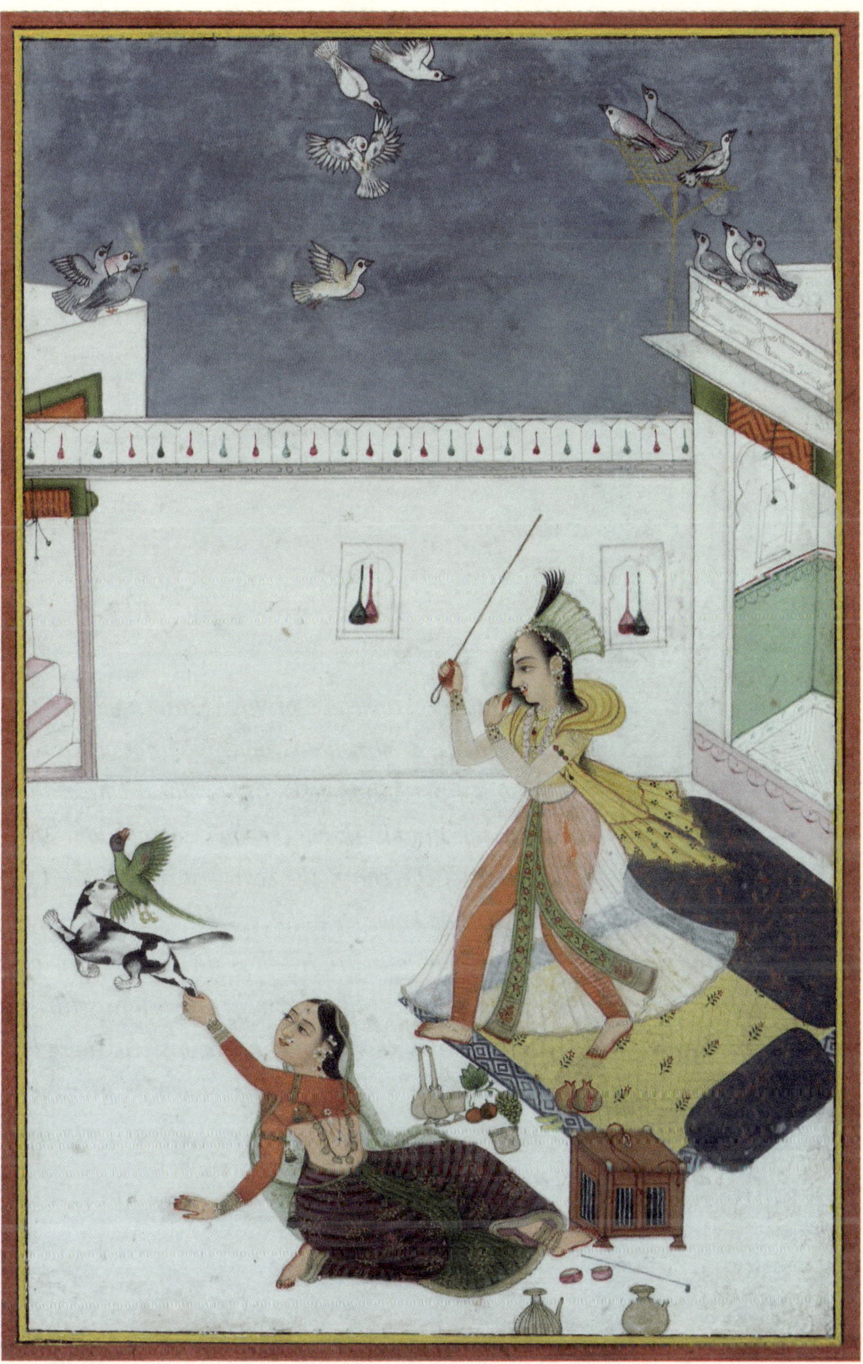

• 36 •

PRINCESS ON A CHAIR WITH A CAT IN HER LAP

Pahari, from a Guler or late Mandi workshop; ca. 1800

[Museum Rietberg, Zurich, acc. no. 2012.162]

The lady is someone of high rank, meant to be seen as a 'firangan' or from another land, perhaps from Europe: the light-coloured hair, the ringlets, the double skirt, the fair complexion, the fancy form of the chair, the seated stance, are all a giveaway. The setting however—the marble courtyard, the flowering shrub at the back, the balustrade—has an Indian air, as does the way she has taken her jutti-like footwear off before settling in the chair. What strikes one is the look of being lost in thought while stroking the back of the cat she holds close. There is affection in the gesture and a feeling of companionability. The cat certainly looks supremely comfortable.

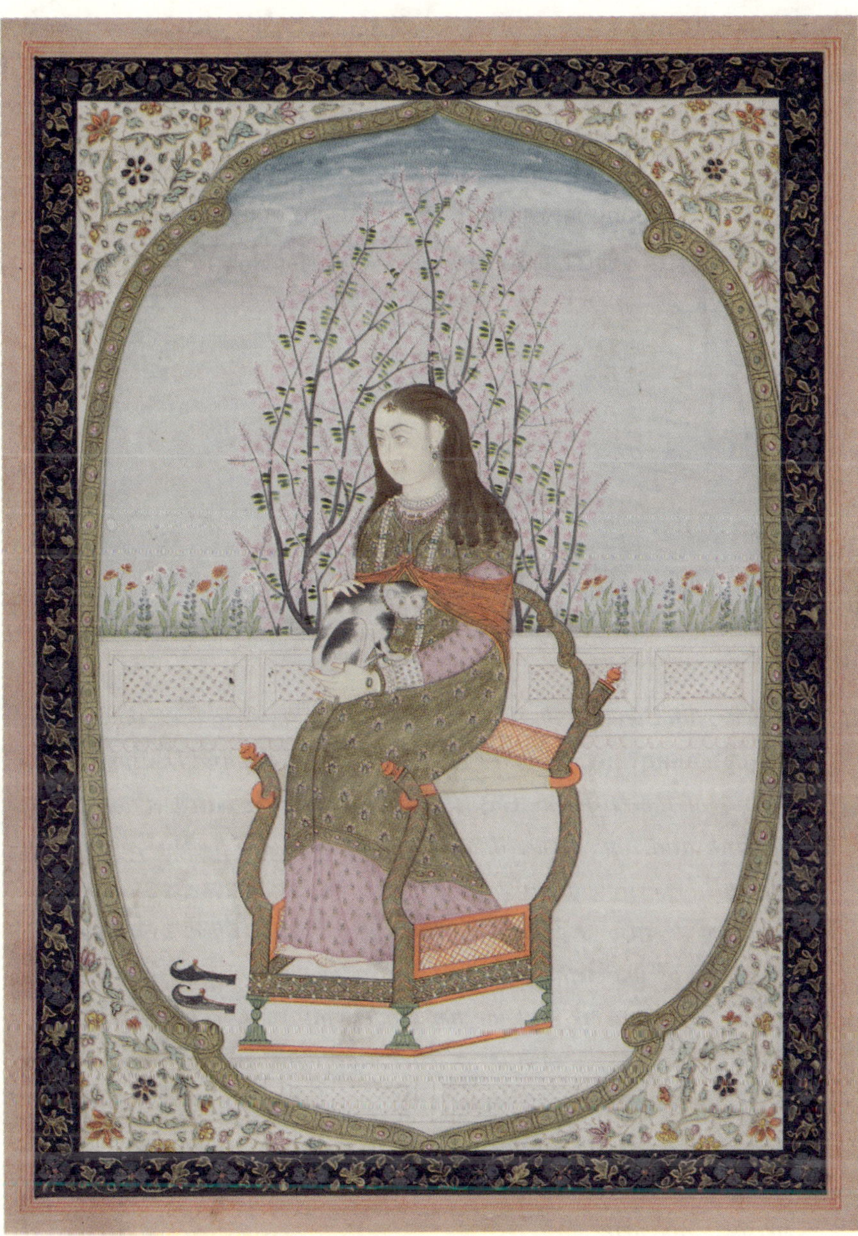

• 37 •

A COURTESAN, DESCRIBED AS A 'BESWA'

Folio from a *Tashrih-al Aqvam* manuscript
Company style; Uttar Pradesh; dated 1825

[The Library of Congress, Washington DC;
acc. no. Rosenwald ms. no. 34]

It was for the redoubtable Colonel James Skinner that the Kitab-i tashrih al-aqvam*, being the History of the Origin and Distinguishing Marks of the Different Castes of India, was prepared. From people of rank and high caste, down to craftsmen and professionals, even menials, everyone figured in it, representing a type. Among those rendered is also a typical courtesan, here described as a 'beswa', meaning of low repute, veshya-like, a woman of pleasure in other words. Here she sits outside her modest quarters, confident looking, smoking a huqqa, while a client approaches her. The beswa's cat—seemingly a standard companion—is not happy with the way it is going. 'No negotiation please', she might be saying, 'not here'.*

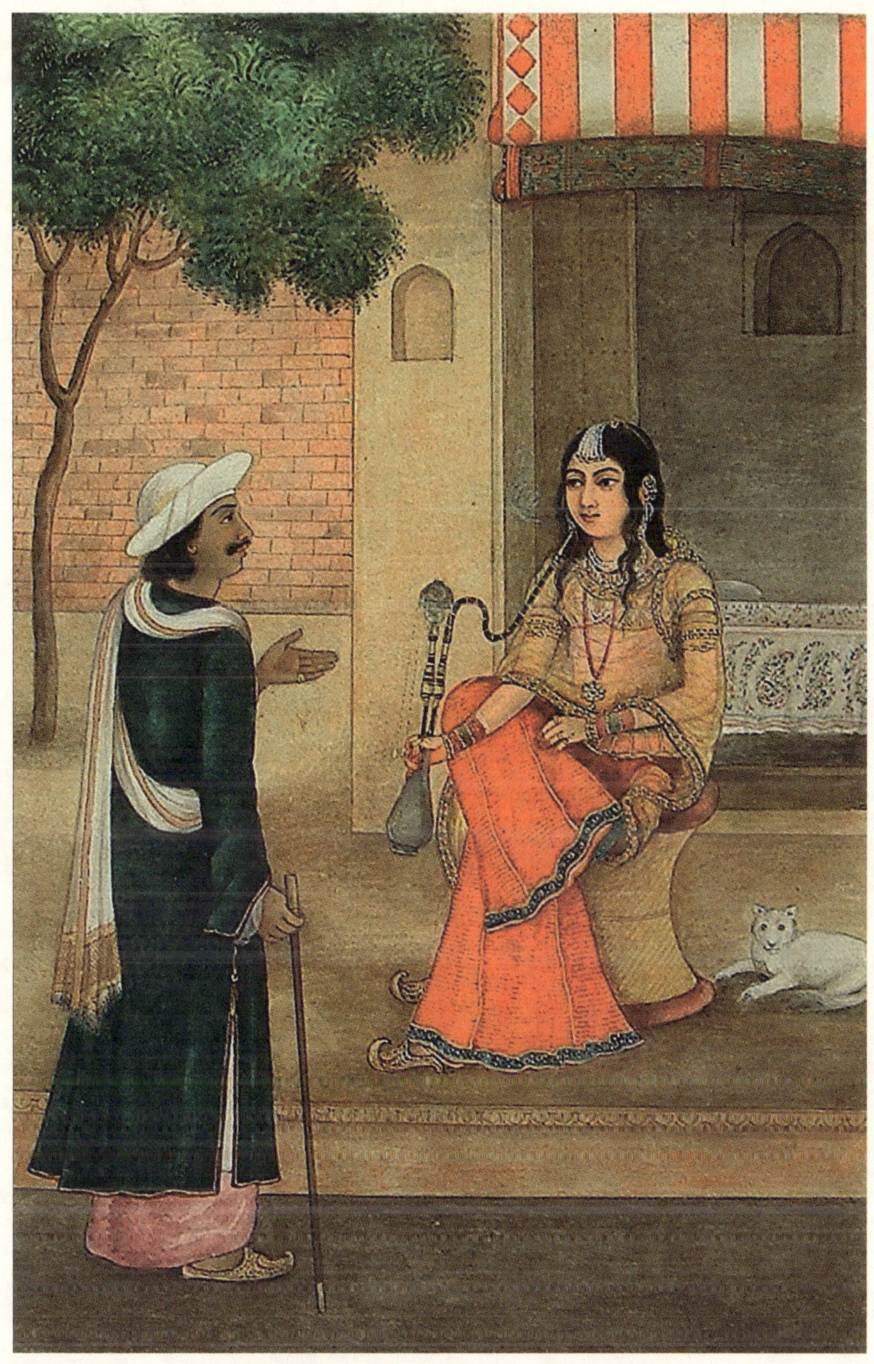

• 38 •

COURTESAN SEATED AGAINST A BOLSTER

Company style; by Faiz Ali Khan; ca. 1840

[Victoria & Albert Museum; acc. no. IS. 71-1977]

The courtesan—there is something about her stance, the look in her eyes, her dress even though tastefully worn, which keeps one from identifying her as a princess—sits against a rich bolster, one leg tucked under, the other bent with one hand resting on the raised knee. The expression on her face—skilfully caught by the Delhi painter, Faiz Ali Khan, is that of innocence, of inexperience. There is tremulous apprehension in the air somewhere. However, the cat by her side, evidently a much-loved companion, considering the collar of rubies (?) she sports, appears perfectly in control and confident, as she looks straight at the viewer, as if posing for a photograph.

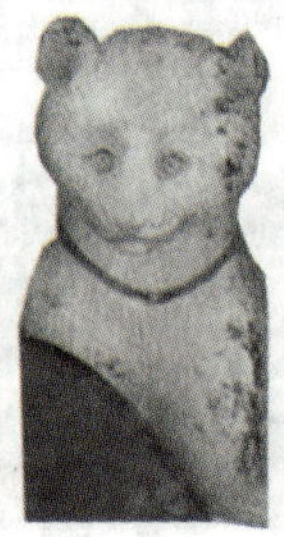

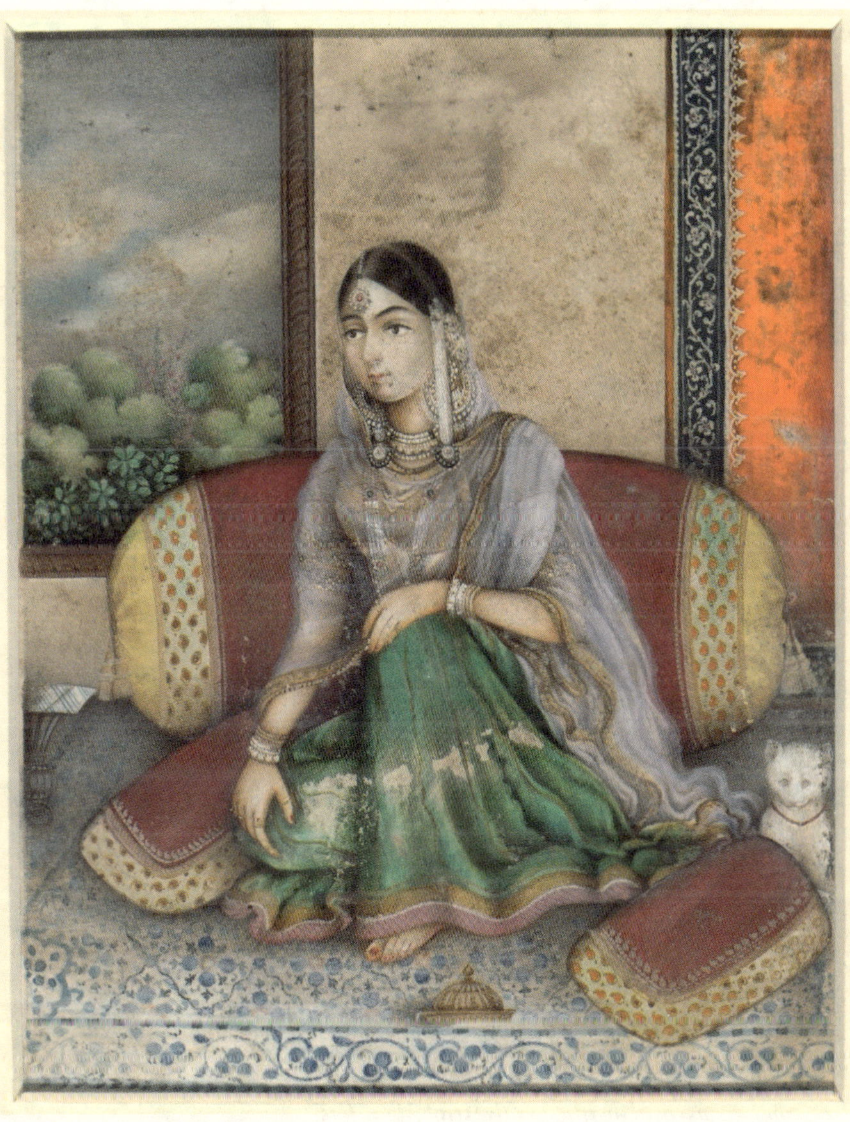

• 39 •

PORTRAIT OF A WOMAN WITH A CAT

Late Mughal; end of the eighteenth century

[Kapoor Galleries, New York]

It is not easy to make out where she is seated, or how, but the young woman is decidedly meant to be seen as a European, possibly Portuguese. The brownish hair worn loose and falling over her shoulders, the dress—the mauve-coloured ruff around the neck, the short jacket and ample skirt, the yellow wraparound—point in that direction. At the same time the aspect is princely: the pearl choker and wristlets, the pendant rubies in the earring, and the feathery sarpesh topping a bejewelled fillet. She is lost in thought, head downward inclined, distant look in the eyes. There is obvious comfort that the furry white cat daintily cradled in her arms and being gently stroked, offers.

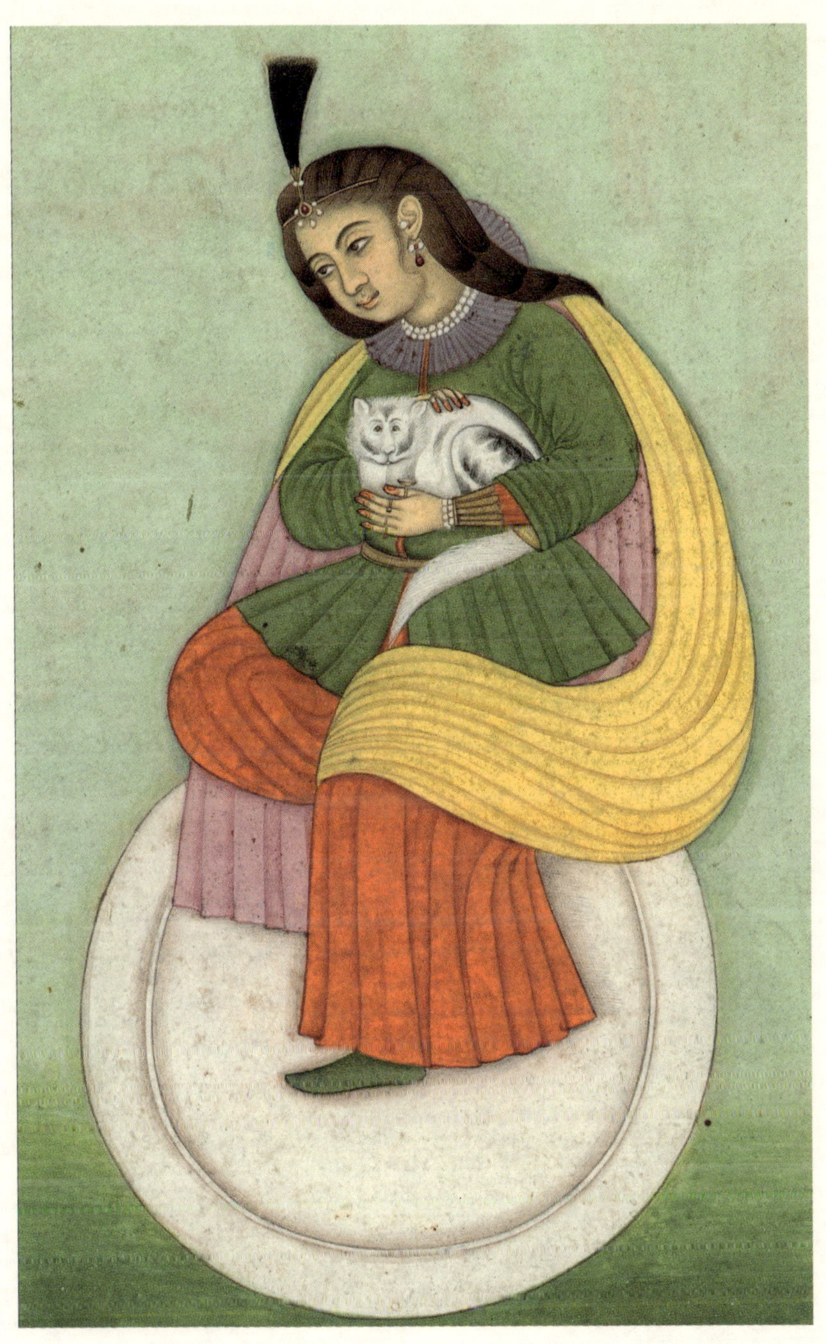

• 40 •

RECLINING COURTESAN CARESSING HER CAT

Rajasthan, possibly from an Alwar workshop; ca. 1850

[Private Collection]

Reminding one in some manner of European odalisques, the young lady stretching out on a carpet, and resting against ample cushions, is lost in thought, bent head supported by a hand, eyes looking at nothing in particular. This, for her, is the hour of leisure and she is all by herself, body relaxed, one bare leg, protruding from under her skirt—absent-mindedly, or is it archly?—bent upwards and touching the other knee. The short choli, the loosely hanging pearl necklaces, the bare midriff, all belong to this moment. But the moment is also mine, the furry cat nestling her head against her mistress's yielding breast, seems to be saying: 'Sheer bliss!'

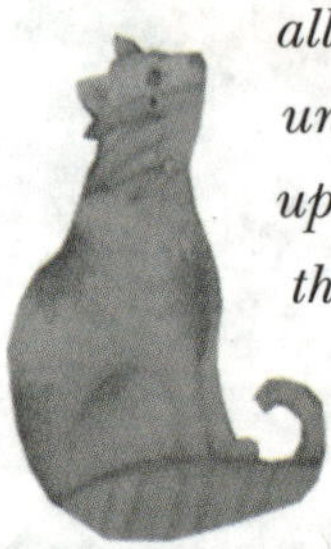

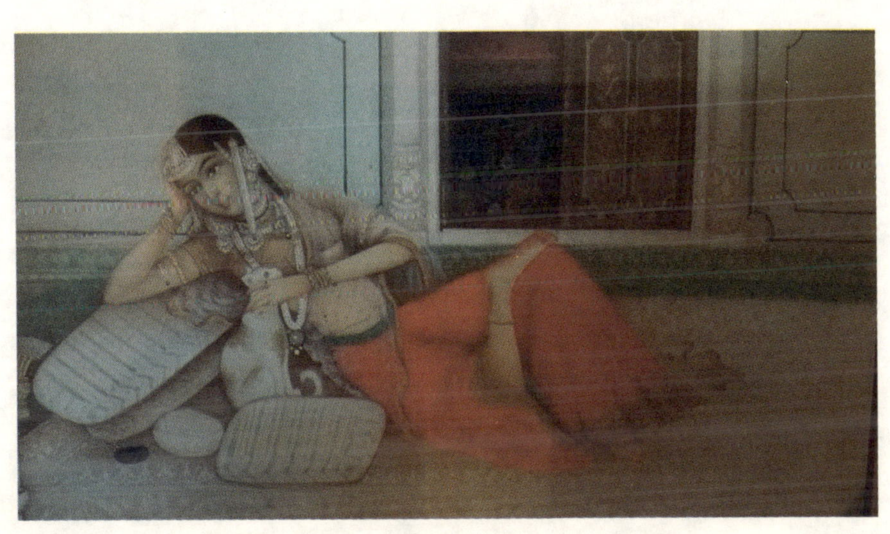

• 41 •

COURTESAN IN A PALACE INTERIOR

Rajasthan, from an Alwar workshop; ca. 1850

[Private Collection]

She seems to be the king's favourite mistress. Resting on a sofa-like divan, upper body upright but the legs, dainty shoes and all, stretching out all along the cushioned surface. As she waits, she is dressed to kill: elegant silk sari which seems to rustle, brief choli to match, diaphanous wrap draped around the torso and high-end jewellery—necklaces, sir-patti, jhoomar, bangles, and wristlets. A portrait, perhaps of the raja, hangs on the wall, the European-looking piece of furniture stands at the back, a flower vase rests on it. The lady holds, elegantly, the stem of a huqqa in her hand and looks ahead, imperiously. Her cat, however, crouching below, appears to have a question in her head.

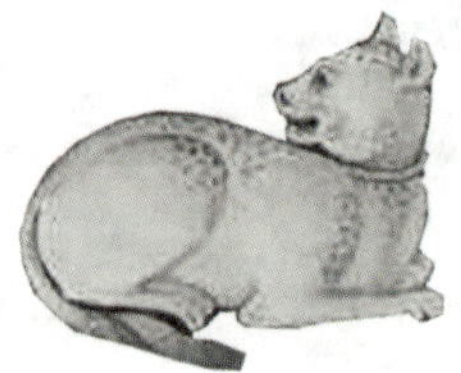

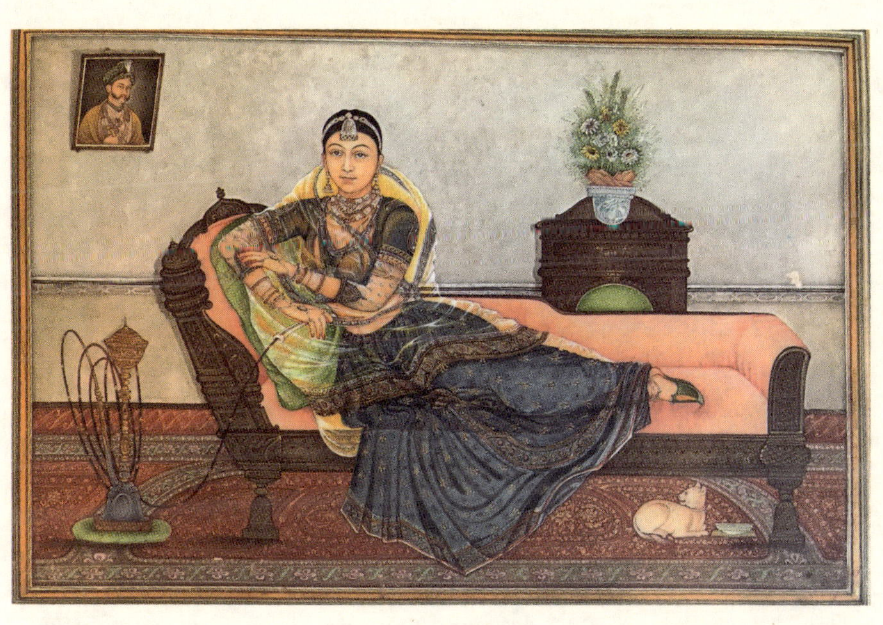

• 42 •

A LADY MEANT TO BE AKHTAR MAHAL, WIFE OF BAHADUR SHAH ZAFAR

Water colour on ivory
Delhi; by Muhammad Fazl; ca. 1850
[British Library; acc no. ADD.OR.5720]

Neither the lady nor the format have very little that seems to be Indian in this bust portrait on ivory. But this is the way things were by the mid-nineteenth century. The young lady, believed to be one of the wives of the last Mughal emperor, Bahadur Shah Zafar, wears here her light-coloured hair loose and no veil covers her head. An inscription gets it wrong by naming her royal by birth: she, in fact, was a concubine who later became the eighth wife of Bahadur Shah. The painting is by Muhammad Fazl, a Delhi painter working in Victorian style, photograph-like, likenesses. The young lady, smiling gently, holds the little unhappy looking, just-weaned, kitten lightly in her hands.

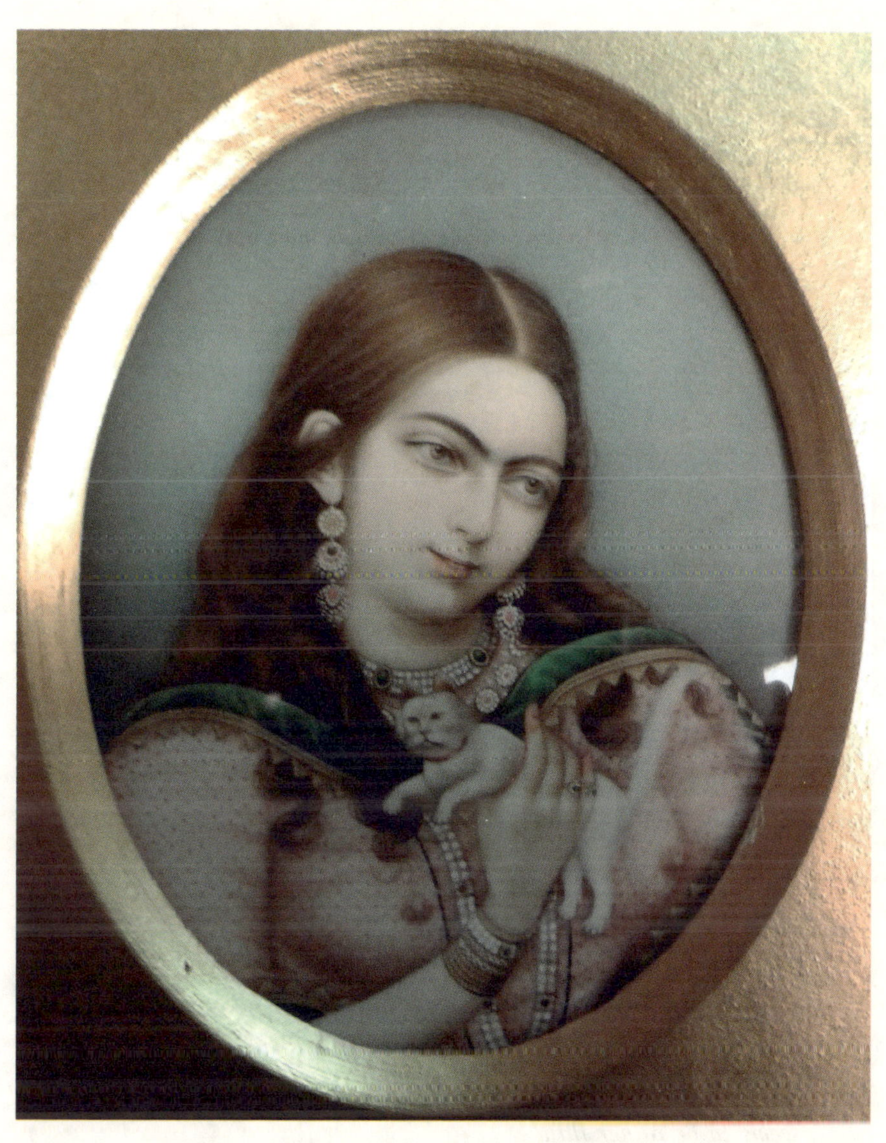

• 43 •

COURTESAN WITH A CAT IN HER LAP

Delhi; ca. 1850

[Francesca Galloway sales catalogue]

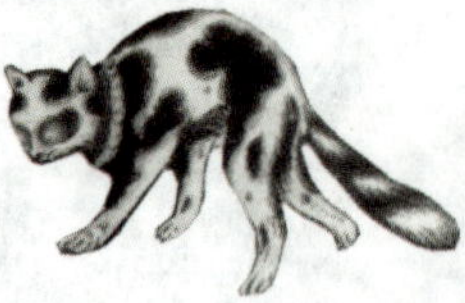

There is loudness in the work: a poster of allure. The young lady, evidently a courtesan, overly made up and bejewelled—one can almost hear the tinkle of her tinselly jewellery—sits on a divan, caressing her hair with one hand. There is a two-candle lamp with tall glass shades on the wall of her rather bare apartment; one can partially see a mirror on a stand near her; a vague view of space opens up at the back; a boldly striped durrie-rug, covers the floor. It all seems like a low-budget setting. A dappled, underfed cat has taken her position on the courtesan's lap, but the connection between her and her mistress seems to be rather thin.

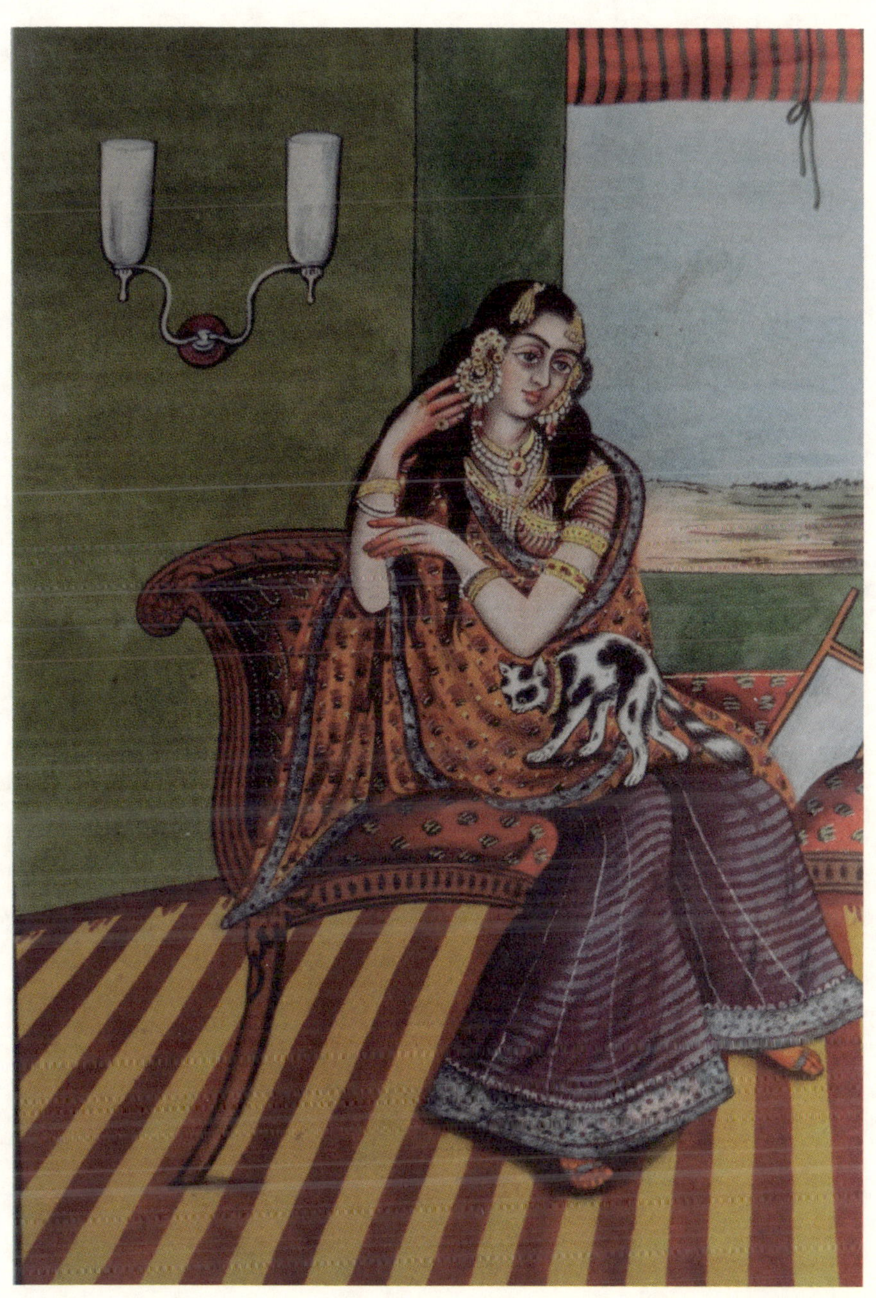

• 44 •

A SUFI, READING

Mughal; attributed to the master painter, Basawan; ca. 1580

[Sotheby's Auction catalogue, 2011, lot 90]

An unglamorous portrait of a scholar, a Sufi perhaps, reading: a book resting on his ample stomach. The person remains unnamed but the scholar's 'wrinkled brow and thoughtful eyes' stay in the mind. 'The physical presence of the figure is such', it has been said, 'that we feel we are not just looking at him, but sitting in the same room'. The room is bare; the man sits on the floor, leaning on a heavy bolster. Only small objects are around. The tethered cat is obviously his, but is completely on her own at this time. She does not seem to mind this, however: 'these have been long hours, and I am tired too', is what we read on her face.

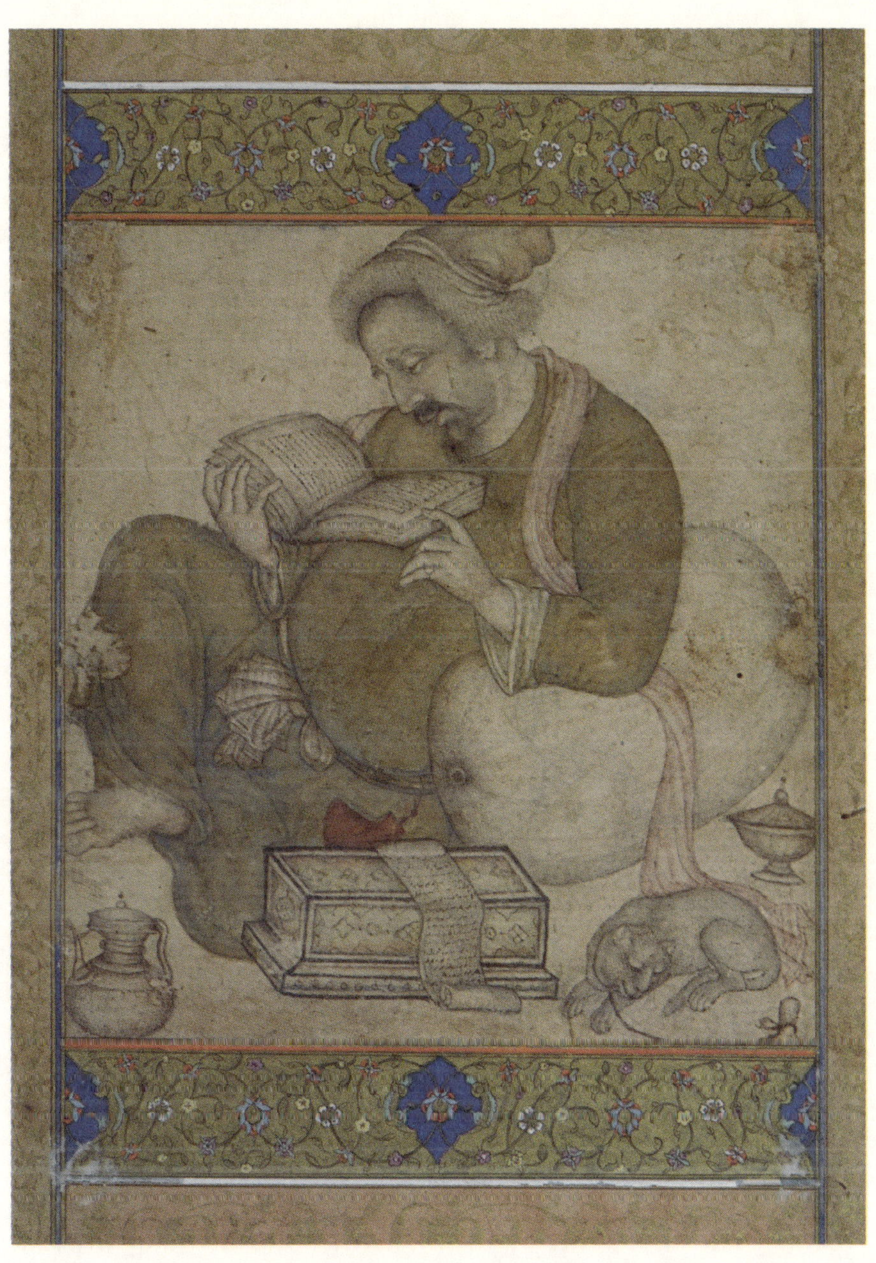

• 45 •

MANY ASCETICS, AND A FAMILY OF CATS

One side of a bi-folio from the *Gulshan Album*
Mughal; first quarter of the seventeenth century

[Staatsbibliothek Berlin; Preussische Kulturbesitz, Oriental Abteilung; Libri Pict. A117, f. 6b]

Not everything is of a piece in this work, but there is so much to see. At the top a loose-robed ascetic facing another, 'superbly turned out' ascetic; in the lower half, one sees under a tree a congregation of yogis, all bare-bodied except for loincloths, all seated around a pile of fire and ashes. But in the left half portion, one also sees, brilliantly rendered, a family of cats: dark-skinned and very alert mother keeping watch over her five offspring who run about, playing games, unconcerned. The pieces of the painting are in no way all connected, but there is some compensation: a rare vignette of a cat family that is hardly ever seen elsewhere.

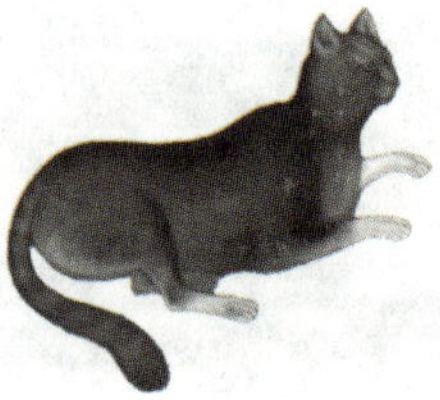

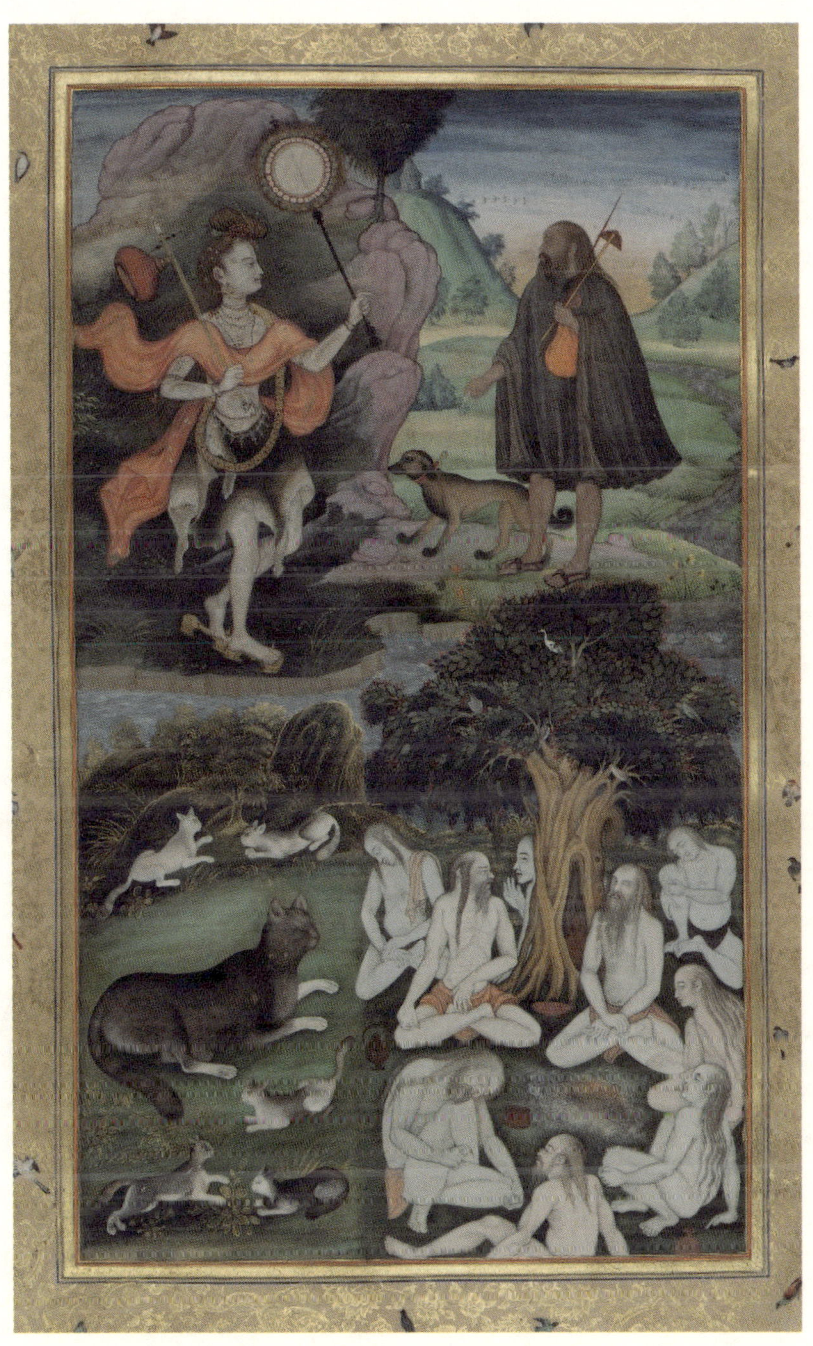

• 46 •

A YOGI SEATED IN THE ALAKH POSTURE

Folio from a *Bahr al-Hayat* manuscript
Uttar Pradesh, Allahabad; ca. 1600–1604.

Chester Beatty Library, Dublin; acc. no. IN 16.17a

A section of this manuscript in Persian on yogic practices—the earliest known illustrated treatise on yoga asanas, or postures—begins like this, mysteriously: '...this body is like a leather bag (anban) full of water, or like a sheep skin (mashk) full of air. If that water or air settles, shrinkage must occur.' Different postures carry different names: this yogi thus is seen in 'alakh': bare-bodied, meditating, seated under a tree, facing a pile of fire and ashes. A cat—evidently a trusted companion—crouches just behind him and seems to be getting into a yogic posture too. 'It is tough, but meaningful. No?"

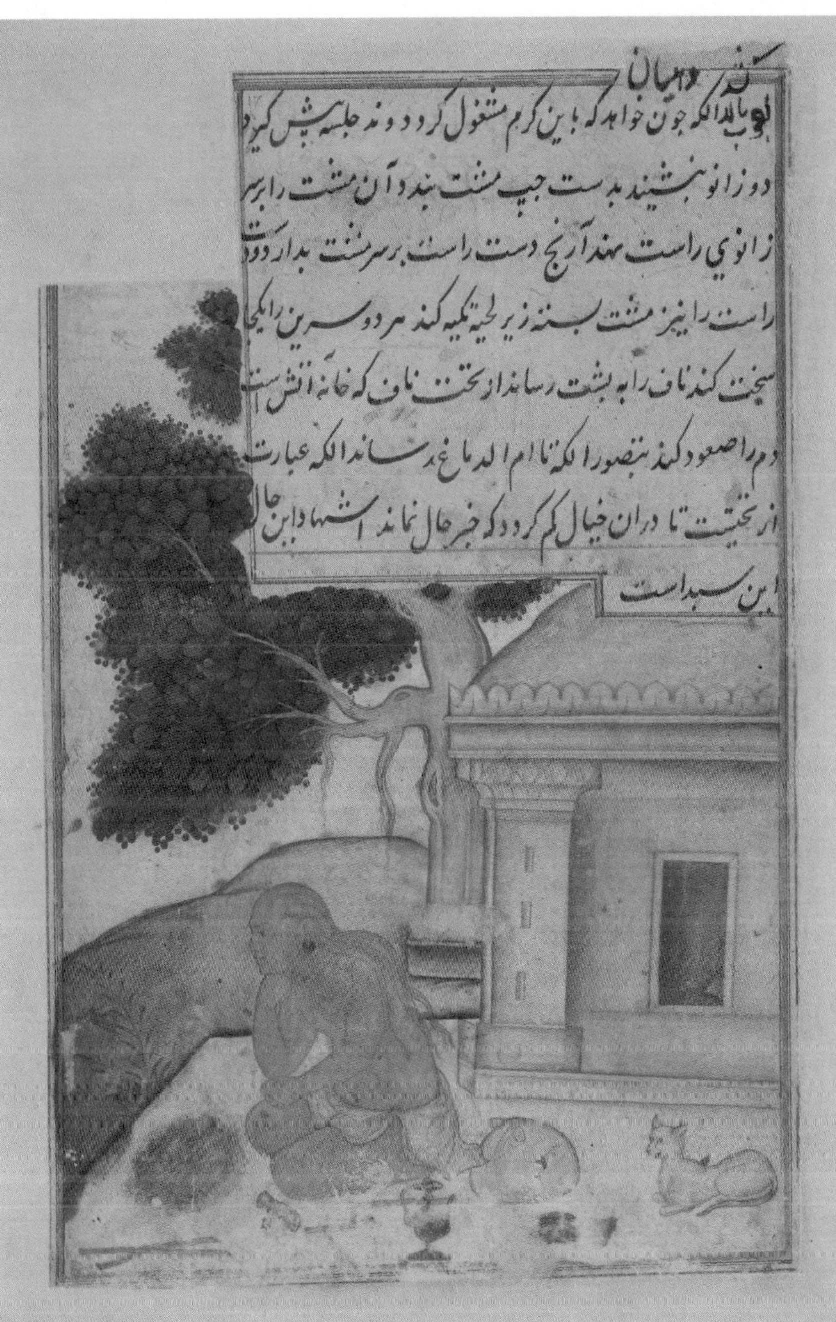

• 47 •

A SANTOOR PLAYER

Mughal; by the painter Jagjiwan; 1590–95

[Chester Beatty Library, Dublin; acc. no. 44.7]

The setting for a musician, seated all by himself, playing on his santoor, is unusual: a chamber in a palace, an elevated platform, elegant bottles placed inside niches and curtains gathered and tied, European fashion, to pillars. It feels as if there might have been a companion to this work, at left, with a patron sitting there, and listening. The musician, naturally bare-footed—his elegant pair of shoes lie just outside—is looking in that direction rather than at his instrument. If there is, on the facing folio, a princely figure, his patron, it is no surprise that the cat sitting in a corner at bottom right is hunching up. After all, she might be in royal presence.

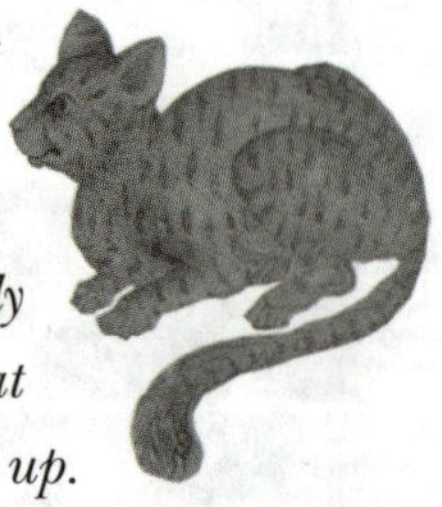

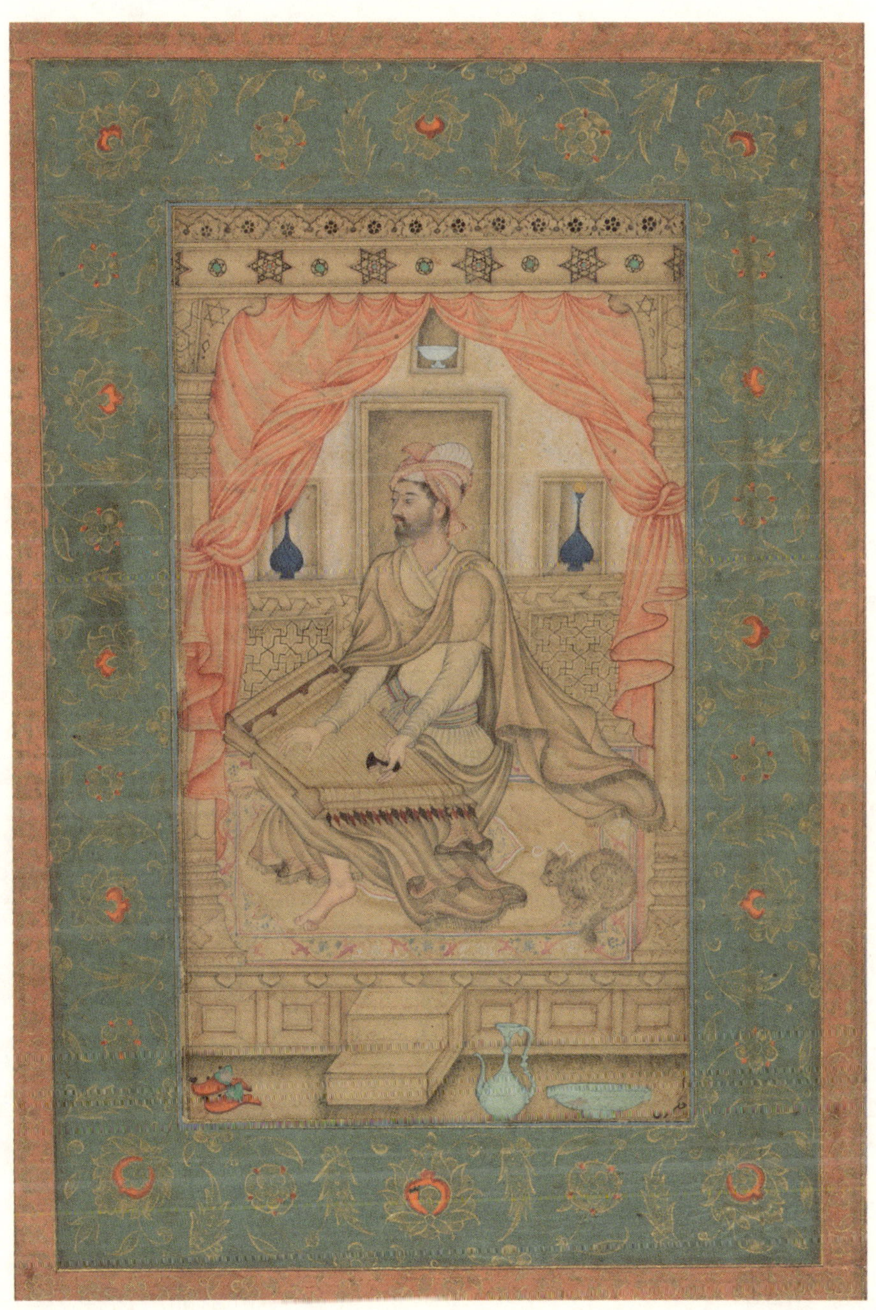

• 48 •

A SUFI SAINT SEATED UNDER A TREE AT A HERMITAGE

Isolated folio cut and pasted on a sheet
Mughal; ca. 1730

[Bonham's auction catalogue, 2011]

The details are all in place: the lone spot; the tree, symbol of growth and enlightenment; the bare, humble surroundings; the deer skin serving for a seat; books lying around. These apart, the venerable figure of the seated saint—identified by a late inscription as 'Hazrat Pir Dastgir' whom one knows from Kashmir—completes the image of a Sufi: long flowing beard, cap covering the head; a robe-like single garment; rosary of beads in hand; and a distant look in the eyes. The saint's little cat sits facing him, alert of stance and look, as if trying to catch the sacred words being recited. Or is it that she is 'seeing' something that is denied to others?

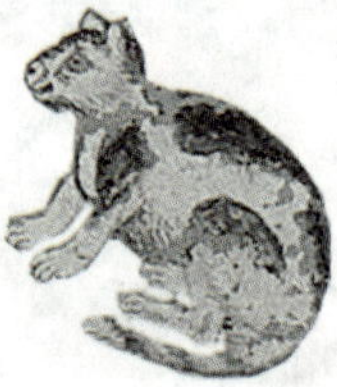

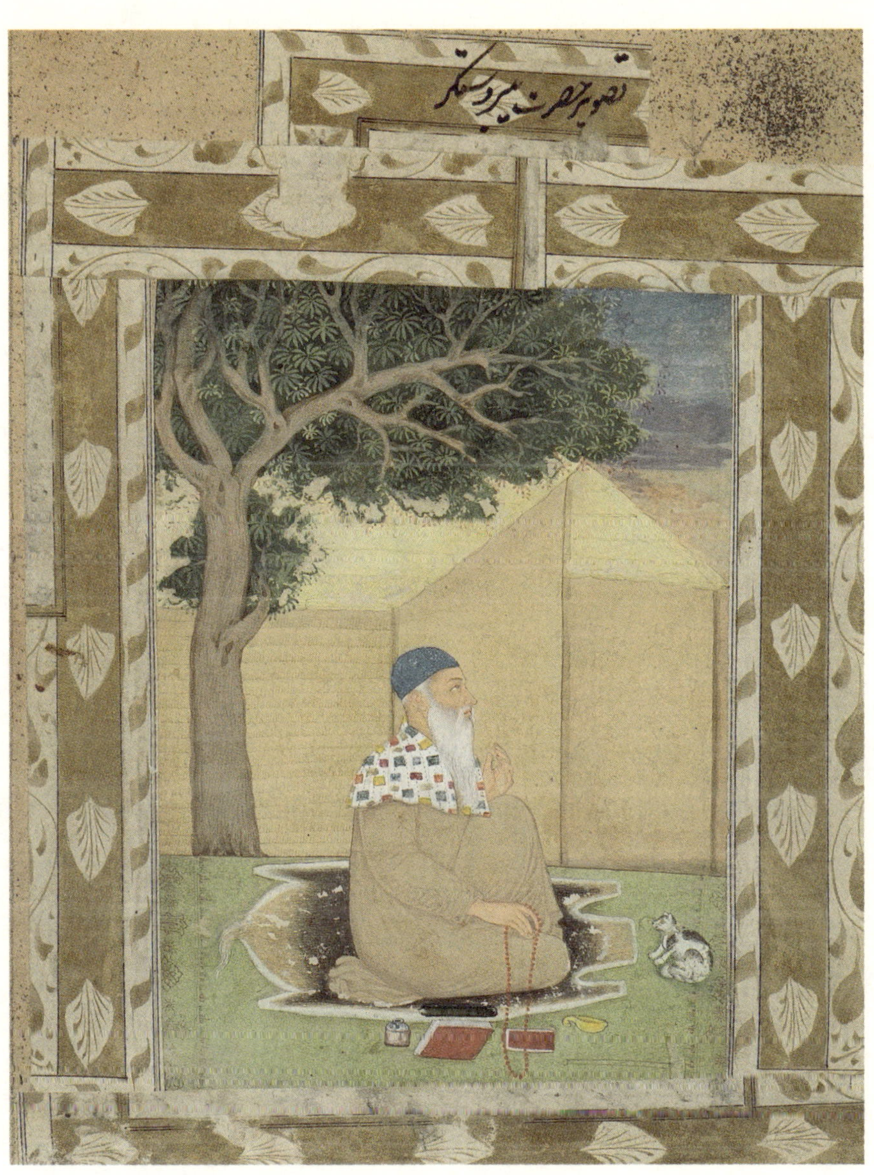
تصویر حضرت میر دستگیر

• 49 •

THE SUFI SAINT HAJI HUSAIN BUKHARI

Folio from the *Shah Jahan Album*; recto, early nineteenth century; calligraphy on verso a late copy of a sixteenth century original

[The Metropolitan Museum of Art, New York; purchase, Rogers Fund and the Kevorkian Foundation Gift, 1955; acc. no. 55.121.10.28]

'There is no restfulness in this heart because my beloved's heart is hard. Patience may be "the wealth of the destitute"; true, but what do I do if my destitute heart knows no patience at all?' This is how the verse on the back reads. These elegant words, however, bear no connection with the Sufi saint. The Haji, elegantly dressed and comfortably seated, is busy reading. The surroundings are serene, and no one intrudes. The cat, paws scratching the beautiful carpet, appears to look straight at the viewer, her stance almost saying that no one should forget that it was lions who used at one time to keep company with Sufi masters, but now, guess who has taken their place?

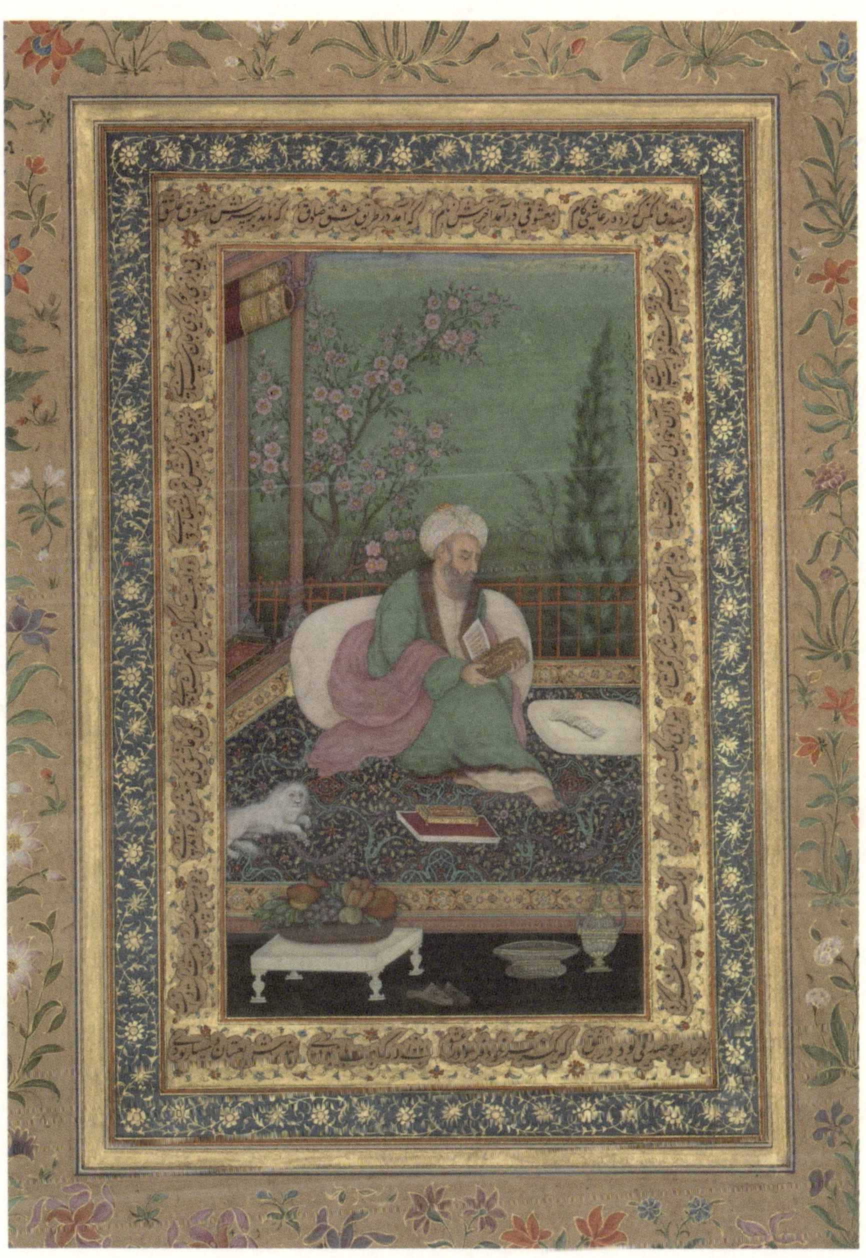

• 50 •

A PAGE FULL OF ANIMALS

Folio from the *St. Petersburg Muraqqa*
Mughal; ca. 1610; by the painter, Abu'l Hasan?
[The Oriental Institute, St. Petersburg; folio 72 recto]

The album of Indian and Persian miniatures which goes by the name St. Petersburg Muraqqa, *now in Russia, springs surprises of its own. On a page, an almost surrealistic omnium gatherum, where animals like lions and elephants, goats and sheep, and bitches with pups, roam around, the pride of place belongs to a large, tethered cat suckling her kitten. The rendering must have been based on decades of devoted study, a scholar has said. Rightly, the catalogue note says: 'Has any artist anywhere rendered livelier, wrigglier kittens? Or a more blissful mother-cat? ...Admire the texture, patterns, colours, tails, and above all the expressions of ecstatic giving and receiving!'*

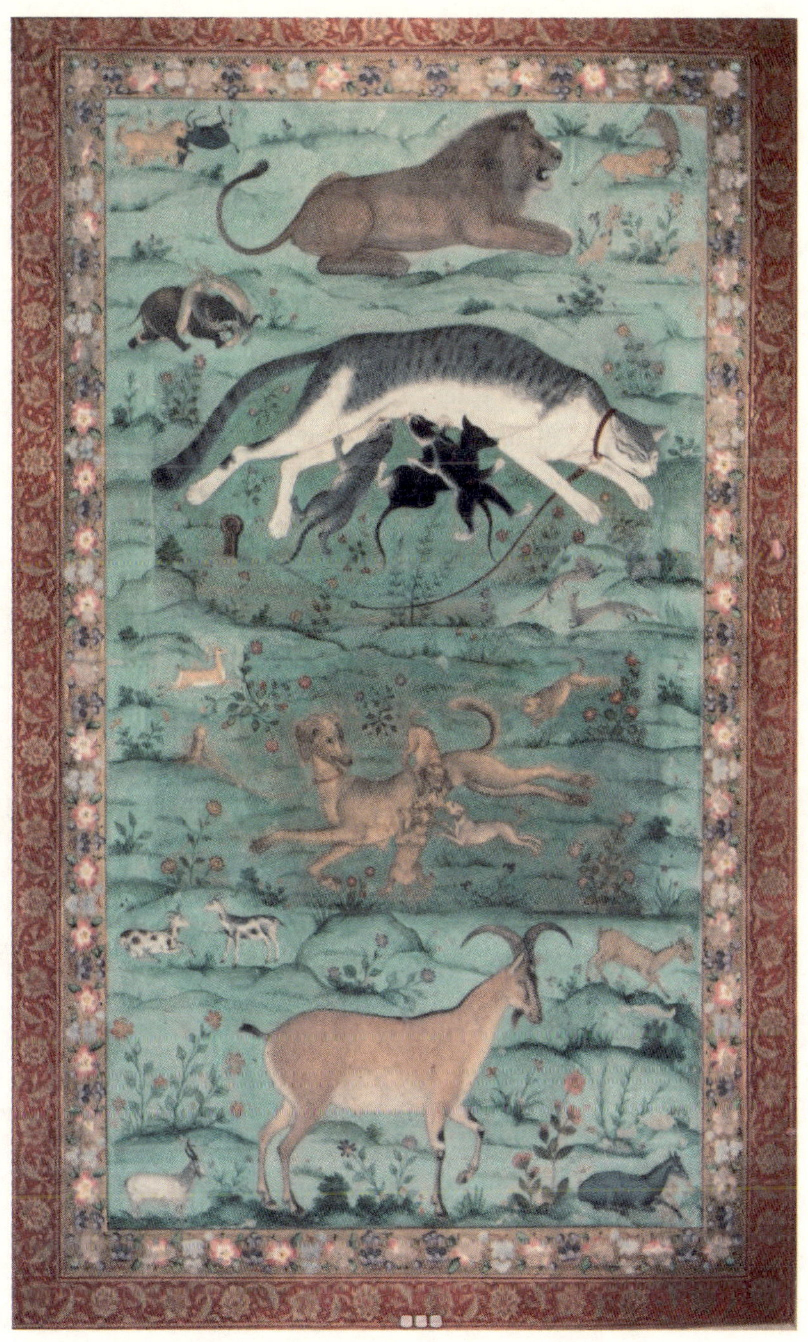

• 51 •

FOUR CATS

Folio from *Book of Dreams*
Rajasthan; from a Mewar workshop; ca. 1730

[Rita Dixit sales catalogue]

Entirely appropriately, for everywhere dreams continue to be a feature of our lives and thoughts, cats figure in them, because they too are a part of ordinary life. In Books of Dreams*—Svapna Darshan, literally 'sights seen in dreams', is often the title—appear sights seen or unseen, familiar or strange. And each time they are interpreted by 'wise men': astrologers, soothsayers, augurs, oracles. They are placed in categories: ashubha, neshta, shreshtha, uttama, etc. Neshta is undesirable, and cats fall in that category. The inscription above forewarns that a dream of cats will lead to obstruction in your plans, render good beginnings meaningless, cause sadness or separation. Four cats of different breeds and appearance are introduced here.*

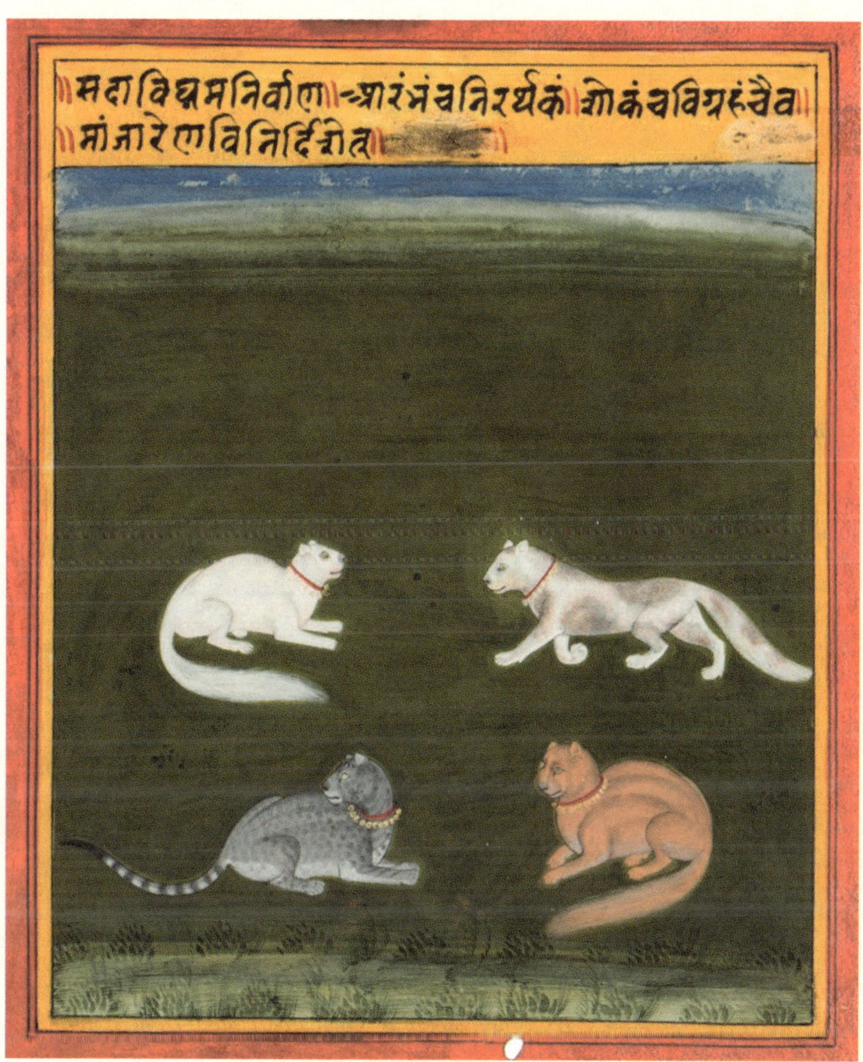
॥ सदा विघ्नमनिर्वाण ॥ आरंभं च निरर्थकं ॥ शोकं च विग्रहं चैव ॥
॥ मांजारेण विनिर्दिशेत् ॥

• 52 •

A CAT

Isolated folio, possibly separated from a series
Lucknow; ca. 1845

[Francesca Galloway sales catalogue;
work from the collection of James Ivory]

Whether this is a real portrait of a cat, or an advertisement for blue 'cat's-eye' gemstones is not easy to tell. But with her golden-retriever like silky-smooth brown coat, she makes an impression. For all her big size one sees her as being of gentle disposition, for that is what one sees in the thoughtful expression. The rendering on the whole is a bit coarse, however, a far cry from the refined brush work of earlier masters. But then even if the work comes from a hastily put together series, she does deserve to have a name. No?

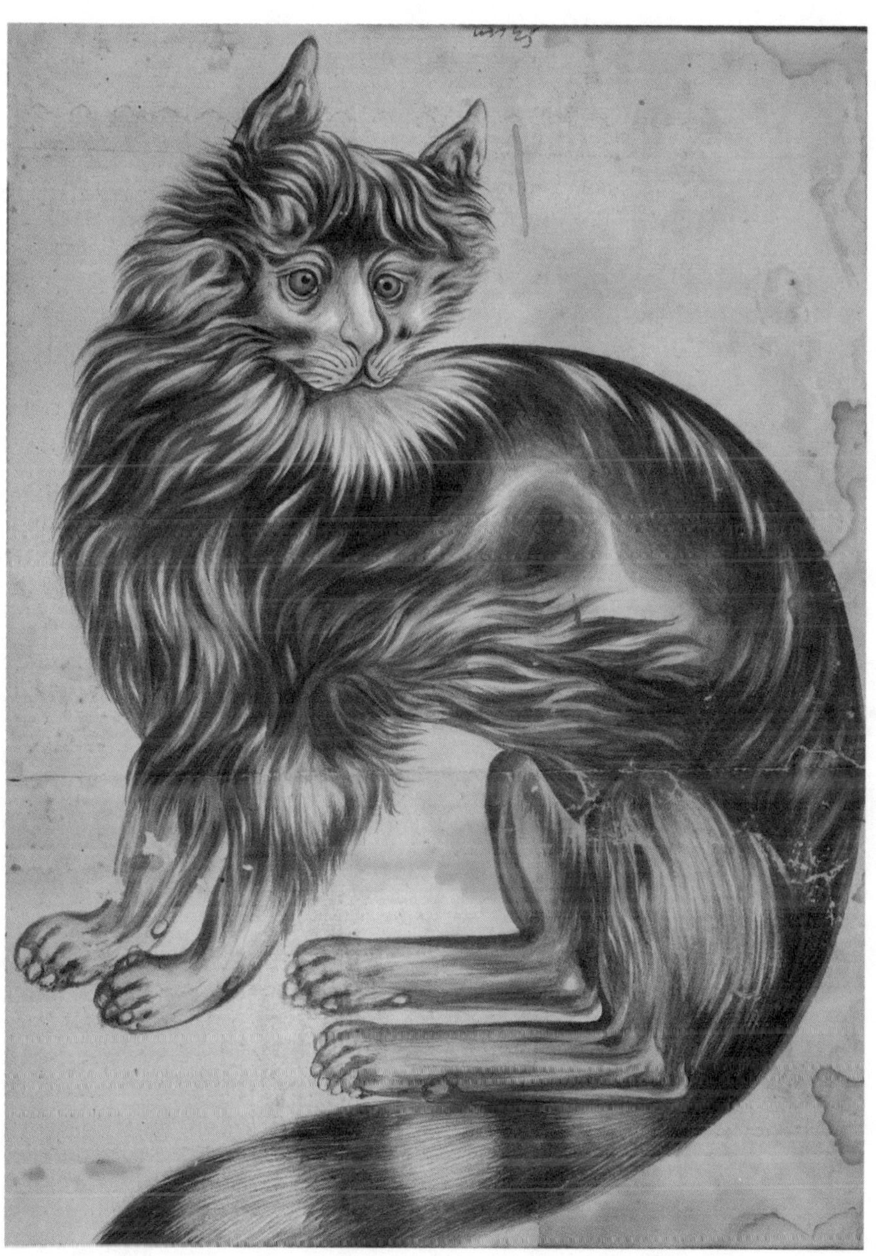

• 53 •

FOUR CATS, ALL FROM SOUTH INDIA

From a manuscript showing animal types
Mysore; second quarter of the nineteenth century
[Private Collection]

Related naturally, but unknown to one another, these four cats seem to have sneaked their way onto a double-page in a manuscript dealing with different types of animals—an inventory of sorts—prepared for the celebrated maharaja of Mysore, Krishnaraja Wodeyar, the third. Brief captions in Kannada identify each type: thus, from top to bottom, Vuru Bekku (common or village cat); the Kiraba jati Bekku (cat of the Kiraba type); Huli Bekku (cat of the tiger type); and the Adavi Bekku (a wild cat). Singularly alert looking, as if, eyes peeled, looking for prey, each stands, all four feet firmly resting on a tiny piece of a grassy mound. Ready for action, or for the painter.

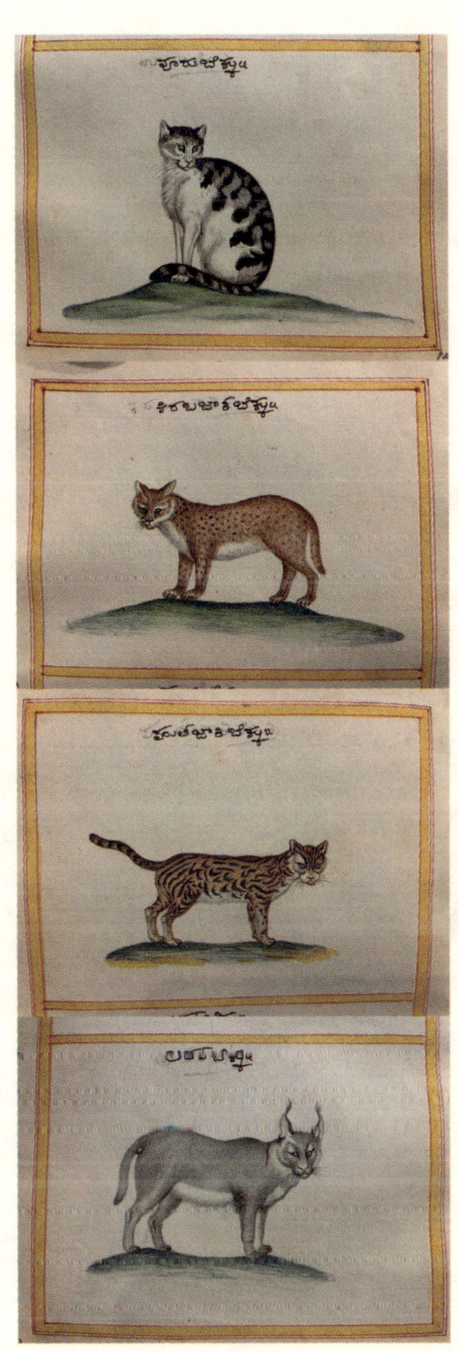

• 54 •

A CAT WITH A STOLEN CRAYFISH

Painted woodcut
Bengal, from a Kalighat workshop; ca. 1900;
by an unknown artist

[Museum of Art and Photography, Bangalore, acc. no. POP.01712]

While this could be a genre image—both fish and cats abounding in Bengal—of a massive cat having gotten away with a crayfish, it could also be a satire on the doings of 'holy men'. Satires on men and manners were a prominent part of Kalighat work, and here the artist could be targeting a segment of Vaishnavas: the vertical u-shaped tilak mark on the forehead is a giveaway, for one thing, as is the predatory look in the eyes of the animal.

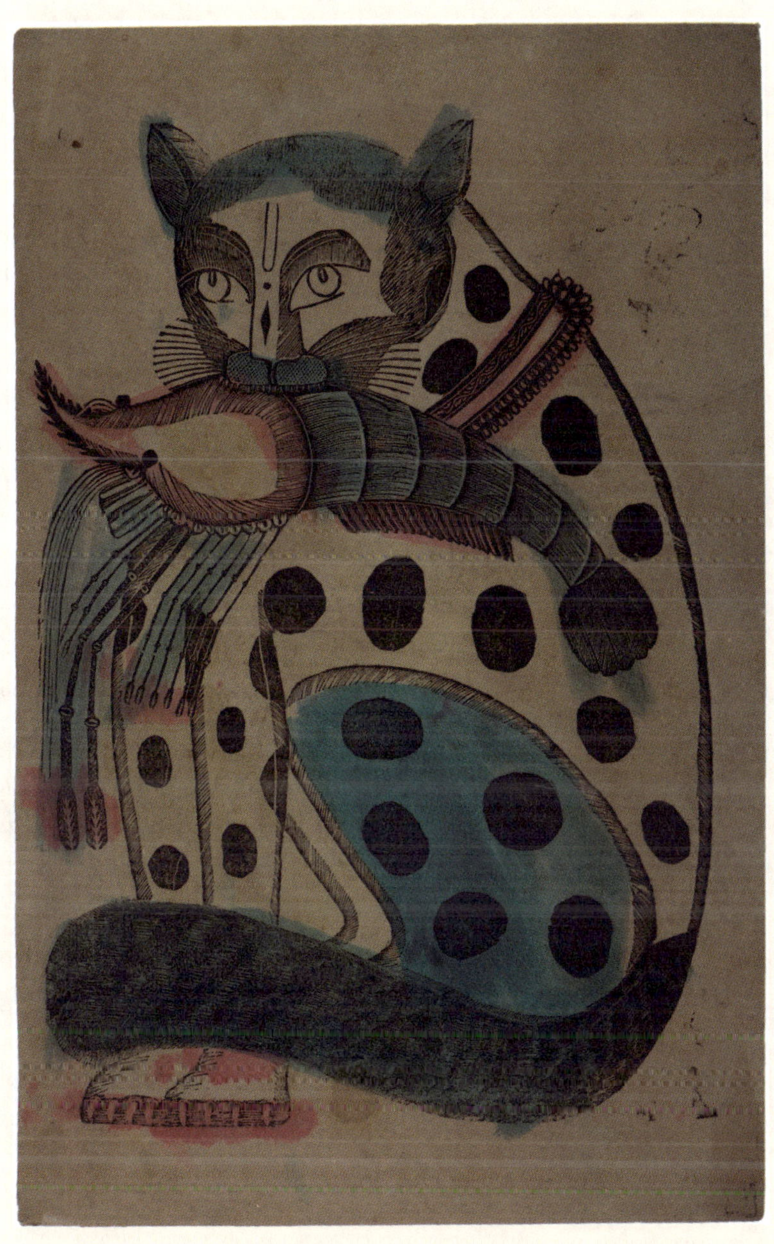

• 55 •

STILL LIFE WITH A FISH

Oil on acrylic sheet
By K. G. Subramanyan; c. 1980

[Museum of Art and Photography, Bangalore; acc. no. M.AC 01359]

Is there a story here, in this luminous, stained-glass like work? There is a fish-seller, a bunch of fish and other sea creatures, a basket with remains of fish, and a large, aggressive-looking he-cat, with a fish skeleton held firmly between his teeth. But the connection is not easy to make, and one concentrates on the figure of the cat with its ungainly look and somewhat fierce aspect. A recollected moment, perhaps, filtered through memory?

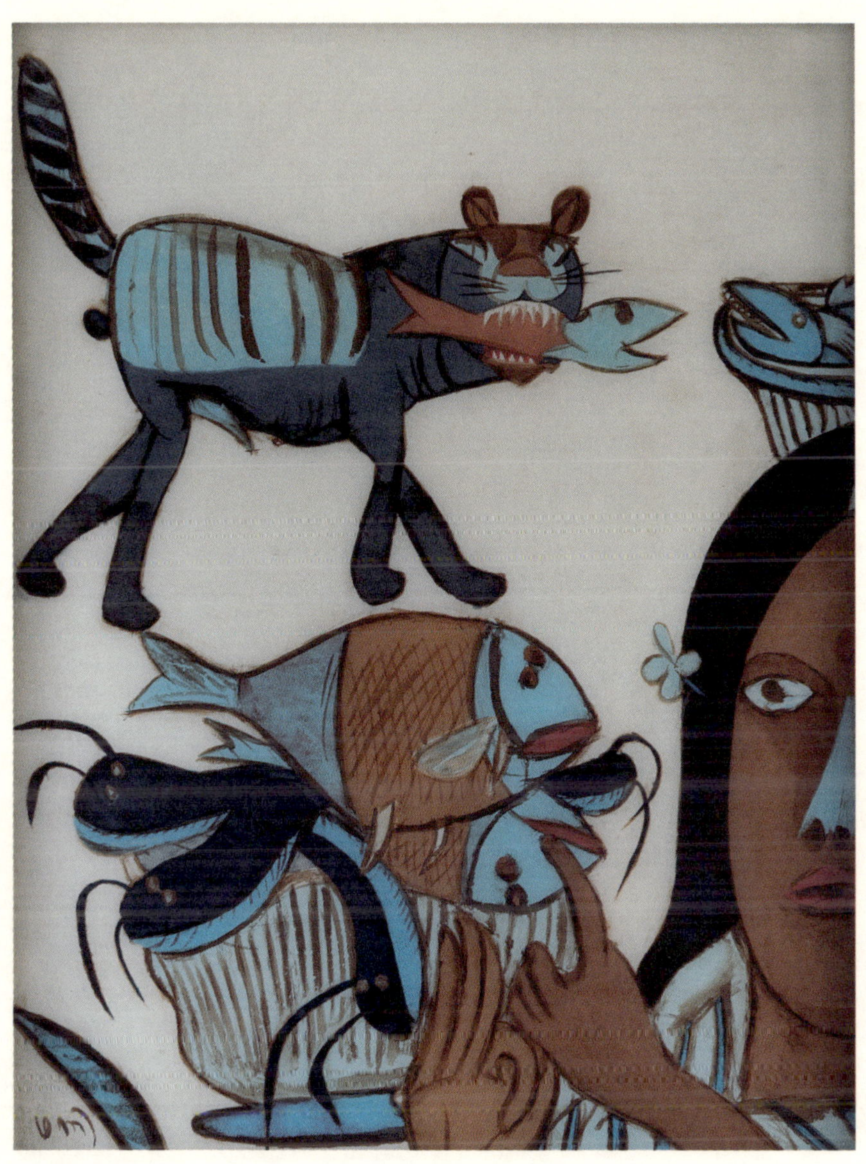

• 56 •

TWO CATS HOLDING A STOLEN LARGE PRAWN

Tempera on board
By Jamini Roy; c. 1968

[Museum of Art and Photography, Bangalore, acc. no. MAC 01364]

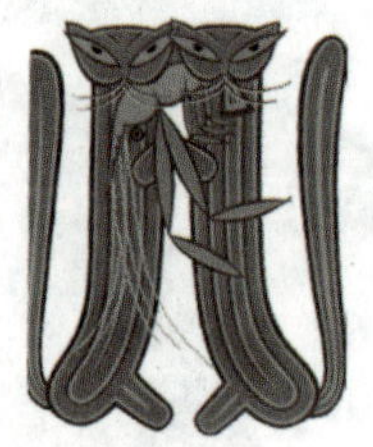

Against a grid pattern in the background, Jamini Roy places two cats in his own, highly stylized fashion, one sees. Everything has been played around with—the slim bodies of the animals, the upright tails, the complete absence of feet, the large 'lotus-eyes' staring at the viewer—merging the image into the folk paintings of Bengal. At the same time, why two cats, and not one? Is there a reference somewhere to the old tale of two cats unable to agree on sharing the catch equally, ultimately landing up with a monkey who cheats them out of their spoil?

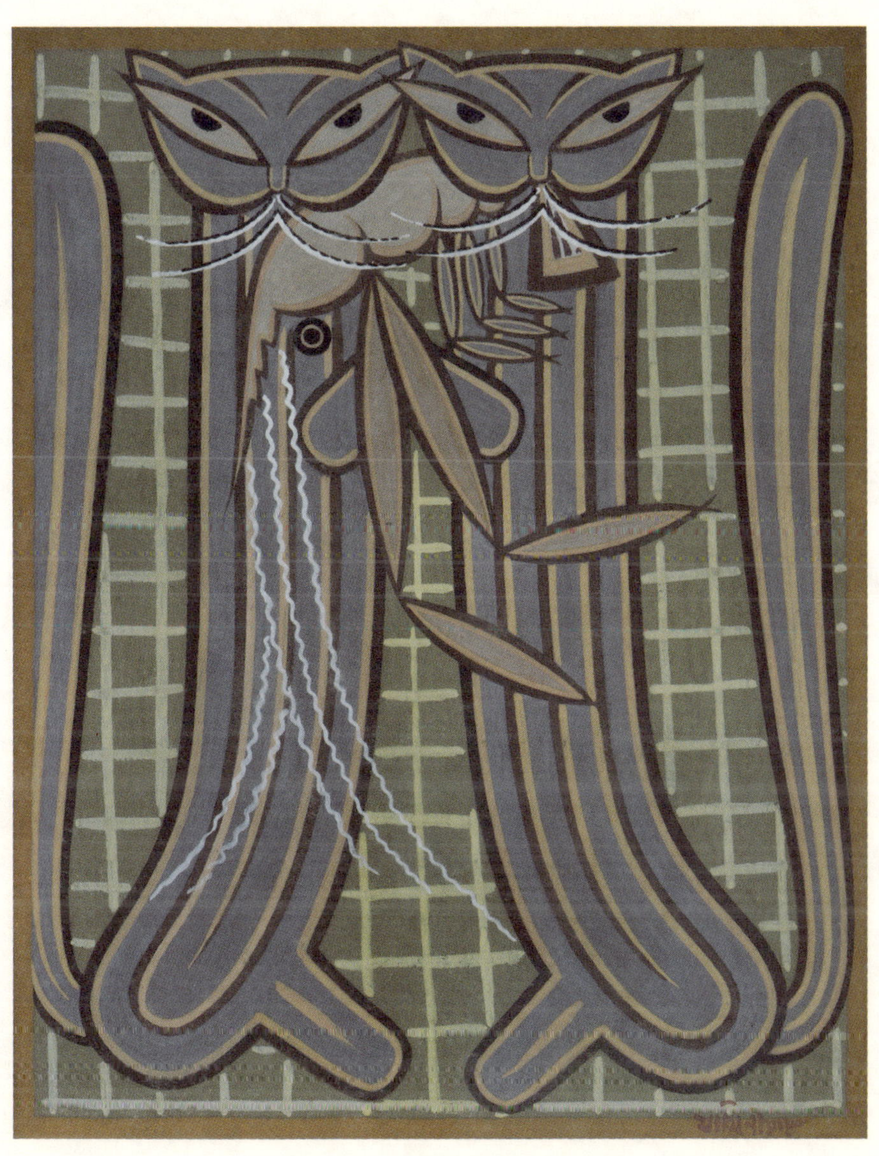

• 57 •

CAT RUNNING WITH STOLEN FISH

Natural pigments on pure silk board
By Mahaveer Swami of Bikaner

[Private Collection]

Harking back to, and continuing to follow in, the tradition of miniature painting, Mahaveer Swami removes all context, all references, and paints here a cat, placing her against a stark, plain ground. One can see, from the way of turning her head and looking over her shoulder, that she is afraid of being pursued, for she has just stolen a fish and is running away with it. Nothing else intrudes, at least here, however. And one can concentrate on the delicate colouring, the texture of the coat, and the look: a mixture of triumph and fear.

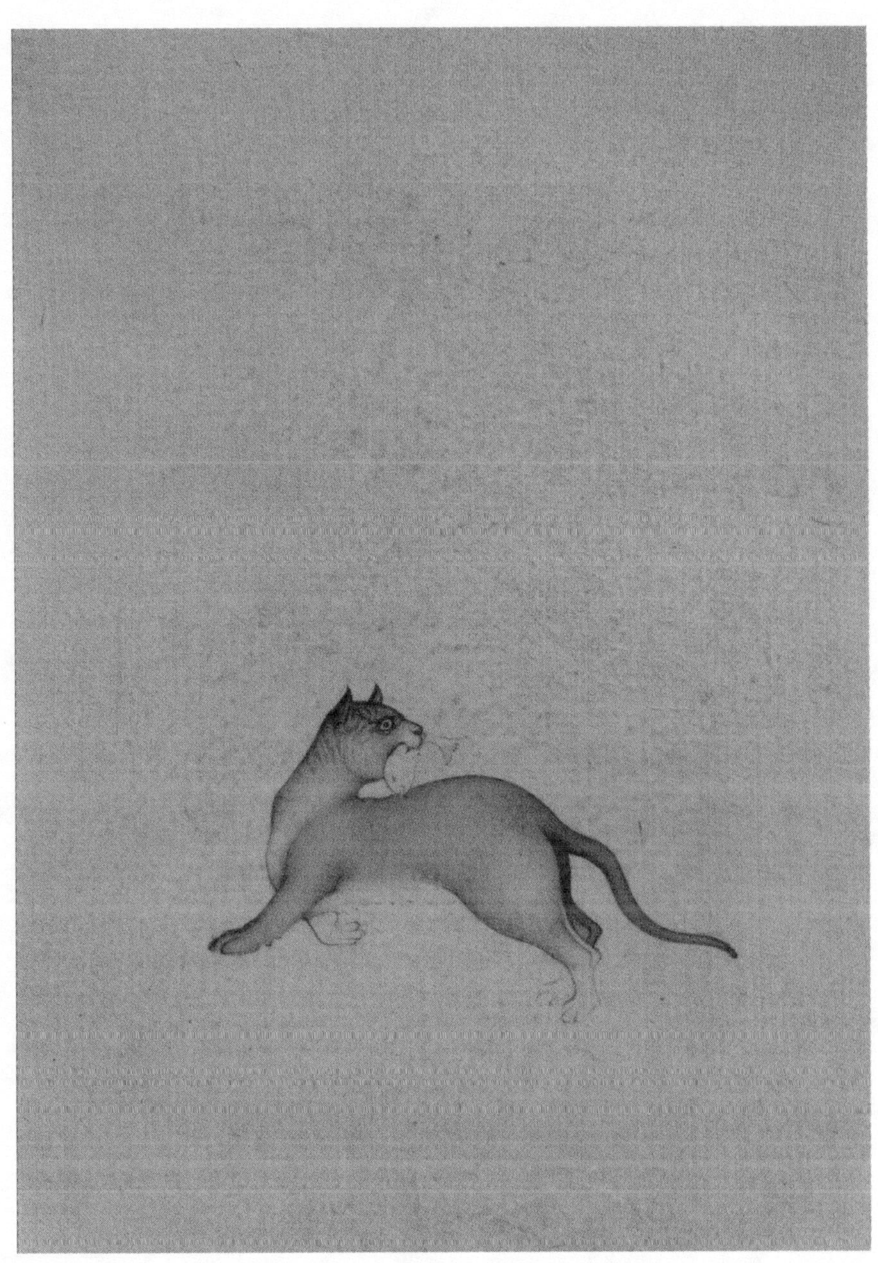

• 58 •

COURTESAN WITH A CAT

From the 'My Cat and I' series
Kalighat style; by Bapi Chitrakar

[Private Collection]

The patuas of Bengal made countless images of courtesans: now embracing clients, now preening themselves in front of mirrors, now feeding their pets, and so on. There was comment in these images of the lives they lead, the changing mores, the place of women in that society. One recognizes that this is an image of a courtesan, not of a woman from a bhadralok background. Painted by a contemporary artist from the patua tradition, here she sits, curvy character, in a cushioned chair, drink in hand, petting her cat which seems to be making eyes at her: 'At least, I am here, Bau'di. No?'

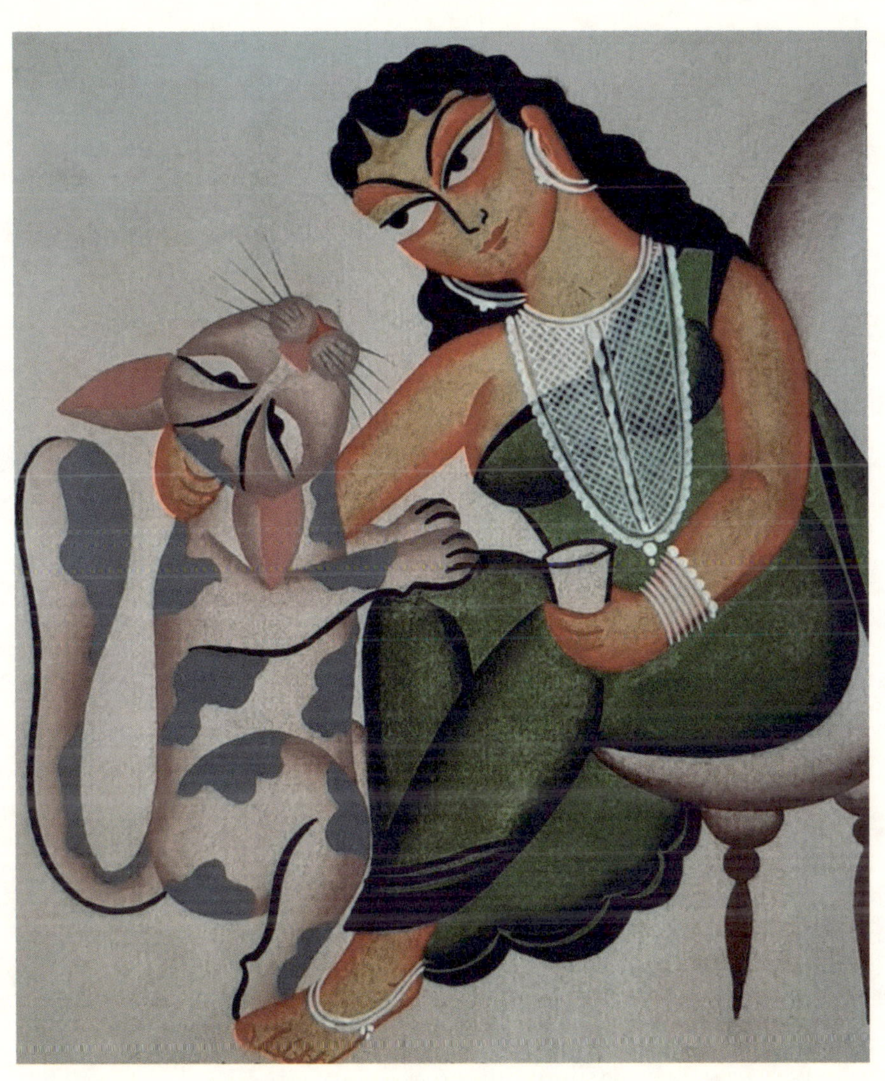

GLEANINGS

From Old Anthologies of Poetic Texts

Among the many ways of seeing cats is the way how ancient poets/philosophers of India brought them into their work. A small sample of this, reproduced here, has been culled from one of the most extensive dictionaries of quotations published by the Vishveshvarananda Vedic Research Institute, Hoshiarpur, over the last couple of decades: the Maha Subhashita Sangraha. *In early literature, there are no poems dedicated to cats; none that feature them as principal subjects or theme, but every now and then they are brought in by great poets—like Bhartrihari, or Magha—into their descriptions of events unconnected with cats. Their cleverness, or hypocrisy, sharpness of sight and observation, or their very nature, are woven both as examples, and as warnings, in a seemingly casual manner. The full context in which the verses were written is sometimes too complex, and one has to make an effort to get into the verse. But, as the discerning reader of the past must have discovered, the effort is worth making.*

The cat has humped her back;
mouth raised and tail curling,
She keeps one eye in fear upon the inside of her house;
her ears are motionless.
The dog, his mouth full of great teeth wide open
to the back of his spittle-jaws,
swell at the neck withheld-in breath
until he jumps her.

—*Shatakatrayadi-Subhashita–Samgraha* of Bhartrihari
[*Maha Subhashita Sangraha*, vol. III, no. 4304]

One should sip water with mantras after speaking to a woman in her
courses, a fallen man, a barbarian, an outcast and his kind;
also having touched a cat or a mouse and on seeing
one answering calls of nature.

—*The Paddhati* of Sharangdhara
[*Maha Subhashita Sangraha*, vol. IV, no. 6690]

By persons who do energetic action results are achieved as in the case of a cat; it never maintains a cow ever since birth, but drinks milk every day.

—*Shatakatrayadi-subhashita-samgraha* of Bhartrihari
[*Maha Subhashita Sangraha,* vol. IV, no. 6880]

A cow, a dog, a lowborn, a cat, a serpent, and a woman not of a respectful stock—all these are declared to be similar.

—*Mahabharata*
[*Maha Subhashita Sangraha,* vol. V, no. 9288]

A cat, being useful, is bought with money, brought from distance, and cherished; but a mouse, being harmful, is carefully destroyed, though it has been nourished in one's house.

—The *Kathasaritsagara* of Somadeva-bhatta
[*Maha Subhashita Sangraha,* vol. VII, no. 11799]

Lord Ganesha praises a cat so as to protect his vehicle, a mouse; even a great person desires to serve a low person due to circumstances.
—*Subhashita-Ratna-Bhandagaram*
[*Maha Subhashita Sangraha,* vol. VII, no. 12587]

As a sportive girl, holding fast a branch of a dwarfish mango tree, in the Gunja-bower, frolicked with a creeper (thereon) and conversed intimately with Krsna, the male cat (close by) scanned every branch (i.e., her body).

—Kr M. Krishnamachariar
[*Maha Subhashita Sangraha,* vol. VIII, no. 13028]

In that city (Dwarka) people mistook as an artificial cat even a real cat which stood with its body extended and still, with a desire to catch the row of artificial birds on the aviaries of houses.

—*Shishupala-vadha*
[*Maha Subhashita Sangraha,* vol. VIII, no. 14246]

Old age lays hold of the youth by the ears, as the old cat seizes on the mouse, and devours its prey after sporting with it for a while.

—*Yoga Vasishtha*
[Book 6, Chapter 7, Verse 21]

POEMS

From the Urdu, Hindi, Persian, Bengali, among Others

MOHINI, THE CAT

Mir Taqi Mir

Translated from the Urdu by BNG

There once was a cat that bore the name Mohini—
'Enchantress'—you might say.
How do I know her? She just strayed into our house one day
and, simply, decided to stay.
She took a liking to us, there is no doubt.
The consequence? She rarely went out.
Then, a wonder, she grew fond of me too
And decided to look up to me for everything: just everything.
Up with the lark was she and soon as she was up
She would saunter into my room
Even ahead of that cat which lurks in the sky:
that heavenly yellow disk that dispels gloom.
You can say that she would come to me at—how do we call it?
—the hour of 'the wolf and the lamb'
And sit there, many watches, just watching my face.
She would eat anything: a piece of dried bread
even a meat scrap, tough and rubbery and stale
And made out as if she enjoyed it.

All to hide my poverty's tale.
...
Time passed, and she began to stir out
Other places, other homes.
She became pregnant; littered several times
But none of her offspring survived.
This happened, again and again,
Again and yet again,
Leaving us sad, devastated
So fond were we of her that now
We began to think hard of ways
To protect and save her womb.
Charms and talismans? Prayers?
Promises made to God?
We would, we promised, give alms in her name
If her kitten lived.
Talismans were procured from holy men
And tied with indigo thread to her belly.
Some wrote sacred words charged with power
On the diet she was used to.
Some wrote talismanic words on the blood from
pieces of rough meat and tripe offered to her
Prayers were addressed to the revered Bi Bila'i;
Other domestic cats were brought in to pray for ours.
Kites were fed pieces of meat
And loaves of magical black beans were cooked.
Young girls were made to sit under cots
To prevent the cat from moving off.
While feeding her bits and pieces, girls
Would open their mouths and meow like cats
In imitation; and then
When heaps of tripe blessed with prayers were
Placed before her, she, blessed soul, would be persuaded to eat.
Prayer after prayer was addressed to God
At midnight, every night, and
Blessings were sought from the Pious Man's cat too.
Some of us made vows to dedicate the merit

Of our good deeds to Abu Huraira, the Prophet's Pious companion.
Many stray cats we began to feed,
Even the cat whom Ubaid used to praise.
Another cat, seeing our state, came in from outside
And would pray and prostrate
Asking Mercy from God for our Mohini.
We would rise early in the morning
Just to seek fortitude from her example
To gain some part of her spiritual strength.
It did bear fruit, all this praying and beseeching:
This time, Mohini gave birth to five kittens
And by the Grace of God they survived, all five of them.
Why would they not in the face of such powerful support?
Bi Bila'i, Abu Haraira, and other holies?

THOSE TWO CATS OF OURS, SOHINI AND MOHINI

Mir Taqi Mir

Translated from the Urdu by BNG

...
In all that pell-mell, that confusion, our Sohini disappeared.
The place was unfamiliar, agitation everywhere.
She, poor thing, must have been completely frightened
And confused.
Suddenly, she was nowhere to be seen; we knew not where she went.
Into the mouth of death, somewhere?
We searched, and searched; looked and looked,
But our beloved cat was not to be found.
I went into the village, asked around, looked into every corner.
Does death come to someone like her, without warning,
Without even the slightest sound of a footstep?
We gave up, eventually. Perhaps it was her destiny that pulled her here.
Was she a cat? Still and serene was she, more like an object painted than alive.
Oh, I still think of her soft fur, 'colour of the time of the wolf and the lamb';
More red than black.
She was so different from the others: sidling up
Only to those whom she warmed to; and then she would look
At them with eyes that said something.
How can her gentle, sophisticated temper be described?
So clean, so tidy.
You wanted to gaze at her forever.
The rosettes on her coat would come alive sometimes

As if surrounded by leaves and flowers.
And her colour? Like a painter would choose it with care,
And apply ever so delicately.
Would she ever even cast an eye on a mouse or a bird?
The Hajj pilgrimage was never on her mind, for she did not need it.
She, our Sohini had a sister too: Mohini.
So different was she: much bolder and less self-restrained
Tearing up any small creature she found, and gobbling it up:
Not just one; she would gobble up four at a time.
As for Sohini; she could not even think of killing someone,
Nothing at all. Why, she would not even sharpen her claws
Or brawl.
Of sensitive temper was she; so different that
Even a field mouse could frighten her
Not like Mohini who would dispatch bandicoot after bandicoot
With her powerful blows.
Sohini would turn tail if she heard even a musk-rat squeak.
Mohini, on the other hand, would start at the slightest noise
Even when she was sound asleep.
Sohini would avert her face even from a gecko
While Mohini, ever rapacious, would not even leave carrion.
Sohini seemed almost like a peri, an angelic creature, as she walked,
And that other one: when she pounced it was like hell breaking loose.
Mountain partridges loved—envied in fact—her gait
And other creatures were in love with her very name.
Such was she, our Sohini. Sorrowed we still are by her absence
Her sudden disappearance.
A cat like her can rarely be found
Even if we scour the whole city of Delhi.
Such was the noble-tempered Sohini
Like a high-born lady.

A FRAGMENT ON HIS CAT

Asadullah Khan Ghalib

Translated from the Persian by BNG

My cat? Noble is she and of gentle temper.
Like a winged fairy she seems to be
When she leaps
Or when she lands, coyly swaying.
Methinks she is some other-worldly being.
Even the prints of her paws on the ground
are like heavenly buds about to open their petals,
So light and mirror-smooth is her frame that
You can almost see the young one she is carrying
Inside her.
As for myself: to a lion's roar is superior her sweet
Purring sound.
Kind of heart that she is, she is moved,
Filled with pity, I know,
at the sight of an animal lying dead.
And if a sparrow were to leave her young one to her care
She will guard it with her life, shooing cock and quail firmly away.
When she licks with her tongue, she can plunge
the Pleiades into envy,
And when she swings her tail,
Everything seems to dance to her rhythms.
Her curls put to shame the locks of the beauteous
May—I pray—that as long as the Sun keeps
Moving through his path in the heavens above,
May my hand keep stroking, gently, her
Soft belly, and that seductive arch of her back.

ON SEEING MY CAT IN SOMEONE ELSE'S LAP

Allama Muhammad Iqbal

Translated from the Urdu by BNG

Come on, love, where did you learn to look with such amour, such seduction in your eyes?
How on earth did you know that these are but guileless beginnings of love?
for each move of yours, each gesture, is soaked in love
and impishness has made your blue eyes its home.
You look at 'her' abashedly now, and now stare at 'her',
one moment you are up, the next you lie down and sleep;
are your eyes like a mirror, full of wonder at all times
or is it that you see with the light that glows inside you?
What coyness! what does this pawing mean:
playfulness? Anger? Or is it just love?
But be careful! If you overdo this, you will lose this dainty lap
if the flower that adorns 'her' bosom falls, you will be in for a beating.

Tell me! What are you seeking, hoping to find?
Ah! Perhaps you have the same questions that I have:
is man alone sensitive to beauty, to love?
or does it reside in all hearts, of all creatures?
Love, I know, is like the choicest wine that a goblet can hold,
it is the soul of the sun, the blood that courses through the veins of moon:
in the weeniest atom, it throbs
it glows in the recesses of the heart of each being
all happiness stems from it, but also all sorrow,
a pearl now, a tear at another time, yet again a dewdrop.

A CAT

Jibanananda Das

Translated from the Bengali by Maitreyee Sen

There is a cat that I come upon, every now and then
Now in the shade of a tree, anon in the sun,
Again under the cover of brown leaves,
Where, after devouring some pieces of fish and their bones,
He reclines, in the skeletal white, parched earth,
Engrossed with himself and his own heart, I see, like the honeybees;
The very next moment he is clawing the trunk of the *gulmohar*
The whole long day he runs, in pursuit of the sun.
He is here now, and then lost again, I know not where.
In the autumn evening, I see him frolicking,
Caressing playfully with his white paws, the soft body of the saffron-hued twilight sun
And then, gathering the darkness into little balls,
He scatters it over all the Earth.

THEY ARE FIGHTING AGAIN, THESE CATS

A reverie by Shafiq-ul Rehman

Translated from the Urdu by BNG

Oh, there they go again:
Cats are fighting. Cats! Cats!! Cats!!!... Caaaa...tsss
Maybe they are fighting in the garden now
There is dusk all around; time of haze
Time to rest
To work
Or just to gaze
And there they go again, these cats
Fighting
Are they four in number or are there only three?
But I cannot rid myself of the thought
That perhaps there are five of them
For they certainly cannot be six.
On the other hand
the night is aglow with light; the moon is shining bright and everything is bathed in moonlight
But all this will not last forever and it will be pitch dark again.
What was I saying? Suddenly, I cannot recall
(What happened to my memory? God only knows it)
Oh yes, I now recall it all! The cats;
They are all there
And they are still fighting in the garden below.

A POEM FOR THE LITTLE GIRL, MUNNI

Ibn-e Insha

Translated from the Hindustani by BNG

'Come, come, little girl!
Where are all your teeth? I don't see them? Where *ARE* they?!'
'I don't know, Dad! Really. But they are all gone.
You know how well I looked after them! For seven long years.
But what could I do, Dad? Some rats came the other day: so big,
Moustaches and all, but meek, and they said: "there is a whole keg of jaggery there
Sweet and delicious
But to bite into it we need some more teeth. Please."
They looked so helpless, Dad. What could I do? I gave them some of mine.'
'Let me ask, again, my little girl! Did you give away all? Or did you lose them somewhere?'
'No, Dad! There also came a cat, sneaking in. Lovely and plump
Like my aunt
On her paws I saw bits of some scraps of sweet, and
on her lips some traces of cream
Cream that she had just licked somewhere.
I loved the sight, and then she spoke to me, in whispers
"I just saw some rats, dear. Dancing on a keg of jaggery: four of them
Making merry.
But I am going to get them, dear. Don't you worry.
When I do, we shall share the spoils. Half-and-half. No?
But I can do this only if you could lend me some teeth."
'Could I have refused, Dad?'

'Come, come, my little girl! You have hardly any left. Did you give away some more?'
'No, Dad! I mean, yes!
When old Moti, our gardener, came and spoke in a piteous voice
His face about to be bathed in tears, I had to listen to him. No?
"Little mistress," he said, "something HAS to be done about that cat.
She comes into the kitchen and does not leave without tasting everything:
Milk and meat: she pounces on everything, right under my nose.
What, however, can I do, old bones that I am? But, wait, I can get after her
If only I had some teeth. Yours?"
'That is how it is, Dad! Some I lent to the rats; some the cat got; and
The rest did our Moti take.'
'All right, all right, my little girl! Do not be upset
But listen!
May I have all that you are left with?
There is a feast tonight holding so much promise:
Chicken legs to bite into, heaps of rice-pilaf, and aubergine pickle
I can make merry with your teeth, Munni. Please.
Or shall I go and knock on some other toothsome door?'
'Of course, Dad! Take all that I am left with.
But do bring them back! I am only lending them for the evening.'

MERI BILLI

Shaheen Iqbal Asar

Translated from the Urdu by BNG

True, no doubt, that my billi cat keeps her belly full
but does she not help keep the kitchen clean?
No, no! no rattling sound, no noise, does she make
while jumping down from the window, my billi cat
if there are any dogs around: even two or three
she makes herself scarce, my billi cat
she even avoids a big well-fed mouse
slyly she slinks away, my billi cat
Meow! meow! meow! meow! she says,
each time that she wants to come in, my billi cat
So? Little ones are scared of a cat without reason
the truth is: it is my cat who is scared of them.

DOGGEREL IN A CHILDREN'S GAME

Anonymous

Translated from the Hindi by BNG

What does a cat say?
Meow! Meow! Meow! Meow!?
No, she says
Main aaoon? Main aaoon? Main aaoon? Main aaoon?
May I come? May I come? May I come? May I come?
(meaning in Hindi)

THAT NIGHT

Anonymous

Translated from the Hindi by BNG

Was I hallucinating, I wonder, or
did I actually see something?
I am sure there was something there
Even now, I think there is.
I did see a shadow, and was afraid, but
'Courage, Man!' I said to myself
and began to look. The thought of
little Chameli who had died two days back
began to roar in my head; was she back?
And I began to look for a protective *mantra*.
So frozen with fear I was that
nothing, absolutely nothing, came to mind.
Unarmed—no *mantra* keeping me afloat—
I took a decision: there was a staff around
also a matchbox, and with those
I headed towards my study.
By this time some fragment of a *mantra*
came sailing into my head and I stammered
it aloud, eyes firmly shut.
When I opened them, what did I find?
A cat. A CAT! Sitting still on my windowsill.
Was it this little creature? I waved the staff in the air.
and she ran, as fast as she could.
Happy at the outcome, I went back to bed.
A triumph? Not really, I think.
For there surely is going to be another time.
Another night; and yet another.

A CAT IS NOT A CAT

S. Ganapathi

A cat is a fallen piece of cloud
rolled up in wakeful sleep.

A mixed metaphor
descending the stairs
with a questioning tail.

THE CAT AND THE COCK

Vikram Seth

Once a certain cat and cock,
Friendship founded on a rock,
Lived together in a house
In the land of Fledermaus.
Each loved music in his way,
And the cock, at break of day
Chanted: 'Cock-a-doodle-do!
Kiki-riki—Kuk-ru-koo!'
While his cat-friend, in the middle
Of the night, would play the fiddle.
Sometimes they would play together
—Handsome fur and fancy feather—
And the pair would dance and sing
While the house with joy would ring.
When the cat would range and roam
Far away from each hearth and home
He would leave his friend the cock
To rewind the cuckoo clock,
Read the papers or a book,
Shine the windowpanes, and cook,
On departing he would say,
'Cocko, have a happy day.
But do not step out of doors:
Don't trust other carnivores.
Please avoid your usual scrapes
You've had many close escapes.

Do things, if you would, my way.'
'Sure…' the cock said. 'Sure, OK.'
But one day a red-tailed fox
Who liked eating hens and cocks
—She had slaughtered twelve or more—
Drooled demurely at the door,
Whispering with a gentle knock,
'It's the postman, Mr Cock.'
'Yes, I'm sure,' the cock replied,
'But I cannot come outside.
As you know, my friend the cat
Says there's no excuse for that.
Slip the mail beneath the door
Like you've always done before.'
For a while the fox was foiled,
But, accents smoothly oiled,
After she had counted ten
She began to speak again:
'Parcel post for you to sign
Here, sir, on the dotted line.
Really sorry, Mr Cock
Would you please undo the lock,
Step outside, and sign, and pay?
Sir, I can't stand here all day.'
'Brother! Brother!' said the cock,
But he did undo the lock,
Step out, and bend down to sign
Neatly on the dotted line.
Quick as quoits the fox's paw
Clamped down on his inky claw,
And she seized him by the comb,
Bit his scruff, and dragged him home.
Now the cock called to the cat:
'Catto, Catto, save my fat!
Save my feathers, save your friend
From a truly wretched end—
Butchered by a vixen vicious

Who finds cocks and hens delicious?'
But the cat was far away
And when at the close of day
He returned, he gasped to find
Pen and parcel left behind,
And red fur, black ink, and blood
Mixed with feathers in the mud.
First he tried to trace the track;
Then he shivered and came back;
Then with head on paw he cried,
For the night was dark outside
And he could not guess or know
What to think and where to go:
'O, dear Cocko, will your claw
Never rest upon my paw?
Will we never dance and sing,
Share our house and everything?
Will I never see your wattle
Rise like dawn above this bottle?'
Then the cat, who had been drinking,
Dried his tears, and started thinking—
Stared at feathers, ink, and fur,
All at once began to purr,
Grabbed his fiddle and a sack,
And set forth upon the track
Leading to the fox's house,
Silent as a yawing mouse.
Now the fox had tied her prey
So he couldn't fly away
And had gone to pay a call,
Dressed in foxgloves, hat and shawl.
She had told her eldest daughter:
'Darling, boil a pot of water.
I will be gone an hour or two.
When I'm back I'll make some stew:
One plump cock, a pound of carrots,
Parsley, and a pair of parrots.

And, all five of you, take care
Of each other, and beware—
Never go out on your own.
Always use the telephone.
Never let a stranger in.
Heed my words through thick and thin:
These are sad and troubled times
Marred by bold and vicious crimes.
Things have changed so much—' she sighed,
'Since the year your father died.
So, my darlings, bolt the lock,
Heat the pot, and guard the cock.'
Off she went, and now the cat
—Glaring at her yellow hat
As it glimmered, gleamed and glowed,
Disappearing down the road—
Tuned his fiddle with a twang,
Coughed, and cleared his throat, and sang:
'Madame Fox's manor hall
Is so splendid, wide and tall.
Her four daughters and her son
Are a match for anyone.
Valentine and Velveeta,
Vera, Violet and Peter—
Come, all five and hear my song—
Step outside and sing along.
Yes, and dance, for I'm a dancer!'
But from inside came no answer.
So he changed the inclination
Of his musical temptation
And, like prince or politician,
Tried to split the opposition.
After counting three times ten,
He began to sing again—
Sing again and sing again
To a modified refrain:
'Madame Fox's manor hall

Is so splendid, wide and tall.
Her four daughters and her son
Are a match for anyone.
Valentine—heart of health—
Meet me, lovely maid, by stealth.
Just for you I'll sing a song—
Come outside, and sing along.'
On and on the cat persisted
Till he couldn't be resisted,
And when finally he spied
Valentine step outside,
Lifting up his fiddle he
Plucked the open string of G,
Gave her nose a frightful whack—
And he popped her in his sack.
'That's the first, and now I've caught her,
I must catch another daughter.'
Said the cat, 'and in the end
I will surely free my friend.
I will surely save his life
From the pot and kitchen-knife.'
Twiddling on a fiddle-string
He began once more to sing:
'Madame Fox's manor hall
Is so splendid, wide and tall.
Her four daughters and her son
Are a match for anyone.
Vera Vixen, fox of truth,
Let me see your grace and youth!
Just for you I'll sing a song—
Come outside, and sing along.'
On and on the cat persisted
Till he couldn't be resisted,
And when finally he spied
Vera Vixen step outside,
Lifting up his fiddle he
Plucked the A-string gallantly,

Gave her nose a frightful whack—
And he popped her in his sack.
'That's the third, and now I've caught her,
I must catch another daughter.'
Said the cat, 'and in the end
I will surely free my friend.
I will surely save his life
From the pot and kitchen-knife.'
Twiddling on a fiddle-string
He began once more to sing:
'Madame Fox's manor hall
Is so splendid, wide and tall.
Her four daughters and her son
Are a match for anyone.
Violet, so fresh and fragrant,
Leave your home and be a vagrant.
Just for you I'll sing a song—
Come outside, and sing along.'
On and on the cat persisted
Till he couldn't be resisted,
And when finally he spied
Violet emerge outside,
Lifting up his fiddle he
Plucked the open string of E,
Gave her nose a frightful whack—
And he popped her in his sack.
'That's the fourth, and now that's done
I must somehow catch the son.'
Said the cat, 'and in the end
I will surely free my friend.
I will surely save his life
From the pot and kitchen-knife.'
Twiddling on a fiddle-string
He began once more to sing:
'Madame Fox's manor hall
Is so splendid, wide and tall.
Her four daughters and her son

Are a match for anyone.
Plucky Peter, per and proud,
Leave your house and join the crowd.
Just for you I'll sing a song—
Come outside, and sing along.'
On and on the cat persisted
Till he couldn't be resisted,
And when finally he spied
Plucky Peter step outside,
Lifting up his fiddle he
Crept towards him silently,
Gave his nose a frightful whack—
And he too went in the sack.
Then the cat skipped round and round,
Making a triumphant sound
—Half miaowing and half mewing,
Half guffawing and half cooing
(This adds up to more than one,
But it really can be done)—
And he heaved the hefty sack
Happily upon his back,
Murmuring—and now his voice
Purred like a well-oiled Rolls-Royce—
'Madame Fox's manor hall
Is so splendid, wide and tall.
Her four daughters and her son
Came outside to join the fun!
Valentine and Velveeta,
Vera, Violet and Peter—
Now I'll cook you in a pot
And I'll serve you piping hot.'
But the little foxes cried
Till the cat grew teary-eyed,
So he let the sack hang free
High upon a willow tree.
'Now get down as best you can,'
Said the cat, and off he ran

To the house to save the cock
From the execution block.
First they hugged, and then the cat
Played a prelude in E flat,
While the cock, concurrently,
Sang a serenade in D.
Then with appetite and ardour,
Commandeering fridge and larder,
Cat and cock both feasted on
Till the fox's food was gone,
Spilled the water on the boil,
Soaked her sheets in mustard oil,
Strained her toothpaste through her comb,
And before they ran back home
Bent the spoons and broke the dishes
'Now,' the cat said, 'heed my wishes.
When we're back at home at last,
Learn a lesson from the past.
Do things, if you would, my way.'
'Sure…' the cock said. 'Sure, OK.'

THE RIGHT TO SPEAK

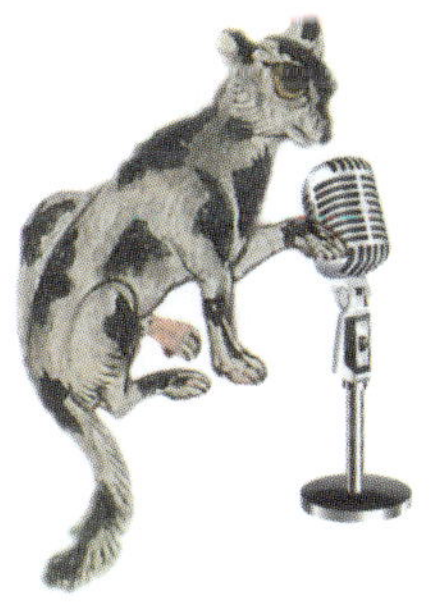

There is all this loose talk about proverbs and sayings and idioms going around, connected with me and my ilk. I am familiar with some, with others not. Most of them are designed to malign me and millions of my siblings, forbears, descendants, whether in India or abroad—Europe and England and United States and wherever else—not to speak of the immediate neighbourhood, where I reside.

I have been elected to speak—or so I think—on behalf of the entirety of my tribe of the past, the present, and the future. My brief is to comment on these sayings. The origin of some of these I will throw light upon—I shall be writing my text in the night when most of you who lean on these sayings, or hide behind them, will not be able to see my drafts—and on others I will comment, respond, confess to, or meow back.

I shall begin with the one which most annoys me, but which most people allow to roll off their tongue without a second thought.

NAU SAU CHOOHE KHA KEY BILLI HAJJ KO CHALI

(Hindi/Urdu)

[*Having made a meal of nine hundred mice, the cat pretends to have turned pious and is off on a pilgrimage to Mecca*]

Let us take this in hand. The proverb is in Hindi or Urdu, but there is a version of it even in Persian, which says:

Gurba'e 'abid namaaz karad

[The cat has turned pious and is now saying her namaz prayers]

All of this goes back to ancient, very ancient, texts, like the Buddhist *Jatakas*, and then continues. True there was a time when instead of running after mice, I would lure them: just pretend that I am a penitent: a mala in hand, I would stand on one leg like a yogi for, I would say, if I were to put all four feet on the ground the earth will not be able to bear my weight; I would keep my mouth open so as to 'eat air', that being the only thing that I consume; and so on. Many would trust me, including hordes of mice, and I would slyly make a meal of one or more of them: see, I have even had the misfortune of being represented like a yogi in a sculpture at Mahabalipuram in South India. Generation after generation has therefore called me a hypocrite, a pretender. The ultimate insult? They made a film song about me: '*Main to chali Kashi, gale mil jaao*' (I am off to Benares; come and greet me for the last time).

The tune is not bad, but to drag me into all this?

I assure you that I have genuinely, honestly, open-heartedly, turned a corner. I am tired of not being trusted. I have not given up hunting or eating mice, I should state, but I do not pretend any more. I am what I am. Be Thyself (or Myself), is what I believe in.

BAKHSHO BI BILLI, CHOOHA LANDOORA HI BHALA

(Hindi/Urdu)

[*Thank you, madam; but I am doing all right without my tail*]

Ah, I remember now. There was this luscious looking mouse, scampering about in the kitchen from one shelf to another, dancing and pirouetting. I kept seeing that for some time, and was tempted to jump him at once, but decided to wait. When the right moment came, I pounced upon him from behind, catching his long, whipping tail in my mouth. But the fellow was too clever, too swift. He took a vigorous leap: off he went and hid in his rathole, leaving his tail behind in my mouth. I was furious with myself, and of course with him, but then what good does fury do?

So, I thought and thought, and decided to try a different track. Slowly I pussy-footed to the mouth of his rathole and in the sweetest voice called out to him. 'I am sorry, dear friend,' I said, 'but that was inadvertent. I would like to return your tail to you if only you were to come out for a trice.' The wretched fellow would not respond first, but when I repeated the delicate offer more than once, he spoke from inside his hole, in a squeaky voice. 'Thank you, madam, but I am doing all right without my tail.'

Cautious little bouncer. Let him stay wherever he is. Tail-less wonder!

BILLI KE BHAAGON CHHEENKA TOOTA

(Hindi/Urdu)

[*What a windfall for that cat: the hanging pot (with milk or yoghurt) fell down on its own*]

It was just the other day: there was this inviting little earthen pot—what else could it have held other than milk or yoghurt, I ask you—that the lady of the house had, very cleverly, suspended from the ceiling with a network of thin strings. When she went out, I jumped, trying to get to the pot: in fact, I jumped and jumped, but the wretched thing was too high. So I gave up. And then, lo! A young boy rushed in with a staff that he had been playing some game with resting on his shoulders. Carelessly, he took a sudden turn and—my luck!—the staff struck the pot, it broke, and fell to the ground. The boy ran out, fearing a scolding, leaving me alone with the goodies that had been in the pot. Sheer luck, I tell you.

A craven old maid saw all this as she came in, and mumbled these words. But who cares? My luck is my own. No?

KHISIYAANI BILLI KHAMBA NOCHEY

(Hindi/Urdu)

[*Thoroughly embarrassed, the cat is now scratching the pillar!*]

The mice had created mayhem, sheer mayhem, in the kitchen. When I showed up—suddenly, for them, (although I had been watching this for a while)—they ran for their lives. Not being able to make my mind up which one to successfully pounce upon, I got a bit distracted. Perhaps even confused. But then there was this last one and I leapt to catch him but, in the flurry of the moment, I did not notice the pillar that was in the way. Bang! I hit that with my head. It took me a while to come to; in this time, the mouse had made off. There was just this pillar and me now. I was red in the face with embarrassment. What was left for me to do? So, I began to scratch that pillar. What could I do? Shamefaced.

Someone saw me in that state, and coined this saying. Unfair, I would say, for hardly ever do I miss....

BILLI KO CHHICHHRON KE KHWAB

(Hindi/Urdu)

[*What does a cat dream of? For scraps of meat of course!*]

This is true, I admit. Equally true is the Persian version of it: '*Gurba hama shab khwab binad dumba*' (A cat dreams all night of a fat sheep's tail). But then why would I not? Especially when I have gone hungry the whole day? What does it cost me, dreaming of those juicy leavings or the fat-rich tail of the neighbour's sheep?

My dreams are mine, and yours are yours. Or, are you a vegetarian?

DABI BILLI CHOOHON SEY KAAN KATWAATI HAI

(Hindi/Urdu)

[*When a cat is under pressure, even mice come and nibble at her ears*]

It will be the rarest of occurrences, I tell you. Me, and pressed down? Pressed down by whom? And how? And why? But, come to think of it, it could happen if I were—goodness gracious! Perish the thought!—I were somehow being pushed down and under pressure as this miserable saying puts it, the mice would be delighted. No? But, let me tell you this: my day is going to come, and it will be their ears, their heads, and their tails, that will be between my teeth. Those pathetic creatures....

HAMARI BILLI, HAMEEN SE MIYAUN!

(Hindi or Urdu)

[*My cat! How does she dare meow back at me!*]

This has nothing to do with me. I have never, ever, spoken back to my keeper or my master. I might not like the food he dishes out, or the fact that he brings me no gifts—like all those fancy cat-vats in palaces wearing collars of golden beads—but I keep all this to myself. It is hard, I know, but obedience, at least visible obedience, is among the first lessons my mother taught me. This way I have a home and keep getting fed, and the master stays happy. As for the meow, I keep it for others or for other occasions.

BAN PAR LAIN GAYI BILARI/MOOS KAHE JE HAMRI JOROO

(Bhojpuri)

[*As soon as the cat went into the jungle, the mouse spoke up, loud: 'that, if you don't know, was my wife'*]

I have heard this before. And I am not only furious but also astonished at the daring of that wretched little mouse. How dare he? Me—ten times his size, ten times cleverer, ten times more handsome—and *his* wife? But wait, I have made enquiries and identified the wretch. He better watch out, for he should know that his days are numbered.

BILLI KHAYE-GI NAHIN TO LURHKAYE-GI

(Hindi/ Urdu)

[*If she does not lap it up, she will topple the vessel*]

There is much truth in this, mixed even as it is with part derision. Of course, I will lap it up, that jug of milk or pot of curds, once I have easy access to it. But if I cannot reach it, I will certainly keep trying—(do you mind?)—and if the vessel gets tilted, my luck; if it does not and falls, my master's (ill-)luck. But I do set an example with my persistence, do I not?

PANCH KAHEN BILLI TO BILLI HI SAHI

(Hindi/Urdu)

[*If all the aldermen say that is a cat, then of course that is a cat*]

I do not know where this comes from, or even what exactly does it mean. It has nothing to do with me in any case: it is about politics, I think. You have to get a group of people to pronounce something, and shout it out loud—true or false—and others will fall in. Far too true, but then that is human frailty, not that of my ilk. We make up our minds on our own. (Unless we are told otherwise, of course.)

BILLI KE SIRHAANE DOODH NAHIN JAMTA

(Hindi/Urdu)

[The milk will not turn into curd if a cat is around: certainly when she sleeps next to it]

Absolutely correct; I have no problem with it. You must understand: it is part of our *sva-bhaav.* Wherever there is even a hint of milk, we shall be there. However much the lady of the house might utter *mantras* or other mumbo-jumbo (we know that each family or tribe has its own, patented formulas) while adding some leavening or curd to a pot of milk in the hope that the yoghurt would set well by the morning, nothing will happen. The milk would have gone by the morning—whether set as curd or has stayed as milk—if we are anywhere close by: awake or asleep.

CHHADEYAAN DE GHAR BILLI AAYI TAN BOLEY 'SHUKR HAI GHAR ZANANA PAIR TE PEYA'

(Punjabi)

[When a cat entered a household of chronic bachelors, they all fell on their knees, and said: 'God be thanked. At long last a feminine presence!']

The usual Punjabi exuberance and nonsense, I say. I just went in, hunting for mice, or looking for some milk or curd, not knowing that it was a household of chronic bachelors. I found nothing there: the sight of a deserted kitchen is all that greeted me. I was about to leave when I found myself surrounded by five pairs of eyes, looking at me almost with affection. Not used to this much of attention from grown-up men, I made as if to leave in a hurry but these men began to make cajoling sweet sounds, almost like whispered whistles, as if to talk to me. So, I lingered for just a little while longer, and then ran. Who would want to be in the company of men starved of feminine company?

I am about to end: it is truly time to wind up. But not before a few short comments on some other phrases/idioms and the like. And certainly before some words on a postscript that I found lying around somewhere. With regard to the comments on phrases and idioms, I will only say True or False; Right or Wrong; or move on to the next one without a comment. First the saying—wise or otherwise—followed by my comment.

BHEEGI BILLI

(Hindi/Urdu)

[Literally, wet cat. Or: see how the cat dragged herself in]

If it means that a cat pretends to be sorry for something she has done or not done, then False. We do get wet sometimes, since we move about a lot.

GURBA'E MISKIN

(Persian)

[Literally, a meek cat. But, metaphorically, a wicked rogue]

Unfair. We do feel humbled sometimes and take comments or treatment meekly. But how does that make us wicked rogues?

A CAT SITS AND MEWS IN THE PALACE ONCE OCCUPIED BY THE ROYAL ELEPHANT.

(Tamil)

Right. But what is wrong with that if this happens? Rightfully, respect is our due.

THE ELEPHANT HAS ITS TIME, THE CAT ALSO HAS ITS TIME.

(Tamil)

Well said.

WHILE SQUATTING, A CAT. WHEN SPRINGING, A TIGER.

(Tamil)

Flexibility, and quickness. That is the key.

WILL THE CAT BE ALARMED AT THE SIGHT OF A RAT?

(Tamil)

Of course not. Is there any question of there even being a match?

DOES THE WILD CAT OBSERVE THE FAST OF SHIVRATRI?

(Tamil)

No. We will be there—hungry and raring to go—when the Lord's 'vehicles' gather.

NOW FOR SOME WORDS ON A 'POSTSCRIPT' WHICH, AS I SAID, I FOUND LYING SOMEWHERE.

Witty, I would concede, but so partial, so unfair. So devoid of taste. But read it for yourself first.

POSTSCRIPT

When you sit there with a cat looking at you, or at nothing in particular, he/she could be in a state—who knows?—of feeling, or having become, one of these:

1. Compunctious: feeling remorse or regret
2. Stomaching: a feeling of bitterness, irritation, or anger
3. Callosity: lack of feeling or capacity for emotion
4. All-overish: vaguely uneasy; slightly indisposed
5. Compathy: shared feeling (as of joy or sorrow)
6. Trepidatious: feeling trepidation
7. Leucocholy: state of feeling that accompanies pre-occupation with trivial and insipid diversions
8. Alexithymia: inability to identify and express or describe one's feelings
9. Desidirium: an ardent desire or longing: especially a feeling of loss or grief

Since, however, cats—most of them, anyway—do not read the *Merriam–Webster Dictionary*, or choose to communicate in its terms, especially if they happen to be in India, how would one know?

A lot of high-flown nonsense, I would say. How about the feelings of closeness, of tenderness, that we bring when you treat us well? Have you never heard our purring that beats in unison with the beating of your heart? Have you never seen the look of melting affection in our eyes as we gaze at you when you are lonesome or distraught? Have you never felt the sensation of sheer comfort when you stroke the silken hair on our backs?

Ask yourself. Seriously.

ACKNOWLEDGEMENTS

While ending the preface to his remarkable, 1895 work, *The Satsaiya of Bihari*, Sir George Grierson wrote: 'The preparation of this book has been no light task, and more than a fair share of my eyesight lies buried in it.' I would not lay any blame at the door of the cats, but I *will* say that the preparation of this book has been 'no light task'.

My struggle to locate material touching upon cats in India turned out to be uncommonly strenuous for hardly anything has been written on them; at the same time while they are there, somewhere, they seem to be almost invisible in the usual range of Indian paintings. So, one had to look for them with an eye sharper than usual: locate material, make sense of it, hammer it into some kind of shape. Fortunately, when I sought it, help, most generous and forthcoming, some from unexpected quarters, poured in from different sources—friends, colleagues, assistants, experts, non-experts, institutions, individuals. And I would like to acknowledge that help here with a deep sense of gratitude. I have so much to be thankful for.

The paintings reproduced here—and there are as many as fifty-eight in number—came for the most part, through the courtesy of museums and auction houses, and the alert assistance of Vrinda Agrawal. Among them, the Cleveland Museum of Art; the Museum of Fine Arts at Boston; the San Diego Museum of Art, San Diego; the Metropolitan Museum of Art, New York; the British Museum, the British Library, the Victoria & Albert Museum, all in London; the Museum Rietberg, Zurich; the Staatsbibliothek, Preussische Kulturbesitz, Berlin; the St. Petersburg Oriental Institute, St. Petersburg; the Library of Congress, Washington DC; the Freer-Sackler Gallery, Washington DC; the Chester Beatty Library, Dublin; the Museum of Islamic Art, Doha. Nearer home: the National Museum, New Delhi; the Chhatrapati Shivaji Maharaja Vastu Sangrahalaya, Mumbai; the Sarabhai Foundation, Ahmedabad; the Bharat

Kala Bhawan,Varanasi; the Museum of Art and Photography, Bangalore; the Jagdish and Kamla Mittal Museum, Hyderabad; the Government Museum and Art Gallery, Chandigarh. This apart, paintings were sourced from helpful auction houses and private galleries, including the Francesca Galloway Gallery, London; Sotheby's, New York; Christies', New York; the Kapoor Galleries, New York; the Rosebery Fine Arts Auctioneers, London; Rita Dixit in London; Brendan Lynch and Oliver Forge, London; Bonhams Fine Arts Auctioneers, London; and the Eberhard Rist Galleries, Stuttgart. Nothing would have been possible without their generous help. I need to make special mention of the warm interest taken in this project by Francesca Galloway and Christine Ramphal at the Galloway Galleries; Caroline Widmer at the Museum Rietberg; Rige Sheba and Khatib-al Rehman at the National Museum;, Abhishek Poddar and Rucha Vibhute at the Museum of Art and Photography; Ashok Mehta and Nigar Gajjar at the Sarabhai Foundation; Cory Woodall and Ladan Akbarnia at the San Diego Museum; Jenny Greiner at the Chester Beatty Library; Seema Gera, Megha Kulkarni and Sangeeta Sharma at the Chandigarh Museum. Franz Joseph Vollmer, Rajiv Rawat, Mahavir Swamy, and Bapi Chitrakar most generously lent images from their personal collections, as did the gifted designer, Jana Kulmatycka, from Warsaw, whose delightful work appears on the cover of this book

I have drawn upon the work of Vikram Seth, Annemarie Schimmel, Shams-al Rehman Faruqi, P. Keshava Murthy, Ashok Bhattacharya, and Maitreyi Sen, reproducing their poetry or their translations and remain indebted to them, as I do to the fantastic teams of Ambar Chatterji and Hemali at the Suitable Agency, and David Davidar and Aienla Ozukum at Aleph Book Company. One could not have asked for a more helpful or a more supportive group of deeply engaged professionals. Aienla in particular deserves my sincere thanks for putting up, with exemplary patience, with my inadequacies at the technical level.

The sensitive drawings of cats, excerpted and adapted from somewhat larger paintings, which go into the catalogue section of this work, owe themselves entirely to the talent of Kaveri Kumar (Peacho to us), and to the technical support of T. J. Their participation in this work has been invaluable, and I remain indebted.

For their gracious warmth, and interest, I owe so much to friends: Eberhard Fischer, William Dalrymple, Cathy Dohrn, Nandini Mehta, Debra Diamond, Prithviswar Sen, Babli Brar

The Parrotia Foundation has, as always, contributed to this effort.

The strenuous task of locating all the material that has gone into this work, bringing order to it, and removing technical hitches of diverse kinds, was left to two tireless associates of mine: Usha Bhatia and Girish Naphade, to whom so much is owed. They were assisted in different ways by Ravinder Singh, Gurcharan Ram, Mahadev, Shiv Ram, and Deepak Rabha, of course, but this does not take away in the slightest the enormous favour they have done to me.

If I have left thanking my family to the last, it is because I find myself struggling to find the words. It has meant everything, everything that is meaningful, to me: the inspiration that was my late wife, Karuna, and the measureless love and support of our two children, Apu and Malavika.

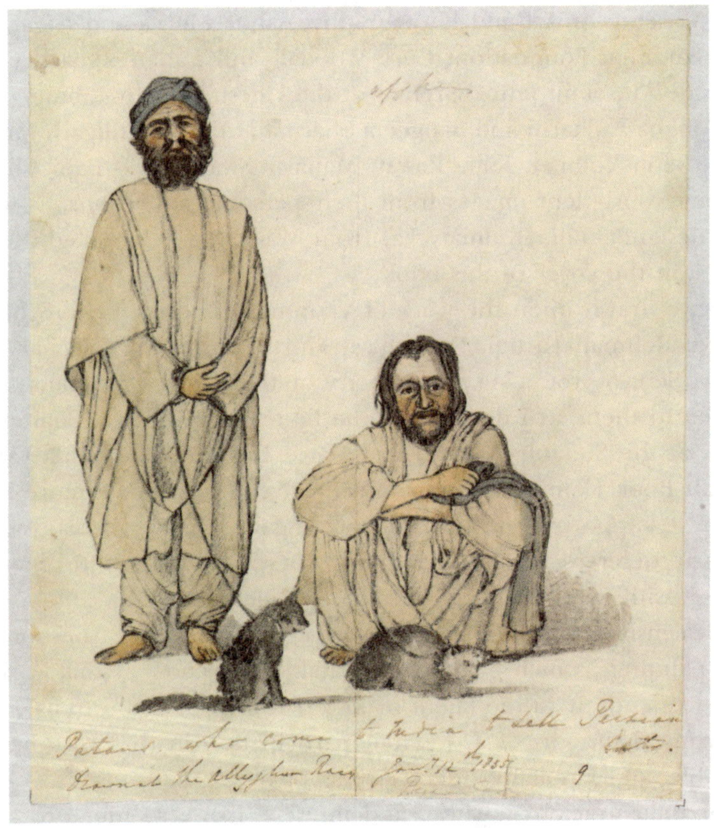

Sketch by G. T. Vigne, 1835. The text on the image reads: 'Pathans, who come to India to sell Persian cats. Drawn at Allyghur Race. January 7, 1935' [Victoria & Albert Museum, London]

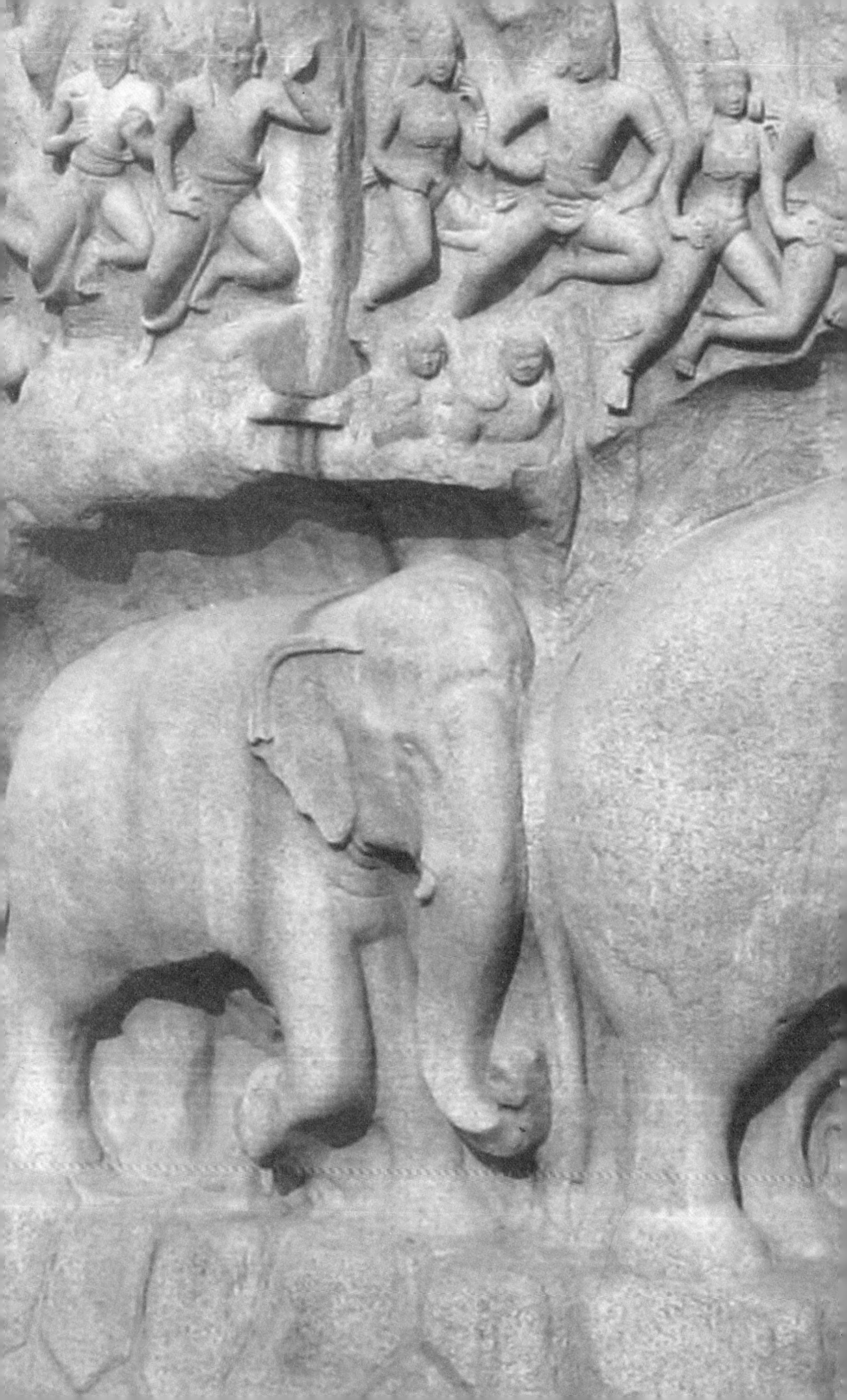